Beyond The Sunset
Life's Journey Now and Forever

WANDA P. THOMPSON

PT Press
Cardston, ALBERTA

Copyright © 2013 by Wanda P. Thompson

All rights reserved. No part of this publication may be reproduced, distributed or transmitted in any form or by any means, including photocopying, recording, or other electronic or mechanical methods, without the prior written permission of the publisher, except in the case of brief quotations embodied in critical reviews and certain other noncommercial uses permitted by copyright law. For permission requests, write to the publisher, addressed "Attention: Permissions Coordinator," at the address below.

Wanda P. Thompson/PT Press
Box 605
Cardston /Alberta, T0K 0K0
www.wandapthompson.com

Book Layout © 2013 BookDesignTemplates.com
ARTWORK © COPYRIGHT 2013 BY WANDA P. THOMPSON
Printed by CreateSpace

Ordering Information:
Quantity sales. Special discounts are available on quantity purchases by corporations, associations, and others. For details, contact the "Special Sales Department" at the address above.

Beyond The Sunset Life's Journey Now and Forever/ Wanda P. Thompson—1st ed.
ISBN: 098807401X
ISBN 13: 9780988074019

Manufactured in Canada
10 9 8 7 6 5 4 3 2 1

Dedication

This book is lovingly dedicated to my Mom and Dad, Chuck and Mary Thompson, to my children Jerry, Jennifer, Mary and Brian. You were a huge source of inspiration and encouragement to me. Thank you for the joy that each of you have given me.

Acknowledgements

I would like to thank my mother Mary Thompson for her encouragement, help in editing, and suggestions.

I am thankful for the inspiration of Heavenly Father. I offer my appreciation to an endless list of family members, friends, Church members and leaders who have taught me and enhanced my gospel learning. To all of these remarkable people, I am both thankful and indebted.

Table of Contents

Dedication iii
Acknowldgements v
Introduction vii
Table of Contents.. vii
Preface ix
Chapter 1. WHICH WAY DO WE GO? 1
Chapter 2. LOVE 11
Chapter 3. MARRIAGE 19
Chapter 4. RESPONSIBILITIES OF CHILDREN 27
Chapter 5. FAMILIES 37
Chapter 6. RESPONSIBILITIES OF PARENTS 43
Chapter 7. GOALS 55
Chapter 8. TEACHING 61
Chapter 9. OBEDIENCE 65
Chapter 10. EDUCATION 69
Chapter 11. TEN COMMANDMENTS 73
Chapter 12. COMPASSION 93
Chapter 13. CONTENTION 99
Chapter 14. HONESTY 103
Chapter 15. PRINCIPLE OF WORK (IDLENESS) 105
Chapter 16. PATIENCE 111
Chapter 17. SERMON ON THE MOUNT 115
Chapter 18. BEATITUDES 119
Chapter 19. VIRTUE 123
Chapter 20. UNSELFISHNESS 127
Chapter 21. PREPARE 129
Chapter 22. HUMILITY 133
Chapter 23. PRAYER 135
Chapter 24. WORD OF WISDOM 141

Chapter 25. TEMPTATION	143
Chapter 26. REPENTANCE	153
Chapter 27. FORGIVENESS	159
Chapter 28. JESUS CHRIST	161
Chapter 29. ATONEMENT	173
Chapter 30. MISSIONARY WORK	179
Chapter 31. BAPTISM	185
Chapter 32. HOLY GHOST	189
Chapter 33. LOYALTY	203
Chapter 34. MEEKNESS	207
Chapter 35. PRIESTHOOD	211
Chapter 36. TESTIMONY	215
Chapter 37. TITHING	221
Chapter 38. SCRIPTURES	231
Chapter 39. TEMPLES	243
Chapter 40. CELESTIAL KINGDOM	253
Chapter 41. HEAVENLY FATHER	265
Chapter 42. TRUTH	271
Chapter 43. FAITH	277
Chapter 44. ENDURANCE	281
Chapter 45. ZION	285
Chapter 46. RESURRECTION	291
Chapter 47. CONCLUSION	297
Appendix	301
The Consequences if there had been no Atonement	
What is Love?	
True Love	317
List of Previous Publications	319
Coming Soon!	
1924 Wembley Rodeo	321
About the Author	323

Preface

From the beginning, marriage has been ordained of God. Adam and Eve were married of the Lord.[1] He told them to be fruitful and multiply and replenish the earth.[2] That commandment has not changed.

Marriage is like a garden. We can plant flowers of all colours and varieties. They need to be cultivated and nourished to grow and blossom. In a marriage we plant the seeds of love, faith, patience and selflessness. We nurture sharing, joys, etc. It is a joy to behold. It gladdens the heart and the eye. However, when all we can see are the faults of one another, marriage becomes a garden of weeds and is very ugly to look upon.

This life is a school. We are here to be tested and tried. We can take comfort that the Lord knows each of us individually. He knows our strengths and weaknesses. He will not try us more than we are able to cope. Sometimes it seems that we are being stretched beyond our ability and that we will break. However, if we put our faith and trust in the Lord, we will be able to endure.

"Surely you cannot study the scriptures without knowing that perilous times are coming. Will you be unaffected? Prepare now! Take steps now to strengthen your family. Spend time together. Establish and maintain family traditions that build happy memories. Maintain a discipline with fair rules and regulations. Express unconditional love to one another through word and act. Develop within each one self-esteem and self-respect by loving and believing in him and having him belong. Provide security that children need. These are the values of which life is made. Establish these, and then we won't need to worry about the frills that too often concern us. As prophetic events unfold, one thing is certain; we will need to be more self-reliant. We will all need to teach more within the walls of our own homes."

---

1 *Genesis 2:21-24; Genesis 3:20*

2 *Moses 5:2*

Introduction

When a new baby comes into this world, he is loved beyond measure and we determine to be the best parents the world has ever known. We want to give this child everything that we did not have, and we want him to be everything that we dreamed of but did not achieve. As a result, we have already made goals for him that, in our mind's eye, is a reality. However, the child is still so tiny and helpless that we do everything for it.

As an infant, we take care of its needs, from feeding and changing the child to loving and protecting him. Even as first time parents, we learn early to distinguish between the child's cries of being hungry, wet, or just wanting to be loved and cuddled. We delight in being needed and loved in return.

As the infant grows, his needs change. He begins to learn to do for himself what we as his parents have hitherto done for him. He learns to feed himself and dress himself. As he continues to grow and develop, he becomes more independent, wanting to spend less time with parents and more time with friends. Throughout this entire process, our needs do not change. We still want to do for our child. We want to protect him from any harm or danger. We still love our child and want what is best for him. We still have the goals that we determined for our child when he was an infant. We still try to direct his paths towards those goals which we have chosen for him.

We grope about in the dark, seeking for ways to teach. We are often discouraged and disappointed with the choices that our child is making. He has a mind of his own and often chooses goals for himself which are contrary to those that you have dreamed of since he was a babe in arms.

However, even though our child still needs to be loved and nurtured as he grows older; it needs to be without the protective mantle that we as parents have thrown about him. We have to learn to let go and trust that we have done the best that we could.

Our most important job in parenting then is to teach our children so that they will be able to return 'honourably and worthily' to our Heavenly home.

What a formidable task! Of all the inventions throughout the history of time, none is as vital or important as that of being a parent! There is nothing to prepare us or to teach us on how to be a good parent. We are flying by the seat of our pants, so to speak, in trying by trial and error those things to teach our children.

We are left completely alone. We do not remember our previous home. We know only what we are familiar with. We either try to teach what our parents have taught us, or we try to avoid the pitfalls that they taught us by avoiding them.

In the pre-existence, we grew up as spirit children of our Heavenly Father and Heavenly Mother. They taught us all that we could learn. We yearned to become like them, so we were willing to come to this Earth, gain a body, and be tested to see if we would do all that our Father asked of us. [3],[4]

Two plans were presented before the Father, the first one presented by Jesus Christ was the Father's plan; in that we would have free agency to choose for ourselves whether we would follow our Father in Heaven. Jesus said, **"Thy will be done and the glory be Thine."**[5] [6] [7]

When we left our former home, our minds were veiled. As such, we do not have any prior knowledge. However, we have **NOT** been left to grope in the dark.

For those of us who earnestly seek, the way is opened. Our Father knew that we needed to have an 'instruction manual' on how to return home. In that manual, it also includes how to raise a family to be able to return

---

[3] Abraham 3:24,25

[4] Hymns of the Church of Jesus Christ of Latter-day Saints, 'Oh My Father' p. 292, published by the Church of Jesus Christ of Latter-day Saints, 1985; Romans 8:16-17; Acts 17:28-29 (22-31)

[5] Abraham 3:27

[6] Moses 4:2

[7] Moses 4:3

home, and most important, what to do to gain exaltation and eternal life. The choice is up to us![8]

The scriptures are abundant with knowledge to teach us how to become worthy to enter exaltation in the celestial kingdom where our Heavenly Parents and Jesus Christ dwell.

---

8 *2 Nephi 2:27*

The present world exceeds our powers of appreciation
and comprehension. It contains beauties we cannot apprehend,
harmonies undiscovered, colors unseen, music unheard
and joys unrealized.

CHAPTER ONE

Which Way Do We Go?

In today's world, there are many new and wonderful inventions and devices to which we may have access. There have always been instructions on how to use them; for example from the horse and buggy to today's vehicles. However, today the instructions seem to have become more complicated and difficult to understand. Commonsense seems to have flown out of the window; at least according to the instructions we have with the article at hand.

Stop! Go! One lane only! One way! Yield! Proceed only when safe to do so. Keep away from moisture. Unplug before servicing. So many directions! Which do we choose? It all depends upon the use for which the item chosen is intended.

From traffic laws and vehicles; to microwave ovens to CD players; refrigerators to televisions to computers; they all come with instructions.

Before we earn the privilege to drive, we must first obtain our learners permit. And how do we do that? An instruction manual! We must study it carefully from cover to cover. Once we are sure that we know the contents, we must take a written test in order to test our knowledge of the laws of the road. Once we have passed the written test, we are given a learners permit which entitles us to drive with another person who has a valid driver's licence. We must then practice what we have learned. When we are confident that we know how to operate a motor vehicle, we then have to take a road test. When we have passed the road test, we are finally issued a drivers licence.

On the front covers of instruction manuals they say, 'READ ALL INSTRUCTIONS BEFORE USE.' Then the instruction manuals go on to give common sense directions. For example, with electrical items; do not expose to water or moisture, it will cause electrical shock which may be harmful or fatal. Unplug appliances before doing any service work.

These basic directions when dealing with electrical appliances may seem to be unnecessary to us, but to some people, they are extremely valuable as they would take unnecessary risks because they are not familiar with the laws of electricity.

But as important as instructions are on how to use and care for our modern inventions, there is something that is much more important that comes with no instruction manual.

We are left to grope in the dark to do the best we can. Sometimes that best is not good enough.

What is more important and comes with no manual? Being a child; growing up; becoming a parent and in turn, raising children to hopefully grow up to become good citizens and honourable adults. In this process of raising our children, we hope we can avoid the mistakes that our parents, and we in our turn, made in raising ours.

When a new baby comes into this world, he is loved beyond measure and we determine to be the best parents the world has ever known. We want to give this child everything that we did not have, and we want him to be everything that we dreamed of but did not achieve. As a result, we have already made goals for him that, in our mind's eye, are a reality. However, the child is still so tiny and helpless that we do everything for it.

As an infant, we take care of its needs, from feeding and changing the child to loving and protecting him. Even as first time parents, we learn early to distinguish between the child's cries of being hungry, wet, or just wanting to be loved and cuddled. We delight in being needed and loved in return.

As the infant grows, his needs change. He begins to learn to do for himself what we as his parents have hitherto done for him. He learns to feed himself and dress himself. As he continues to grow and develop, he becomes more independent, wanting to spend less time with parents and more time with friends. Throughout this entire process, our needs do not change. We still want to do for our child. We want to protect him from any harm or danger. We still love our child and want what is best for him. We still have the goals that we determined for our child when he was an infant. We still try to direct his paths towards those goals which we have chosen for him.

WHICH WAY DO WE GO?

We grope about in the dark, seeking for ways to teach. We are often discouraged and disappointed with the choices that our child is making. He has a mind of his own and often chooses goals for himself which are contrary to those that you have dreamed of since he was a babe in arms.

However, even though our child still needs to be loved and nurtured as he grows older; it needs to be without the protective mantle that we as parents have thrown about him. We have to learn to let go and trust that we have done the best that we could.

In the pre-existence, we grew up as spirit children of our Heavenly Father and Heavenly Mother. They taught us all that we could learn. We yearned to become like them, so we were willing to come to this Earth, gain a body, and be tested to see if we would do all that our Father asked of us. [9],[10]

Two plans were presented before the Father, the first one presented by Jesus Christ was the Father's plan; in that we would have free agency to choose for ourselves whether we would follow our Father in Heaven. Jesus said, "Thy will be done and the glory be Thine."[11] [12] [13]

Lucifer's plan put forth would force all of us to do right; therefore he would bring all of his Father's children home to him.[14] However, the price to be paid was that Lucifer wanted all the glory for himself. [15] [16]

Our Father chose the first, Jesus Christ, and Lucifer rebelled and took a third of the hosts of heaven after him. There was a great battle and Lucifer and his followers were cast out of heaven.[17] Because of their decision to follow Lucifer and reject the Father's Plan of Salvation for the exaltation of his

---

9 Abraham 3:24,25
10 Hymns of the Church of Jesus Christ of Latter-day Saints, 'Oh My Father' p. 292, published by the Church of Jesus Christ of Latter-day Saints, 1985; Romans 8:16-17; Acts 17:28-29 (22-31)
11 Abraham 3:27
12 Moses 4:2
13 Moses 4:3
14 Moses 4:1
15 Moses 4:3,4
16 Moses 4:1
17 Abraham 3:27

children[18] for those who would follow Jesus Christ, Lucifer and his followers lost the right and privilege to gain a body and eventually receive exaltation.[19]

As a result, they are continually trying to deceive us and lead us astray.

As we leave our Heavenly home to come into our mortal bodies, a veil is drawn across our minds so we will not remember our previous existence. This is part of our testing. We know that by our being here on this earth, in mortal bodies, we have kept our 'first estate'. Our 'second estate' is our time here on earth. How we respond to the trials and temptations we are given, will determine our 'third and final estate.'

Our most important job in parenting then is to teach our children so that they will be able to return 'honourably and worthily' to our Heavenly home.

What a formidable task! Of all the inventions throughout the history of time, none is as vital or important as that of being a parent! There is nothing to prepare us or to teach us on how to be a good parent. We are flying by the seat of our pants, so to speak, in trying by trial and error those things to teach our children.

We are left completely alone. We do not remember our previous home. We know only what we are familiar with. We either try to teach what our parents have taught us, or we try to avoid the pitfalls that they taught us by avoiding them.

'Experts' have written volumes on child-rearing. They have become rich because parents are trying to do the best they can. Most parents acknowledge their inadequacy in dealing with the super task of bringing a child into this world and then raising that child the best they know how.

We are left to the opinions of these so-called 'experts' in raising the most important possession we will ever have; our children.

They do not know the mind and will of our Heavenly Father. They do not know the grand plans He has for each of His children; to be exalted and to return to Him. Even if they did, they do not know the detailed plans to enable this great event to be accomplished.

---

18 *Moses 1:39*
19 *Abraham 3:26*

When we left our former home, our minds were veiled. As such, we do not have any prior knowledge. However, we have **NOT** been left to grope in the dark.

For those of us who earnestly seek, the way is opened. Our Father knew that we needed to have an 'instruction manual' on how to return home. In that manual, it also includes how to raise a family to be able to return home, and most important, what to do to gain exaltation and eternal life. The choice is up to us![20]

That is very scary. We can choose. We can know. We can do. The manuals that our Father has given to us are priceless. To the unobservant, to casually gaze upon them, their value is hidden and locked away. Their price is beyond rubies and gold. Our Father has also given us a key to unlock these manuals.

What are these priceless manuals? They are the scriptures and the words of the holy prophets; the Bible, the Book of Mormon, the Doctrine and Covenants and the Pearl of Great Price. What is the key to unlock the fountain of knowledge? It is the Holy Ghost. Our Father has not forgotten us. He loves us. We are his children. He has entrusted us as parents to prepare our children, given to us, to teach and prepare them to return home and gain exaltation.

What a tremendous responsibility! What an overwhelming task! Where do we begin? Do we wait until our children are 8, 9, or 10? Do we wait until they are older? Or younger? What does the Lord say?

'And again, inasmuch as parents have children in Zion, or in any of her stakes which are organized, that teach them not to understand the doctrine of repentance, faith in Christ the Son of the living God, and of baptism and the gift of the Holy Ghost by the laying on of the hands, when eight years old, the sin be upon the heads of the parents.

'For this shall be a law unto the inhabitants of Zion, or in any of her stakes which are organized.

'And their children shall be baptized for the remission of their sins when eight years old, and receive the laying on of the hands.

---

20 *2 Nephi 2:27*

'And they shall also teach their children to pray, and to walk uprightly before the Lord.'[21]

From the beginning, Adam and Eve were a family. When they were cast out of the Garden of Eden,[22] Adam ate his bread by the sweat of his brow;[23] and Eve, his wife, laboured with him.[24] The Lord commanded them to multiply and replenish the earth.[25]

'And Adam and Eve blessed the name of God, and they made all things known unto their sons and daughters.'[26]

The history of Israel begins with the family of Abraham. He is highly esteemed of the Lord as a father and teaches his children properly.

Family life is safeguarded with such divine commandments referred to as the Ten Commandments found in Exodus 20. Through the prophet Abinadi, the Lord again taught the people on the North American continent as found in Mosiah 13:12-24 in the Book of Mormon. As the Book of Mormon was prepared by the Lord for us in our day,[27] here and now, the Lord is also speaking to us.

'Thou shalt have no other Gods before me';[28] 'Thou shalt not make unto thee any graven image';[29] 'Thou shalt not bow down thyself to them nor serve them';[30] 'Thou shalt not take the name of the Lord they God in vain';[31] 'Remember the Sabbath day, to keep it holy';[32] 'Six days shalt thou labour and do all thy work;[33] 'Honour thy father and thy mother';[34] 'Thou

---

21 *D&C 68:25-28*
22 *Genesis 3:23*
23 *Genesis 3:19*
24 *Moses 5:1*
25 *Moses 2:28*
26 *Moses 5:12*
27 *Mormon 8:14-16*
28 *Exodus 20:3; Mosiah 12:35*
29 *Exodus 20:4; Mosiah 13:12*
30 *Exodus 20:5; Mosiah 13:13*
31 *Exodus 20:7; Mosiah 13:15*
32 *Exodus 20:8; Mosiah 13:16*
33 *Exodus 20:9; Mosiah 13:17*
34 *Exodus 20:12: Mosiah 13:20*

shalt not kill';[35] 'Thou shalt not commit adultery';[36] 'Thou shalt not steal';[37] 'Thou shalt not bear false witness against thy neighbour';[38] 'Thou shalt not covet'.[39] The Lord said, "That thy days may be prolonged, I have given unto thee these commandments."[40]

The Lord continues speaking, "And again, I say unto you, I give unto you a new commandment, that you may understand my will concerning you; or in other words, I give unto you directions how you may act before me, that it may turn to you for your salvation."[41]

When Jesus Christ was born in the meridian of time, He fulfilled the Law of Moses,[42] and gave us a higher law.[43] What are some of the other things we need to teach our children? We need to teach them to respect one another, to be kind, loving, compassionate, honest, virtuous, and unselfish. We need to teach our children to walk uprightly before the Lord. What does that mean?

We need to teach our children about repentance, faith in the Lord Jesus Christ, baptism by immersion for the remission of sins and the laying on of hands for the Gift of the Holy Ghost. They need to understand how to pray and that praying opens the way for us to talk to our Heavenly Father. We need to study the scriptures with our children and ask for guidance so that they too may come to understand and love them.

All these things and more we do by example. They will not learn if we say one thing and do another.

We need to teach our children to avoid contention because Lucifer is the father of all lies.[44] Where there is contention, the Holy Ghost and the Spirit of the Lord cannot stay.

---

35 *Exodus 20:13; Mosiah 13:21*
36 *Exodus 20:14; Mosiah 13:22*
37 *Exodus 20:15; Mosiah 13:22*
38 *Exodus 20:16; Mosiah 13:23*
39 *Exodus 20:17; Mosiah 13:24*
40 *D&C 5:33*
41 *D&C 82:8,9*
42 *Matthew 5:17*
43 *D&C 41:5; Matthew 7:24; Mosiah 3:17,18*
44 *Moses 4:4*

When there is no contention, the Lord will perform mighty miracles.

The Lord tells us, 'And ye will not suffer your children that they go hungry, or naked; neither will ye suffer that they transgress the laws of God, and fight and quarrel one with another, and serve the devil, who is the master of sin, or who is the evil spirit which hath been spoken of by our fathers, he being an enemy to all righteousness. But ye will teach them to walk in the ways of truth and soberness; ye will teach them to love one another, and to serve one another.'[45]

This cannot happen overnight. It takes years to teach. Therefore, we must begin when our children are still small. We need to teach them on their level so that they may understand.

While they are yet small, teaching needs to be simple. As they grow in understanding, we can teach in greater depth.

The Lord says, 'Wherefore, they cannot sin, for power is not given unto Satan to tempt little children, until they begin to become accountable before me.'[46]

The Lord also tells us, 'And all thy children shall be taught of the Lord; and great shall be the peace of thy children.'[47]

'I have commanded you to bring up your children in light and truth.'[48]

'And again, inasmuch as parents have children in Zion, or in any of her stakes which are organized, that teach them not to understand the doctrine of the gift of the Holy Ghost by the laying on of the hands, when eight years old, the sin be upon the heads of the parents.

'For this shall be a law unto the inhabitants of Zion, or in any of her stakes which are organized.

'And their children shall be baptized for the remission of their sins when eight years old, and receive the laying on of the hands.

'And they shall also teach their children to pray, and to walk uprightly before the Lord.'[49]

---

45 *Mosiah* 4:14-15
46 *D&C* 29:47
47 *Isaiah* 54:13
48 *D&C* 93:40
49 *D&C* 68:25-28

The scriptures are abundant with knowledge to teach us how to become worthy to enter exaltation in the celestial kingdom where our Heavenly Parents and Jesus Christ dwell.

The scriptures teach us what we must do as parents and how we must teach our children. They also teach children what their responsibilities are. It is not enough that parents struggle to do what is right and the children ignore their parents. Children too, have a responsibility to learn.

"Beyond The Sunset Life's Journey Now and Forever", will explore and show how families are part of God's plan for us; not only now but also in the eternities to come. It will show how we can have love and peace within our families now and also for eternity.

CHAPTER TWO

Love

'AND THIS IS MY WORK AND MY GLORY, TO BRING TO PASS THE IMMORTALITY AND ETERNAL LIFE OF MAN.'[50]

'FOR GOD SO LOVED THE WORLD THAT HE GAVE HIS ONLY BEGOTTEN SON, THAT WHOSOEVER BELIEVETH ON HIM SHOULD NOT PERISH, BUT HAVE EVERLASTING LIFE.'[51]

'GREATER LOVE HATH NO MAN THAN THIS THAT A MAN LAY DOWN HIS LIFE FOR HIS FRIENDS.'[52]

In the pre-existence where the Father's plan was presented and accepted, we all shouted for joy. Our Father must have had mixed feelings, knowing that His Only Begotten Son was to be crucified in order for the atonement to be brought about. Jesus Christ was the only perfect being. He alone could atone for the sins of all mankind. Everyone, whether they chose evil or good, would gain salvation. However, only those who would accept and follow Jesus Christ could gain exaltation in the celestial kingdom. He alone could unlock the keys of death that would bind the rest of the human race. Jesus knew what was expected of him and he accepted gladly. Because of that love, we have the free agency to choose to return to our Heavenly Father in the Holy Courts on high.

Our Father knew that in order for the rest of his children to have the opportunity to choose good over evil, thereby exercising their free agency

---

50 *Moses 1:39*
51 *John 3:16*
52 *John 15:13*

and returning home, Jesus Christ's mission was vital. He therefore, was foreordained to become the Saviour[53] of the world.

We, each of us, still have our free agency to choose which way we will go. If we choose to ignore the path the Saviour has shown us, we too must suffer as did He in the Garden of Gethsemane. Jesus said that, 'For behold, I God, have suffered these things for all, that they might not suffer if they would repent; But if they would not repent they must suffer even as I; Which suffering caused myself, even God, the greatest of all, to tremble because of pain, and to bleed at every pore, and to suffer both body and spirit—and would that I might not drink the bitter cup, and shrink—nevertheless, glory be to the Father, and I partook and finished my preparations unto the children of men.'[54]

Unless we repent, we too must suffer as He; which suffering caused Him, even the greatest of all, to suffer and bleed at every pore because of pain.'[55] Our Saviour, Jesus Christ does not want that to happen to us because he loves us. He suffered for our sins and died and was resurrected so that one day, we too may return to our Heavenly home.

When one of your children leaves home, you feel a sense of loss. You are excited for them, and yet at the same time you feel emptiness. You worry about them. You worry that they will forget all that you have taught them and become caught up in the cares and follies of the world.

I can imagine that is how our Father feels as he sends each of his precious children here to earth. Not only have they had a veil drawn across their minds, but they are sent to parents who are inexperienced in the knowledge of raising children. How he must worry about each of us, not only the children, but we as parents as well. I know that He desires to teach us, and comfort us. He knows that this earth life and the experiences we will face will not be easy. We can take comfort from the knowledge that he was once in the position that we now are.

---

[53] *Isaiah 43:11; D&C 76:1; Abraham 3:24-26*
[54] *D&C 19:16-19*
[55] *D&C 19:16-19*

'For as man now is, God once was and as God now is, man may become.'[56]

We have the potential to become like God. We are the literal spirit offspring of our Heavenly Father. We are gods in embryo. Just as we desire for our children to become like us and follow in our footsteps, so too does our Father in Heaven desire for us to learn to become as He. We need to learn what his attributes are and then emulate them and teach them to our children. In the process, we are becoming as God would have us be when He says, '**Be ye therefore perfect, even as your Father in Heaven is perfect.**'[57]

Where do we find the attributes of our Heavenly Father and Jesus Christ? How do we know what to do to become like them? We need to search the scriptures for in them we will find eternal life. Jesus Christ said, '**And this is life eternal, that they may know Thee and Jesus Christ whom Thou hast sent.**'[58]

Our Father knows the heartbreak, the disappointments, the sorrows and the joys we will face. He also knows of the temptations and trials we will encounter as we travel through this life. He overcame them. He is perfect. What a perfect example! We are told to '**Be ye therefore perfect, even as your Father in Heaven is perfect.**'[59]

How do we go about teaching this perfect unconditional love? What is unconditional love? Unconditional love is charity. And what is charity? It is the pure love of Christ.[60] Charity is the highest, noblest, strongest kind of love, not merely affection; the pure love of Christ. It is never used to denote alms or deeds or benevolence, although it may be a prompting motive.

'Charity suffereth long, and is kind; charity envieth not; charity vaunteth not itself, is not puffed up,

'Doth not behave itself unseemly, seeketh not her own, is not easily provoked; thinketh no evil;

---

56 *Teaching of the Prophet Joseph Smith, 1977 Edition, Deseret Book Company, Salt Lake City, Utah p. 345-346*

57 *Matthew 5:48*

58 *John 17:3*

59 *Matthew 5:48*

60 *Moroni 7:47*

'Rejoiceth not in iniquity, but rejoiceth in the truth;
'Beareth all things,
'Charity never faileth…'[61]

'Wherefore, the Lord God hath given a commandment that all men should have charity, which charity is love. And except they should have charity they were nothing.'[62]

'And now abideth faith, hope, charity, these three; but the greatest of these is charity.'[63]

'And charity…beareth all things, believeth all things, hopeth all things, endureth all things.'[64]

There will be many times when our children do things contrary to the teachings they have been given. We must learn to differentiate between the child and the thing which they have done. We do not love that which the child has done wrong, but we **do** love the child. We must communicate with our children so that they will understand the difference. So many times when children are disciplined, they associate that which they have done wrong as being that they are bad. This is not so. They cannot separate the two, the action and the individual, as being entirely distinct. They feel that they are one and the same.

God is love. As we strive to become like Him, we too will develop this attribute of God in our pursuit of 'becoming as He is.'

The Lord said, 'And we will prove them herewith, to see if they will do all things whatsoever the Lord their God shall command them.'[65]

When we have unconditional love, there are no strings attached. Jesus Christ's love was not exclusive. In other words, he did not love only a select few. He loved all. It did not matter that we were imperfect. Christ's love was given without restraint.

If love is to be continuing, there must be action. We cannot sit idly by and expect love to flourish and grow. We must constantly nurture it.

---

61 *1 Corinthians 13:4,8*
62 *2 Nephi 26:30*
63 *1 Corinthians 13:13*
64 *Moroni 7:45*
65 *Abraham 3:25*

Having a Godlike love means to hold others in high esteem - to love them as we love ourselves. Love cannot be forced; love cannot be coaxed and teased. This principle of love is a basic essence of the Gospel of Jesus Christ.

If we do not learn to have charity, we cannot be saved in the kingdom of God. Neither can we be saved if we do not have faith or hope.[66] It is vital that we learn how to possess these attributes.

"Let love, and peace, and the Spirit of the Lord, kindness, charity, sacrifice for others, abound in your families. Banish harsh words, envyings, hatreds, evil speaking, and obscene language and innuendo, blasphemy, and let the Spirit of God take possession of your hearts. Teach to your children these things, in spirit and power, sustained and strengthened by personal practice. Let them see that you are earnest, and practice what you preach...Not one child in a hundred would go astray; if the home environment, example and training, were in harmony with the truth in the gospel of Christ, as revealed and taught to the Latter-day Saints."[67]

President N. Eldon Tanner has suggested how we should view others in order to develop pure, loving hearts: "By seriously trying to apply the Golden Rule that the Saviour gave to us, we will find greater joy, success, satisfaction, and friendship as we go through life, and we will enjoy the love of others and the Spirit of our Father in heaven. If we will always look for the best in others, in our friends, in our wife, in our husband, in our children, they will turn out to be the most wonderful people in the world. On the other hand, if we are looking for their weaknesses and faults and enlarge upon them, these same people may become even despicable."[68]

Elder A. Theodore Tuttle has emphasized some aspects of family life that will fortify us and strengthen the bonds of love: "Surely you cannot study the scriptures without knowing that perilous times are coming. Will you be unaffected? Prepare now! Take steps now to strengthen your family. Spend time together. Establish and maintain family traditions that build happy memories. Maintain a discipline with fair rules and regulations. Express

---

66 *Moroni 10:21*
67 *Joseph F. Smith, Gospel Doctrine, p. 302*
68 *Love One Another p. 2*

unconditional love to one another through word and act. Develop within each one self-esteem and self-respect by loving and believing in him and having him belong. Provide security that children need. These are the values of which life is made. Establish these, and then we won't need to worry about the frills that too often concern us. As prophetic events unfold, one thing is certain; we will need to be more self-reliant. We will all need to teach more within the walls of our own homes."[69]

'There is no fear in love; but perfect love casteth out fear: because fear hath torment. He that feareth is not made perfect in love.'[70]

'If you treat a man the way he is, he will remain that way. However, if you treat him as he ought to be, he will become that way.'[71]

As you love your husband or wife, children, neighbours, friends, acquaintances, you are being an example of the Gospel of Jesus Christ. If you treat them as the children of our Heavenly Father, they will one day act as children of divine deity. As we treat them with the potential we know they have within themselves, we too are growing and changing to achieve the same goals, that of becoming more Christlike. Often times we are not aware of the growth and change within ourselves. This is humility.

---

69 *(Conference Report, October 1979, p. 39; or Ensign, November 1979, p. 28)*
70 *Moroni 8:16*
71 *Author unknown*

LOVE

Salt Lake City Temple

CHAPTER THREE

Marriage

From the beginning, marriage has been ordained of God. Adam and Eve were married of the Lord.[72] He told them to be fruitful and multiply and replenish the earth.[73] That commandment has not changed. It is in this way that the spirit children of our Heavenly Parents can come to this earth, gain a mortal body, be tested and prove themselves worthy to return to their home on high. Our time here is but a small moment in the time span of eternity. Marriage is sacred.

Marriage lays the foundation for worlds, for angels and for the Gods, for intelligent beings to be crowned with glory.

The children of Zion love in proportion to the heavenly knowledge which they have received - for love keeps pace with knowledge - and as one increases, so does the other and when knowledge is perfected, love will be perfected also.

Marriage is like a garden. We can plant flowers of all colours and varieties. They need to be cultivated and nourished to grow and blossom. In a marriage we plant the seeds of love, faith, patience and selflessness. We nurture sharing, joys, etc. It is a joy to behold. It gladdens the heart and the eye. However, when all we can see are the faults of one another, marriage becomes a garden of weeds and is very ugly to look upon.

Love is the most practical thing in the world.[74]

'Someday after we have mastered the winds, the waves, the tides and the gravity, we will harness for God the energies of love, and then for the second time in the history of the world, man will have discovered **fire**.'[75]

---

72 *Genesis 2:21-24; Genesis 3:20*
73 *Moses 5:2*
74 *Matthew 22:36-39*
75 *Unknown French scientist*

There are many different elements to marriage. Once we have found the 'perfect' partner, we then need to keep alive the love that has sprung up. There will be many times when we wonder if we have chosen the 'right' partner. Our patience will be tried to its limit.

There is a joy in oneness with one another. Marriage is the perfect place to learn patience. We need to have a sense of humour. Many rough spots can be gotten through and smoothed over. We need to learn to be forgiving. We are not perfect, and neither is our spouse. We both have much to learn.

Our spouses should not only be our lovers, but also our closest friends with whom we share our most innermost selves. We need to respect one another. The differences between us are what make each of us a unique and individual person. If we can remember that they too are children of God in embryo, we can help them to attain and become the best they can be. In the process, we are growing and helping ourselves as well.

Marriage can be difficult at times. It can also be the most rewarding and fulfilling achievement. During the difficult periods, we need to learn to empathize with the disappointments. We need to be able to trust our partner implicitly.

There is one other partner that no marriage should be without. That is the Lord. We need to ask for his help and blessings on a daily basis. We do that through daily prayer. We need to have individual prayer as well as prayer with our partner. With the Lord's help, we **will** become all that God has meant for us to be.

As we pray, we should ask for the spirit to help us say what needs to be said; and then listen and be sensitive to what we are feeling.

To achieve a joy in oneness through marriage, there are seven 'C's' which I would like to share.

1. <u>Compassion</u>

The dictionary defines compassion as being tender-hearted; suffering with another; sympathy; pity.[76] As we become selfless instead of selfish, we learn to have compassion on those around us. We want to lift their burdens.

---

76 *The New Webster Encyclopedic Dictionary*, 1980 Edition, Avenel Books, New York, p. 168

MARRIAGE

2. <u>Covenant</u>

When we take our marriage vows, we make solemn covenants to our mates. We promise to love, honour and cherish them all the days of our lives; in sickness and in health; till death do us part. When we marry in God's holy temples, we are not married for time only. We are married for time and eternity. There are additional promises made to each couple who live worthily. It is this 'New and Everlasting Covenant' or marriage for time and all eternity in the temples that will allow us to enter into the highest degree in the Celestial Kingdom. Surely it is worth all the struggles we face and sacrifices we have to make!

"Cleave unto the covenants which thou hast made."[77] What motivates thousands of Latter-day Saints to leave home, school, and work to serve missions? To take the time to serve in temples? To make the rearing of righteous families their top priority? To serve in a multitude of ways that enriches the lives of others?

One major reason is covenants. A covenant is a sacred, enduring contract and promise. It may be between God and an individual, such as the covenants we make at baptism, during the sacrament, or in the temple. Or it may be between God and a group of people, such as God's promises to Abraham and Sarah and their righteous posterity.[78] For each covenant, the Lord outlines the blessings we can obtain and the things we must do to merit those blessings.

We find "the covenants of the Lord, which he hath made unto the house of Israel"[79] in the scriptures. The Lord tells us that the Book of Mormon is a covenant for Latter-day Saints, "to do according to that which I have written."[80] He defines the gospel as the new and everlasting covenant.[81]

As Latter-day Saints, we make many covenants. At baptism, we commit to become witnesses before the Lord that we "will serve him and keep

---

77 *D&C 25:13*
78 *Abraham 2:8-11; Genesis 17:19*
79 *1 Nephi 13:23*
80 *D&C 84:57*
81 *D&C 22:1; D&C 66:2*

his commandments."[82] Each Sunday thereafter we partake of the sacrament to witness again that we will "always remember him and keep his commandments."[83]

Our observance, or non observance of the covenants which we make, is an unerring measurement of our attitude toward the Lord.

If you live a normal life span, you will probably renew the sacrament covenant more than 3,000 times before you die. That covenant must be highly important to the Lord or he would not ask us to repeat it so often. But if we make the same covenant that many times and then fail to keep it, what will he say to us when we meet him? On the other hand, if we keep it, we will obtain those blessings which are 'the most desirable above all things.'

Keeping our covenants helps us become more Christ like. Keeping our covenants can also influence our attitudes about Church service. Elder Boyd K. Packer of the Quorum of the Twelve tells of a released stake president who said, "I was happy to accept the call to serve as stake president, and I am equally happy to accept my release. I did not serve just because I was under call; I served because I am under covenant. And I can keep my covenants quite as well as a home teacher as I can by serving as stake president."

Elder Packer said: "This president understood the word covenant...He had learned that exaltation is achieved by keeping covenants, not by holding high positions..."

"Ordinances and covenants become our credentials for admission into the Lord's presence. To worthily receive them is the quest of a lifetime; to keep them thereafter is the challenge of mortality."[84]

3. <u>Commitment</u>

When we marry, we commit ourselves to our partner, as well as to the Lord when we marry in the temple. We also consecrate ourselves to the building up of the kingdom of God. Consecration is the giving of one's time, talents and means to care for those in need - whether spiritually or temporally.

---

82 *Mosiah 18:10*
83 *D&C 20:77*
84 (*Conference Report, October 1979, p. 39; or Ensign, November 1979, p. 28*)

4. <u>Compliment</u>

It is very important for the self-esteem of each individual in the marriage covenant to keep their marriage fresh and vibrant. No one likes to be taken for granted. During the courtship, each partner should endeavour to make the other feel special and needed. That should not change at the onset of marriage. If anything, it should be in more abundance. After all, this is the person with which we have chosen to spend the rest of our lives; and if we are worthy, the rest of eternity. Compliment one another daily. Let the other know that you love and appreciate them. Sometimes when there have been particularly trying times, just hearing your partner tell you they love you, or a small gesture of kindness, is all that it takes to be able to cope with a situation.

5. <u>Complement</u> - Reach our highest potential with the help of our partner.

Each of us is different. We have different needs and wants. We have different likes and dislikes. Life would be boring indeed if we were all identical. Each of us has weaknesses and strengths. When we help our partner, we are helping ourselves. We are striving together to reach our goal in the Celestial Kingdom.

6. <u>Compromise</u>

Life is a series of compromises. None of us can have what we want all the time. Particularly is this true in marriage. There will be times when we want to throw up our hands in despair and quit. If we sit down and discuss what it is that each of us wants or needs, then a compromise can be reached. Perhaps you may wish to take turns or both can give a little to come to a compromise. Marriage teaches us not to be selfish. By giving of ourselves, we learn to become unselfish. We learn to serve. We learn to love unconditionally. We need to learn to love one another as our Heavenly Father loves us.

7. <u>Communication</u>

Communication is vital. Without it, we cannot succeed. We need to communicate with our spouse as well as our Heavenly Father.

We have to communicate with our spouse what our needs and wants are. They are not mind readers.

We need to love one another as Heavenly Father loves us. He knows that we are not perfect. He is patient with us. He knows we will make mistakes. He forgives us as we repent. So too must our attitudes be with our spouse. We are both trying to achieve the same goals. We usually have different ideas on how to go about it.

One of the great blessings of marriage is to be co-creators with our Heavenly Father in bringing children into this world. Some children which are sent to earth have extra special needs. Parents may wonder what they have done. They may feel guilty or that somehow it is their fault. To this Heavenly Father says no. These special spirits are sent here for our benefit; and also so that the Lord's miracles may be manifest.

THE ROAD AHEAD
(By JoAnne Burkhart)

The road ahead of them is long; its obstacles are high,
The reason they're succeeding is - They're not afraid to try.
No matter what the effort, that's required to succeed,
They push ahead, determined, to satisfy each need.
Sometimes it's necessary, that theirs' is a slower pace,
But that does not prevent them, from entering the race.

With handicaps and problems, their lives are complicated,
But for each deficiency, it seems, Somehow they've compensated.
To make up for their "quiet" legs, They've developed many charms,
Like loving looks and dimples, and Herculean arms.
They're clever little people, and more-than-average smart,
And if you're not careful, they captivate your heart.

They manipulate those wheelchairs, braces, crutches, walkers,
Anywhere they go - And all of them are talkers!
Through countless operations, Medications, casts, infections,
They patiently recover, in spite of past reflections.
We wonder what their secret is, of courage through it all,

MARRIAGE

Through faith they'll "make it somehow",
Though now and then they fall.

They grit their teeth and all the while they're looking up above,
Perhaps that's why, with every breath, their lives exhibit love.
They take just one day at a time; one step begins the miles,
And, be the battle great or small, they light the way with smiles.

CHAPTER FOUR

Responsibility of Children

GOD HAS ENDOWED US WITH ALL OF HIS POTENTIALITIES AS WELL AS HIS TENDENCIES. THAT IS, WE POSSESS WITHIN OURSELVES THOSE NATURAL INBORN QUALITIES OF INTEGRITY, JUSTICE, HONOUR, FAIRNESS AND TRUTHFULNESS. OUR MISSION IS TO DEVELOP THESE TRAITS TO THEIR UTMOST. TO REPLACE EVIL WITH GOOD IS THE REASON WE ARE.[85]

MAN POSSESSES QUALITIES OF SPIRIT AND ATTITUDES OF MIND WHICH GIVE HIM A POTENTIAL GODLIKE STATUS.[86]

WHAT IS MAN IN THIS BOUNDLESS SETTING OF SUBLIME SPLENDOUR? I ANSWER YOU HE IS GREATER AND GRANDER THAN ALL THE SUNS AND STARS IN SPACE. HE IS MORE PRECIOUS IN THE ARITHMETIC OF GOD THAN ALL THE PLANETS. FOR HIM THEY WERE CREATED. THEY ARE HIS HANDIWORK AND MAN IS HIS SON. WHAT A DISTINCTION![87]

How precious is each of us! What glorious possibilities we have! We, each of us, are special. Our Father loves us and wants us to return home. He has given us the free agency to choose and act for ourselves. Sometimes we will make the wrong choice. He has given us the principle of repentance. He has given us parents who love us. They are to teach the children so that they too may become exalted.

---

85 *Elder Sterling W. Sill*
86 *Hugh B. Brown*
87 *James E. Talmage*

But what about the children? Do they have a responsibility to listen and learn? The Lord says an emphatic **yes**.

Children are to Honour their Father and Mother.[88] They are to listen and obey them.

'O, remember, my son, and learn wisdom in thy youth; yea, learn in thy youth to keep the commandments of God.'[89]

THE PARENTS I CHOSE
Before I knew Earth, in a world high above,
I lived in a place full of soft light and love.
The mother who loved me shone warm with deep pride,
And the father who loved me kept me close by his side.
In the haven of my parents I knew safety and peace,
Yet loss filled their eyes when a child was released.
I desperately hoped to never see the day,
When my absence put pain in their hearts that way.
Then all at once, my mother's sweet light
Clouded over with sadness, and try as I might,
I could not understand her bittersweet tears;
When she kissed me goodbye, my heart leapt with fear.

Father took my hand and we slowly walked away.
He said, "My little one, 'tis time to face the day.
You will leave this world and go forth to learn.
For your mother and I, yes my child, you will yearn.
While your time down on Earth will be open and free,
There is just one thing that you must promise me.
Please always strive to do what is right,
And keep your heart close to the truth and the light."

As a tear trickled down he let go of my hand,

---

88 *Mosiah 13:20; Exodus 20:12*
89 *Alma 37:35*

RESPONSIBILITY OF CHILDREN

And I heard him say, "Sweet child, please come back when you can."
Then Heaven was gone and I heard a strange noise,
Felt strange, warm arms, and heard a strange voice.
It was soft, called me angel, and was filled with pure joy.
And said. "A girl! I was so sure you were a boy."
Then another voice, lower, spoke tender, warm words,
A voice I was sure I had just barely heard:

"My precious little baby, you must promise please,
To always stay close to your mama and me."
The great love I felt, that in Heaven abounds,
Was no different on Earth, just closer to the ground.
And now as I kneel by my bed every night,
I know the choice that I made was so right.
I miss you dear Father, but you and I know,
There are no better people than the parents I chose.[90]

'Children, obey your parents in all things: for this is well pleasing unto the Lord.'[91]

SATURDAY'S WARRIOR
By William Wordsworth
"From a pre-mortal dawn he came,
Trailing clouds of glory,
Born on the last day of the world,
He entered life's battlefield.

Nearly vanquished, he rises,
Reaching for the victor's crown -
The rediscovery of himself
And who he really is."

---

90 *Author unknown*
91 *Colossians 3:20*

Each of us has been born into the Saturday evening of time. All is at stake; the crown of eternal life for those who are faithful, or to be cast into the lake of fire and brimstone with Satan and eternal damnation. The choice is up to us. The Lord will not interfere. He is there to help us when we ask.

However, Satan has no qualms about enticing us to choose evil. He makes the very appearance of evil seem good. In the Book of Mormon, the Lord has forewarned us about the tactics of Satan. Satan does not want anyone to succeed. He wants all to fail, thereby becoming as miserable as he.

At this time in the Saturday evening history of the world, Satan and his followers, mortal as well as those who chose to follow him after the war in heaven, are out in full force. They are raging upon the earth. There has never been so much wickedness as there is now. They know that they have very little time left to persuade the children of men to seek not after righteousness, but to seek after their own pleasures. He wants us to be full of pride, greediness, selfishness; to seek after those things which will take us further away from the truth. He binds us with flaxen cord, strand by strand, until we can no longer escape. We are then bound as Satan's, for Satan to do with us as he pleases.

All around us, from the billboards to television, from books to movies, Satan uses deceitful tactics.

As children honour and obey their father and mother, they are learning what they need to do and know to be prepared to return to their Heavenly home.

Satan knows that were he to come right out and offer someone to do something wrong, he would be refused. Therefore, he is very subtle, gradually leading us astray. By reading or watching something that is inappropriate, by doing something wrong 'just because everyone else is doing it', peer pressure, flattery, among other tactics, he is gradually weakening our resolve. Before we know it, we have stepped over the 'line'. We then wonder what happened from our resolve to do right, to the crossing of the 'line'. It does not happen overnight. There are many gradual steps downward. Often times we do not even realize that we are not headed in the same direction. Let me give an example.

RESPONSIBILITY OF CHILDREN

Once there were a group of teenagers who attended their Sunday meetings every week. They attended seminary and young women's and young men's. They were strong in the gospel. A new boy moved into town. Wanting to befriend this new individual and make him feel a part of their crowd, they asked him to several activities. Each time he declined saying that he did not feel comfortable.

He then asked if any of them would like to go to a party that was being held by his old friends where he used to live.

After talking about it, the group of teenagers decided that it would not be wise. They had heard that there would be alcohol and drugs at this party. One girl spoke up in defence of the boy. She said, "We have asked him to all of our activities and he has constantly turned us down. Don't you think that we should support him? If we go to his party, maybe he will come to ours."

"What about the drugs and alcohol?"

"What about it?" the girl asked. "We know what is right and wrong. We don't have to drink or anything. Let's just go to show him we care."

After much debate, the girl was still the only one to want to go.

"All right," she said. "I'll show you that nothing will happen."

That night she went with the new boy. As they arrived at the party, it was in full swing. The music was blaring out words and messages which were inappropriate and offensive. There was nothing familiar. People were shouting profanities back and forth. Bottles of beer and other alcoholic beverages were in every hand. Cigarette smoke and other funny smelling odours wafted through the air.

Frightened, the girl wanted to leave. As she turned to the boy, he caught hold of her arm and dragged her towards the house.

"I want to go......" she started to say.

The boy interrupted her. "Come meet my friends. You'll like them." He continued pulling her up the steps.

As the others saw who was coming, they shouted, "Great to have you back," slapping him on the back as he pushed his way through the crowd, pulling the girl with him.

As the night wore on, drinks and cigarettes and the other drugs were pushed upon her. Each time she refused. After a while, the boy said, "Come on, just one. It won't hurt you. You're making a spectacle of yourself. Everyone is staring."

Looking around, the girl, uneasy to begin with, saw that everyone was giving her funny looks.

"See, what did I tell you. If you won't drink it, then just hold it. That way no one will know that you are not drinking. Ok?"

Giving in, the girl agreed to hold a glass of beer. "I won't drink it," she said. "I will only pretend to when someone is looking."

"That's my girl."

Reluctantly, the girl accepted the glass.

After a while, the boy again approached the girl. "Why don't you just take a little sip? Everybody is wondering why you haven't had your glass refilled. Just sip a little, ok?"

Again the girl gave in. Just a little sip. It wouldn't hurt anything.

Before she knew it, her glass was empty. Someone took the empty glass and replaced it with a full one, this time larger.

The music and speech which had been repulsive to her upon her arrival now didn't seem so bad. In fact, it was kind of neat. Even though the words weren't the best, it had a beat that was catchy.

By the end of the evening, all the resolve of the girl to give support to a new friend had turned into disaster. Gradually, she had been enticed to do those things which she knew were wrong; all so that she would fit in with the crowd and not seem out of place.

By small seemingly innocent means were her resolves to stand up for what she knew was right taken away. Little by little were they whittled down until she finally submitted.

She still knew the gospel was true. She still attended all of her meetings including young women's. But now there was a difference. Satan had worn down her resolve. It would now be easier to get her to find reasons to quit attending young women's, then church, until he finally has her where he wants her, to feel that because of her wrong choices, she is no longer worthy.

RESPONSIBILITY OF CHILDREN

Her self esteem has dropped. She will no longer 'hang out' with those who encouraged her not to go. She feels uncomfortable now with the teachings of Christ because she is not living them. So instead, she turns to that lifestyle where she does feel comfortable.

Little by little, strand by strand, Satan binds us with flaxen cord. We need to shun the very appearance of evil. We need to hold fast to that which we know is true and good.

'Pray without ceasing.

'Prove all things; hold fast that which is good.

'Abstain from all appearance of evil.

'And the very God of peace sanctify you wholly; ....your whole spirit and soul and body be preserved blameless unto the coming of our Lord Jesus Christ.'[92]

Our Father in Heaven knows the tactics and ways which Satan will try to deceive us. Heavenly Father has warned us:

'Pray always, lest you enter into temptation and lose your reward.'[93]

Through prayer and the guidance of the Holy Ghost we can overcome all things.

"Right decisions are easiest to make when we make them well in advance. When I was young, I made up my mind...that I would never taste tea, coffee, tobacco, or liquor...

"The time to decide on a mission is long before it becomes a matter of choosing between a mission and an athletic scholarship. The time to decide on temple marriage is before one has become attached to a boyfriend or girlfriend who does not share that objective. The time to decide on a policy of strict honesty is before the store clerk gives you too much change. The time to decide against using drugs is before a friend you like teases you for being afraid or pious. The time to decide that we will settle for nothing less than an opportunity to live eternally with our Father is **now**."[94]

---

92 *1 Thessalonians 5:17, 21-23*
93 *D&C 31:12*
94 *President Spencer W. Kimball*

President Spencer W. Kimball also says, "Oh, if our young people could learn this basic lesson: to always keep good company, to never be found with those who tend to lower our standards. Let every youth select associates who will keep him on tiptoes, trying to reach the heights."

'And again, believe that ye must repent of your sins and forsake them, and humble yourselves before God; and ask in sincerity of heart that he would forgive you; and now, if you believe all these things see that ye do them.'[95]

'When there is quarrelling and arguing in the home, reverence is not possible. Children who are obedient to their parents help to bring a reverent atmosphere into the home that is pleasing to the Lord.'[96]

As each of us, children or adult, face our weaknesses, we grow. If we choose to blame others for our problems, we will remain spiritually and emotionally stagnant.

Eternal life is eternal growth and endless progression. We need to constantly be aware of the battle for our souls. We cannot hope to win that battle and win the victory if we are not constantly vigilant. Eternal life is worth all the sacrifice which we may endure during our mortal probation. We need to make correct decisions, for every decision is taking us towards our goal, whether it is eternal life or hell.

In the 1985 LDS hymnbook, the hymn on page 303 aptly tells us what we must do and the rewards for doing so.

KEEP THE COMMANDMENTS
Keep the commandments, keep the commandments!
In this there is safety; in this there is peace.
He will send blessings; He will send blessings.
Words of a prophet: Keep the commandments.
In this there is safety and peace.

'Pray always, that you may come off conqueror; yea, that you may conquer Satan, and that you may escape the hands of the servants of Satan that do uphold his work.'[97]

---

95 *Mosiah 4:10*
96 *Elder Vaughn J. Featherstone*
97 *D&C 10:5*

RESPONSIBILITY OF CHILDREN

Children will display many emotions. Many negative emotions are:
-anger
-apathy
-boredom
-sadness and depression
-guilt
-fear and anxiety
-stress

As we heed the prophets and obey the commandments of the Lord, as we study the scriptures and help our children to understand the scriptures on their level, these feelings and emotions will disappear. They will be replaced with love, understanding, compassion, and selflessness as they serve one another and put into practice what they have learned.

Dear Children,

I remember well the day you left my side, wandered through the veil and ventured forth to fulfil your earthly mission. I had a tear in my eye each time I clothed your spirit in a cloak of love and sent you off to school. Be assured that my thoughts are with you now as always. I love you with all my heart. I know of your lives, the good and the bad, your grief, your disappointments, your unrewarded efforts, your frustrations and temptations, but always remember. . . . . . ALL THAT I HAVE IS YOURS, if you will only come home again.

Children realize that in each of you I placed a bit of heaven, no one was exempt. I love you all. Each of you has some blessed gift, some talent, and some small part of me in you. Search for it, develop it, use it and most importantly share it with others. If you really love me, help others find themselves, and lead them to me; show your love by serving others.

Repent of your failings and humble yourselves. Make yourselves ever teachable and continually strive to improve. I gave you weaknesses to help you to be humble, please don't let discouragement engulf you. I'll come if you need me.

My children cease your idle contentions. Be peacemakers; it breaks my heart to see so many of my children fighting. If they only could see what I have hoped, planned and desired for them (My heart breaks as I watch them), but you, my faithful children, **are** my hope.

It is through you that my work must proceed. You haven't much time and there is so much to be done. I beg you to get started. Accomplish the mission I gave you before you left me, I'll help you. I'm never too busy or too far away to come to you. I'm nearer to you always than you might think. Come to me often in prayer, I love to talk to you my beloved children. Be diligent in my work and my kingdom will be yours. I'd love to take you in my arms but I too, must wait patiently, for that time will come. Until then, I leave you with my peace, my blessing, my love and never forget I am nearby if you need me.

I love you and miss you so very much, and oh how I am looking forward to your return again to me and your mother.

With all my love, Your Heavenly Father[98]

If our Father in Heaven were to write a letter to us personally, it might read something like this. He is pleading for us to come home. As we search the scriptures and obey the commandments, we can return to our home on high. He knows each of us personally. He knows our names, our strengths and weaknesses. He will help us. It is up to us to ask and then to listen as He leads us.

---

[98] *Unknown author*

CHAPTER FIVE

Families

Families are forever. That is what the Lord intended.

'FOR ALL WHO WILL HAVE A BLESSING AT MY HANDS SHALL ABIDE THE LAW WHICH WAS APPOINTED FOR THAT BLESSING, AND THE CONDITIONS THEREOF, AS WERE INSTITUTED FROM BEFORE THE FOUNDATION OF THE WORLD.

'AND AS PERTAINING TO THE NEW AND EVERLASTING COVENANT, IT WAS INSTITUTED FOR THE FULLNESS OF MY GLORY; AND HE THAT RECEIVETH A FULLNESS THEREOF MUST AND SHALL ABIDE THE LAW, OR HE SHALL BE DAMNED, SAITH THE LORD GOD.

'AND VERILY I SAY UNTO YOU, THAT THE CONDITIONS OF THIS LAW ARE THESE: ALL COVENANTS, CONTRACTS, BONDS, OBLIGATIONS, OATHS, VOWS, PERFORMANCES, CONNECTIONS, ASSOCIATIONS, OR EXPECTATIONS, THAT ARE NOT MADE AND ENTERED INTO AND SEALED BY THE HOLY SPIRIT OF PROMISE, OF HIM WHO IS ANOINTED, BOTH AS WELL FOR TIME AND FOR ALL ETERNITY, AND THAT TOO MOST HOLY, BY REVELATION AND COMMANDMENT THROUGH THE MEDIUM OF MINE ANOINTED, WHOM I HAVE APPOINTED ON THE EARTH TO HOLD THIS POWER (AND I HAVE APPOINTED UNTO MY SERVANT JOSEPH TO HOLD THIS POWER IN THE LAST DAYS, AND THERE IS NEVER BUT ONE ON THE EARTH AT A TIME ON WHOM THIS POWER AND THE KEYS OF THIS PRIESTHOOD ARE CONFERRED, ARE OF NO EFFICACY,

VIRTUE, OR FORCE IN AND AFTER THE RESURRECTION FROM THE DEAD; FOR ALL CONTRACTS THAT ARE NOT MADE UNTO THIS END HAVE AN END WHEN MEN ARE DEAD.'[99]

"Let love and peace, and the Spirit of the Lord, kindness, charity, sacrifice for others, abound in your families. Banish harsh words, envying, hatreds, evil speaking, obscene language and innuendo, blasphemy, and let the Spirit of God take possession of your hearts. Teach to your children these things, in spirit and power, sustained and strengthened by personal practice. Let them see that you are earnest, and practice what you preach...Not one child in a hundred would go astray; if the home environment, example and training, were in harmony with the truth in the gospel of Christ, as revealed and taught to the Latter-day Saints."[100]

How do we combat the world today of immorality, crime, the degeneration of families? How do we strengthen our own families to be able to cope with and rise above the problems which exist in our society? How can we be a spiritual strength to our families?

We need to have family home evening on a weekly basis. By so doing, we are building ties that are bound and knit together in love. With each family member taking time out from their busy schedules, they are showing to each family member that they are most important. Families with small children are showing and teaching them that they are children of a Heavenly Father who loves them, and has given them parents that love them too. As we take time for family home evening, we are closing the doors of the world around us outside. Inside, there is warmth and love and a concern for each individual.

Family home evenings can be exciting times where there are fun activities planned for each age group to participate. They can be times of quiet spiritual learning and growth. Service projects can be enjoyed where there may be elderly people in their neighbourhood or community who need help

---

99 D&C 132:5-7
100 Joseph F. Smith, Gospel Doctrine, p. 302

with yard work, housework, or just to visit. Elderly and lonely individuals can be invited to join in their family home evening.

The Lord has told us that '**when ye are in the service of your fellow beings, ye are only in the service of your God.**'[101]

In this way, through family home evening, children are being taught the importance and value of the family. They will desire to have their own families for eternity.

Family prayer is another strength to build upon. As we pray within our families, we are asking our Heavenly Father to protect us and to keep us strong. We are asking for His guidance to do all those things which are right before Him. As we ask for these blessings, our children are witnessing the power of the Lord in helping them to make everyday decisions. The Holy Ghost is with them to aid and comfort.

Becoming worthy to attend the temple is another way we can spiritually strengthen our families. Within the walls of the temple, the outside world is left behind. For a short time, we feel that we are no longer part of the world we are familiar with. We feel the love that our Saviour and Heavenly Father have for each one of us and we yearn to be able to have their arms encircled around us. We are important to them. They want us to return home to them. As we attend the temple we are strengthened to cope with the trials this life has to offer. We are blessed with more spirituality within our homes, our children are more obedient and there is more harmony within our homes. The temple is a small taste of heaven. The more often we attend, the more desire we have to be worthy to return to our home on high; to teach our children to have the same desires as we, and to become all that our Heavenly Father would have us be.

We cannot attain spirituality in one day, or a week or a month. It is an on-going journey. It takes a life time, one day at a time. As we prepare ourselves to be spiritually in tune by daily individual and family prayer, studying the Book of Mormon and the other scriptures daily, we will find ourselves in a position to enjoy the promptings of the Holy Ghost. We will also be worthy to receive personal revelation pertaining to ourselves and our families.

---

101   *Mosiah 2:17*

As we prepare ourselves to be spiritually in tune, the spirit of the Lord is manifested to us and we feel greater spirituality.

As we are called to various callings, we need to accept them and magnify those callings. We need to make Jesus Christ the centre of our teachings. Children need to be taught to understand and obey the doctrine of the Gospel of Jesus Christ. They need to feel united as their family commits to the Gospel. As Joshua put it in the Old Testament, '**As for me and my house, we will serve the Lord.**'[102]

We need to call upon our husbands frequently as they honour the priesthood to give blessings to their wives and children. Because of the power of the priesthood, Satan is constantly trying to wear the brethren down with discouragement and procrastination. As a result, they need to constantly work hard to become spiritual strengths to their families. Through the power of the priesthood, their families can be blessed. As blessings are bestowed, they themselves are strengthened of the Lord.

As wives and mothers in Zion, we need to support and strengthen our husbands. At times, we may need to be the spiritual leader in our home. We are not to take over the responsibilities of our husbands. Far from it! We are to encourage them to take up their duties and perform them as they should. We should never nag, but be loving and encouraging. We need to ask the Lord for his help and guidance. We cannot be exalted without our husbands, nor can they be exalted without their wives.

We are living in a great era of the world's history. We are living in a time when all prophecy will be fulfilled. It is also the time of the greatest wickedness upon the face of the earth. We need to fortify our families against the wiles of the devil, to know his tactics and how to overcome them. He does not want us to succeed. He wants each of us, as well as our families to fail. Therefore, he puts every obstacle in our path, trying to thwart our progress and distract us from our goals of eternal life. In so doing, he gradually leads us down to hell.

We are a Royal Generation! The Lord has saved us for this day because of our faithfulness and valiantness in the pre-existence. Let us not let our Heavenly Father and Jesus Christ down! They are depending upon us! They are there to

---

102 *Joshua 24:15*

help us if we will only ask. The Book of Mormon was written for us in our day. In it the Lord has provided what we need to do and know to combat the wickedness around us and be victorious! We need to study the Book of Mormon daily and ask the Lord to open our minds so that we may understand.

Husbands and wives are to honour one another. As they do so, their children will grow in an environment of love.

'Likewise, ye wives, be in subjection to your own husbands; that, if any obey not the word, they also may without the word be won by the conversation of the wives;'[103]

'While they behold your chaste conversation coupled with fear.'[104]

'Whose adorning let it not be that outward adorning of plaiting the hair, and of wearing of gold, or of putting on of apparel;'[105]

'But let it be the hidden man of the heart, in that which is not corruptible, even the ornament of a meek and quiet spirit, which is in the sight of God of great price.'[106]

'For after this manner in the old time the holy women also, who trusted in God, adorned themselves, being in subjection unto their own husbands:'[107]

'Likewise, ye husbands, dwell with them according to knowledge giving honour unto the wife, as unto the weaker vessel, and as being heirs together of the grace of life; that your prayers be not hindered.'[108]

'Finally, be ye all of one mind, having compassion one of another, love as brethren, be tender-hearted, be courteous.'[109]

'Not rendering evil for evil, or railing for railing: but contrariwise blessing; knowing that ye are thereunto called, that ye should inherit a blessing.'[110]

---

103 1 Peter 3:1
104 1 Peter 3:2
105 1 Peter 3:3
106 1 Peter 3:4
107 1 Peter 3:5
108 1 Peter 3:7
109 1 Peter 3:8
110 1 Peter 3:9

As husbands and wives, we need to learn to be patient with one another. We are to be tender-hearted, compassionate, united with one another to seek after the kingdom of God. We are not to retaliate when one partner does something that is contrary to the commandments. Rather, we are to love them, and have compassion for them. Christ loves each of us unconditionally. So too, must we love our spouses.

We are not to be swayed by outward appearances. How a person looks on the outside is not important. Rather, what the individual is on the inside. If a person has a pure heart and a gentle spirit, then is the individual of great worth. It is not the outward appearance that counts, it is the inward self. Man judges the outward whereas God knows the innermost self of the individual. God loves each of us, we are of infinite worth. The worth of souls is great in the sight of God.

CHAPTER SIX

Responsibility of Parents

'WHEREFORE TEACH IT UNTO YOUR CHILDREN THAT ALL MEN, EVERYWHERE, MUST REPENT, OR THEY CAN IN NOWISE INHERIT THE KINGDOM OF GOD, FOR NO UNCLEAN THING CAN DWELL THERE.'[111]

'Wherefore, be not weary in well-doing, for ye are laying the foundation of a great work. And out of small things proceedeth that which is great.'[112]

'Organize yourselves; prepare every needful thing; and establish a house, even a house of **prayer, a house of fasting, a house of faith, a house of learning, a house of glory, a house of order, a house of God.**'[113]

As parents, it is our responsibility to teach those children entrusted to our care. They are dependant upon us for their food, shelter, protection, love and learning.

The roles of fathers and mothers, though different, are both extremely important. A child needs both of his parents.

To be a mother is the highest calling that she can attain to. It has more value than fame or fortune, although the world would have one think otherwise. The effects of motherhood reach far into the eternities. The teachings that a mother instils into her children, will be felt for generations to come. Her example and love will be taught by her children to their children. Therefore, everything that a mother does will be felt some where along the path towards her posterity.

---

111 *Moses 6:57*
112 *D&C 64:33*
113 *D&C 88:119*

How blessed will she be when her posterity rise up and call her blessed! All the sacrifice that she has endured will be worth it.

'Who can find a virtuous woman? For her price is far above rubies.

'The heart of her husband doth safely trust in her, so that he shall have no need of spoil.

'She will do him good and not evil all the days of her life.

'She seeketh wool, and flax, and worketh willingly with her hands.

'She is like the merchants' ships; she bringeth her food from afar.

'She riseth also while it is yet night, and giveth meat to her household, and a portion to her maidens.

'She considereth a field, and buyeth it: with the fruit of her hands she planteth a vineyard.

'She girdeth her loins with strength, and strenghtheneth her arms.

'She perceiveth that her merchandise is good: her candle goeth not out by night.

'She layeth her hands to the spindle, and her hands hold the distaff.

'She stretcheth out her hand to the poor; yea, she reacheth forth her hands to the needy.

'She is not afraid of the snow for her household; for all her household are clothed with scarlet.

'She maketh herself coverings of tapestry; her clothing is silk and purple.

'Her husband is known in the gates, when he sitteth among the elders of the land.

'She maketh fine linen, and selleth it; and delivereth girdles unto the merchant.

'Strength and honour are her clothing; and she shall rejoice in time to come.

'She openeth her mouth with wisdom; and in her tongue is the law of kindness.

'She looketh well to the ways of her household, and eateth not the bread of idleness.

'Her children arise up, and call her blessed; her husband also, and he praiseth her.

'Many daughters have done virtuously, but thou excellest them all.

RESPONSIBILITY OF PARENTS

'Favour is deceitful, and beauty is vain; but a woman that feareth the Lord, she shall be praised.

'Give her of the fruit of her hands; and let her own works praise her in the gate.'[114]

Oh, that all mothers could say of their children, "I have no greater joy than to hear that my children walk in truth."[115]

We need to prepare our children for the world, to be in the world but not of the world. They need to understand that even though they will be faced with many temptations and trials, they can remain true and steadfast in their testimony of Jesus Christ. He will be with them to he\lp them succeed. When they do make mistakes, they need to understand that it is through the atonement of Jesus Christ that repentance is possible. Through Jesus Christ, their sins can be made white, and they can be worthy. It needs to be sincere repentance.

'And I give unto you a commandment that you shall teach one another the doctrine of the kingdom.

'Teach ye diligently and my grace shall attend you, that you may be instructed more perfectly in theory, in principle, in doctrine, in the law of the gospel, in all things that pertain unto the kingdom of God, that are expedient for you to understand;

'Of things both in heaven and in the earth, and under the earth; things which have been, things which are, things which must shortly come to pass; things which are at home, things which are abroad; the wars and the perplexities of the nations, and the judgments which are on the land; and a knowledge also of countries and of kingdoms...

'That ye may be prepared in all things when I shall send you again to magnify the calling whereunto I have called you, and the mission with which I have commissioned you.'[116]

There are many things which the Lord expects us, as parents, to teach our children to prepare them, not only how to succeed in this life, but also

---

114   *Proverbs 10:10-31*
115   *3 John 1:4*
116   *D&C 88:77-80*

how to prepare them to receive their exaltation in the heavenly courts on high.

As these special spirits leave their heavenly home, our Father has placed great responsibility on us as parents to teach our children how to avoid the pitfalls of this life, to be happy, to learn what we must do and know, to be able to return to our heavenly home on high.

Children need to be taught to pray and to walk uprightly before the Lord. They need to learn to prepare and be worthy to go to the Holy Temple of the Lord to receive further light and knowledge.

A child's mind is like a sponge. He will absorb everything that is around him. We, as parents, have until they are eight years old to teach them to understand the basic principles of the gospel. When they reach the age of eight, they can then be baptized and receive the gift of the Holy Ghost for additional guidance and help.

Satan has no control over a child under eight years of age. This is why it is so vital to install principles of righteousness within them. Once Satan can reach them, they already need to have the understanding of right from wrong. As they grow, they can be taught in greater detail and depth.

'Train up a child in the way he should go: and when he is old, he will not depart from it.'[117]

This does not tell us that our children will be perfect and not make any mistakes, but rather that if we have taught them correct principles, they, like Enos in the Book of Mormon, will remember the things which they have been taught.[118] They will have a desire for repentance and to come back to the presence of the Lord.

A WOMAN'S PRAYER
By Joy Saunders Lundberg
Dear Father, how I want to be
All that thou designed for me,
For in thy plan I know I'll find

---

117 *Proverbs 22:6*
118 *Enos 1:3*

RESPONSIBILITY OF PARENTS

The joy that brings true peace of mind.
Please help me build within my soul
A gentleness with self-control.
And help me ever be aware
Of others who may need my care.
Oh, help me learn the gracious art
Of living with a happy heart,
And open up my eyes to see
Thy blessings here on earth for me.
Please cleanse my soul of all past sin,
Let sweet forgiveness enter in,
That I may know the fullness of
My Saviour's pure atoning love.

Dear Father, help me see my worth,
And find a balance here on earth,
Then in each season's time fulfil
The goals that match thy holy will.

And when the world calls out to me
Please help me turn my heart to thee
That I may never sacrifice
The things that matter most in life.

Help me remember who I am,
And, somehow, fully understand
That I'm a daughter born of thee,
Divine offspring of deity.

Fathers, too, have a mission to fulfil in the raising of children. Where the mother's role is to be nurturing her children and teaching them spiritually, the father is to be the breadwinner. He is to provide a home for his family. Because he is the head of the house, and the priesthood bearer, he has additional responsibilities. He is to be a support to his wife, the mother of his children. He also needs to help nurture his children, as a partner with his wife.

'No power or influence can or ought to be maintained by virtue of the priesthood, only by persuasion, by long-suffering, by gentleness and meekness, and by love unfeigned;

'By kindness, and pure knowledge, which shall greatly enlarge the soul without hypocrisy, and without guile-

'Reproving betimes with sharpness, when moved upon by the Holy Ghost; and then showing forth afterwards an increase of love toward him whom thou has reproved, lest he esteem thee to be his enemy;

'That he may know that thy faithfulness is stronger than the cords of death.

'Let thy bowels also be full of charity towards all men, and to the household of faith, and let virtue garnish thy thoughts unceasingly; then shall thy confidence wax strong in the presence of God; and the doctrine of the priesthood shall distil upon thy soul as the dews from heaven.

'The Holy Ghost shall by thy constant companion, and thy sceptre an unchanging sceptre of righteousness and truth; and thy dominion shall be an everlasting dominion, and without compulsory means it shall flow unto thee forever and ever.'[119]

To both men and women, as they grow from childhood to adulthood, their ways and understanding must change from those of a child to those of an adult. They cannot teach their children of higher values and goals if they are still acting and thinking like children. Therefore:

'When I was a child, I spake as a child, I understood as a child, I thought as a child: but when I became a man, I put away childish things.'[120]

'But ye will teach them to walk in the ways of truth and soberness; ye will teach them to love one another, and to serve one another'[121]

What type of parent are we to be? Should we be permissive? Or should we pamper our children, giving them whatever it is they desire and want? Or

---
119 *D&C 121:41-46*
120 *1 Corinthians 13:11*
121 *Mosiah 4:15*

should we make them do what is right by making sure that what they, the parent says, is done by being autocratic?

Where do we draw the line? What does it mean to be each of these different types of parents? Let's review a few examples.

1. <u>Permissive Parents</u>

Permissive parents are afraid of conflicts. Therefore, they avoid them at all costs. They feel that they are powerless against their children. The problems and activities of their children overwhelm them. They therefore, avoid setting limits and guidelines as they believe that these guidelines will hamper their children's development and growth.

Disrespect and discouragement are bred by permissiveness, thereby inviting rebellion. It creates havoc in family life and is a vicious cycle which is difficult to break.

2. <u>Pampering Parents</u>

Pampering permissive parents believe that the love of their child will be lost if they do not give in on most issues. By giving in, they believe that they will be loved and respected.

Pampering parents will pick up after their children. They clean their rooms; pick up their clothing, wherever it is that has been deposited in the home. They make excuses for their children, taking responsibility for household chores which have been assigned to their child. The parent will call the child when it is time to get up; reminding them what time it is for various activities and speaking for their child. Curfew times are disregarded and allowed by parents.

3. <u>Autocratic Parents</u>

Autocratic parents are critical of their children's performances. They are demanding and threatening. Punishments or rewards are used as a means of manipulating. They are constantly reminding and nagging. They believe that there is only one right opinion, theirs, the parent's, and as a result, they do not trust or respect their child.

When parents use the autocratic approach, they lose the respect of their children. The child also suffers as he loses his own self-respect. The child learns only to please and conform rather than to think for himself and to make informed decisions. Where then do we draw the line? Is there no other way? Yes! Within this method, parents and children do not struggle for power. Effective parenting is equated with equality and respect. All family members, regardless of age, learn to live as equals. No one tries to be superior, seize power, punish or talk down to other members in the family. The relationship is one of democracy; respect replacing rebellion, and cooperation replacing coercion.

How do we go about achieving an equal relationship, one of love and respect?

There needs to be mutual trust, respect, concern and caring; empathy and compassion for one another's sorrows and problems and a willingness to help draw family members closer together. As emphasis is focused upon each other's qualities rather than faults, the atmosphere of trust is fostered and nurtured. Thoughts and feelings can be shared without feeling that those deep feelings will be mocked.

Support of goals, whether personal or as a family are shared. Each individual member of the family knows that they are an important, integral part of that family. They accept that there will be times of trial, that although no one within their family is perfect, they are still accepted, wanted and loved.

As we teach our children, there are skills we as parents need to learn to help with this important task. Many times our children will do things contrary to that which they have been taught. They need to understand from us that even though we do not approve of what they have done, we still love them as individuals. They are still children of Heavenly Father. He, as well as we, loves them unconditionally. We as parents need to accept our children and empathize with them when they make mistakes. For example, if our children have practised hard for a contest but did not do well, we need to let them know that we know that they worked hard. Help them to see where their mistake was and encourage them to keep trying. Do not put them down. Children will feel that because they are the ones at fault, they are worthless but not because of what they did. We need to let them see and know that it is who they are that is important. They each are priceless and they have infinite value to us and to Heavenly Father.

RESPONSIBILITY OF PARENTS

Focusing on our children's strengths instead of weaknesses helps to build their self-esteem. As their self-esteem increases, so too does their desire to improve themselves and do better, whatever the situation.

As we look for the positive results in different situations which our children are involved with, no matter how bad the situation is, we are helping them to see different ways to view each situation. We are helping them to learn something good from the bad experiences.

Focus on the effort and improvement your children have made. It does not matter that they do not perform as well as someone else's child. What is important is that they feel that they themselves are important to you; that you appreciate the hard work and effort which they are expending.

The following is a brief summary of the above points:

1. Discouragement is the basis for most failure.
2. One of the major roles of a parent is to be an encourager.
3. Encouragement is the process of focusing on an individual's resources in order to build self-esteem.
4. Learn to recognize some positive aspect in every trait.
5. Encourage your children to pursue their own goals, provided the goals are socially acceptable.
6. Methods of encouragement:
    a) Showing faith
    b) Building self-respect
    c) Recognizing effort and improvement
    d) Focusing on strengths and assets
7. Praise is a reward given for an achievement. It fosters competition and fear of failure. Encouragement is given for effort and improvement. It fosters cooperation and self-esteem. It inspires confidence and acceptance.
8. Recognize your own strengths by valuing yourself as a person, not only as a parent.
9. Strategies for encouraging children:
    a) Give responsibility.
    b) Show appreciation.
    c) Encourage participation in decision making.

d) Ask your children for opinions and suggestions.

e) Accept that mistakes will be made. After all, neither we, nor our children are perfect.

f) Emphasize that it is the process, not just the end product, which is important.

g) Liabilities can be turned into assets. Point out the positive in every situation.

h) As you show confidence in the abilities of your children to make decisions, their self-confidence will grow and blossom. Small decisions made will encourage good judgements of larger more important decisions.

i) Expect that your children will do well. Be positive about their achievements.

j) Develop alternative ways of looking at situations. Make them teaching opportunities.

Avoid pampering your children. Let them do those things which they are able to do for themselves. Parents and children are of equal human worth. Our Heavenly Father loves each of us. Mutual trust and respect are the basis for an equal relationship.

Only by changing their own attitudes can parents change the relationships with their children. As children grow, they need to learn that independence and responsibility go together.

Avoid the inclination to control; stay away from power struggles. Parental force invites resistance.

As children grow, develop realistic expectations which will help your children to establish their own standards. Learn to recognize when your children are attempting to control you with their actions of attention, power, and revenge, displays of inadequacy, excitement, superiority, and peer acceptance.

The following guidelines will help in responding to the four basic types of misbehaviour:

<u>Attention</u>

Never give attention on demand - even for positive behaviour.

RESPONSIBILITY OF PARENTS

Power

Bow out of power struggles. Let your children experience the consequences of their misbehaviour. Win your children's cooperation by enlisting their help, opinions and suggestions. Let them feel that they are an important part of your family.

Revenge

Avoid the feelings of hurt. Strive to build a relationship based on trust instead of seeking revenge in turn.

Display of Inadequacy

Encourage any positive efforts your children make. To you it may seem small and insignificant, but to them it is very important. By so doing, you are helping to build their self-esteem. Do not criticize. Constant criticism encourages feelings of low self-esteem. There is a time for constructive criticism, but not when they have accomplished something which they feel is important and for which they are proud.

As you strive to create a positive relationship with your children, you will be rewarded as they seek to pursue positive goals of cooperation, involvement, self-reliance and responsibility.

Many times children will display a variety of emotional misbehaviours in the hopes to manipulate their parents.

When anger is shown, often times the child is trying to win; to get control or to get even. Refuse to be intimidated. Do not give in or fight. When there is a calmer atmosphere later, discuss the problem with your child to come to an acceptable solution for both the parent and child.

Apathy is common in all of our children, especially teenagers. They are trying to demonstrate that they have power in that they will only do those things they want to do when **they** want to do them. They only want to do enough to get by, nothing more. As parents, we want to throw up our hands in despair.

Invite your child or teenager to participate in decisions within the family. Show him that his ideas and opinions are important, that he can contribute towards the goals of his family. As he sees that he is a valued member of the family, his apathy will dissipate. Let him have responsibility for something important that you as a parent would normally handle. Let him become responsible by having responsibility.

Who hasn't heard, 'Mom, I'm bored. There's nothing to do!' With older children, they will often use this excuse to avoid being involved with others or participating in life.

Help your child to find activities that they may not have thought of. However, if your child continues to stay bored, then leave him to work it out for himself. Often, as parents do not pamper to their whims, and they have to think for themselves, they will get bored with being bored! They will then go find something themselves to do.

Sadness and depression are often used to control other's feelings, avoid responsibility, and gain pity or to get revenge. Show your child that you understand and empathize with him. Help him to solve his problem. If your child wants to remain sad, let him work it out for himself. Do not pity him. Do not take over your child's responsibilities. He still has to perform his responsibilities. If the depression and sadness lasts for any length of time, consult professional help.

Satan uses all these tactics and more. As we learn and understand them for what they are, we can help teach and prepare our children better. We can help them see that the unhappiness of each individual is the goal of the adversary. We can thwart his evil designs by knowing what they are and where they come from.

CHAPTER SEVEN

Goals

Without goals, we go nowhere. We can daydream about what we would like to do or accomplish, but without plans or goals, they are only dreams.

In the pre-existence, Heavenly Father and Jesus Christ had a goal or plan for each of us. What is that goal?

'FOR BEHOLD, THIS IS MY WORK AND MY GLORY---TO BRING TO PASS THE IMMORTALITY AND ETERNAL LIFE OF MAN.'[122]

We want to reach exaltation in the Celestial Kingdom and return to live with our Heavenly Father and Jesus Christ. What is exaltation?[123]

"And again, verily I say unto you, if a man marry a wife by my word, which is my law, and by the new and everlasting covenant, and it is sealed unto them by the Holy Spirit of promise, by him who is anointed, unto whom I have appointed this power and the keys of this priesthood; and it shall be said unto them---Ye shall come forth in the first resurrection; and if it be after the first resurrection, in the next resurrection; and shall inherit thrones, kingdoms, principalities, and powers, dominions, all heights and depths— then shall it be written in the Lamb's Book of Life, that he shall commit no murder whereby to shed innocent blood, it shall be done unto them in all things whatsoever my servant hath put upon them, in time, and through all eternity; and shall be of full force when they are out of the world; and they shall pass by the angels, and the gods, which are set there, to their exaltation

---

122   *Moses 1:39*
123   *D&C 132:19*

and glory in all things, as hath been sealed upon their heads, which glory shall be a fullness and a continuation of the seeds forever and ever."[124]

How do we go about it?

There must be a place prepared for us to dwell[125] and be tested.[126] There must be a plan of salvation that we may choose to reach that goal.[127] There must be specific steps along the way to guide us and help us. We must have our free agency to choose good over evil[128].

For each phase of the earth's creation, Jesus Christ and Heavenly Father planned it first.[129] The formation of the earth, the creation of all living plant matter, animal life of every kind, the heavens and the earth, the sun, moon and stars, and mankind. Every living thing was commanded to multiply and replenish the earth.[130] Adam was formed and given a companion. They too, were commanded to multiply and replenish the earth.[131]

The temptation for Eve to eat of the forbidden fruit was part of the plan of salvation. Without Eve and then Adam partaking of it, the spirit children would not have been able to come to this earth.

When Satan was cast out of Heaven and sent to this earth, it was not by accident. In order for us to have our free agency, there must be good and evil to choose from.[132] Our Heavenly Father knew this. It was part of the plan for us to be tested to prepare us for exaltation.

So it is with us. We should have as our goal, the celestial kingdom. The Lord is explicit in what we should do and what we must have in order to obtain that goal. It is worth any price we have to pay or any sacrifice we have to make to achieve it.

---

124 *D&C 132:19*
125 *Abraham 3:24*
126 *Abraham 3:25*
127 *Abraham 3:26, 27*
128 *2 Nephi 2:11*
129 *Moses 3:5*
130 *Moses 2:28*
131 *Genesis 1:28*
132 *2 Nephi 2:11; 2 Nephi 2:15,16*

GOALS

> 'FOR IF YOU WILL THAT I GIVE UNTO YOU A PLACE IN THE CELESTIAL WORLD, YOU MUST PREPARE YOURSELVES BY DOING THE THINGS WHICH I HAVE COMMANDED YOU AND REQUIRED OF YOU."[133]

How do we go about setting goals? The following guidelines are effective for any goal that is chosen.

First of all, the goal needs to be visualized. Picture yourself as already having achieved the goal. Before you can visualize your goal, you need to be specific. Know what you want. Secondly, your goals need to be realistic and attainable, but they also need to be a challenge. For some, setting your goal to reach the celestial kingdom may seem out of reach. Set short term goals. If you sit down and take it one step at a time, it will be much easier to accomplish. We do not need to become perfect in this lifetime. We will have opportunities to progress and reach our goal in the next life. However, we need to be working toward it now. For short term goals, break them down into daily goals.

Third, believe in yourself. You are important.[134] Each of our Heavenly Father's children is important. He loves you and wants you to succeed. He will help you. All you have to do is to ask for his help.[135]

Fourth, you need to plan. Write down your goal. Then write down specific ways you can reach your goal. This helps it to become real. Read through your goal every day, morning and night. Put it in a place where you will see it often. Read it before you go to bed at night. Without a plan, all goals will fail because they are only vague. You must be specific. Set small goals along the way that will help you achieve your major goal. In this way you can see your progress.

Fifth, set a target date. For each goal you need to set a date whereby you have something to reach for. If you fail to accomplish it by then, reset the date and try again. The only time you will completely fail is if you don't try.

---

133   D&C 78:7
134   D&C 18:10
135   D&C 88:63; D&C 75:27; D&C 49:26

Sixth, evaluate yourself every so often. This way it will help you to keep on track. As you evaluate yourself, you may find that you need to make adjustments to your goals.

Seventh, plead your case before the Lord.[136]

Eighth, exert yourself mentally, exercise your faith.[137] Qualify yourself by obedience and the Lord is bound.[138] **Don't** take your eyes off your goal.[139]

Ninth, Avoid distractions - Satan will do all he can to distract us. He wants us to fail. He wants to give us feelings of low self-worth, discouragement and failure. When we give in to these feelings, we find it much more difficult to keep our eyes on the goals we have set.

Tenth, reward yourself. As you complete each step towards short term and long term goals, reward yourself. It gives you a feeling of self-worth and accomplishment. When things may get difficult, it will be easier to stay on track because you have already accomplished a portion of the goal.

As Latter-day Saints, we can set personal worthiness goals that are attainable in this world. We can gauge our progress towards our Heavenly Father by the way in which these goals are met.

1. I pray in private regularly
2. I seek the guidance of the Spirit
3. I honour my father and mother
4. I am morally clean
5. I obey the Word of Wisdom, including not using tobacco, alcoholic drinks, coffee, tea, or harmful drugs
6. I am honest in thought, word, and action
7. I pay my tithes and offerings
8. I respect and support the priesthood
9. I obey the laws of the land
10. I apply the principles of repentance and forgiveness
11. I help make my family life better

---

136 *Alma 37:37*
137 *D&C 6:36*
138 *D&C 82:10*
139 *Philippians 3:14; Matthew 17:22; Matthew 14:28-31*

12. I refrain from swearing, gossiping, criticizing others, and other unworthy speech

13. I avoid all immoral and suggestive materials and entertainment

14. I am an example of the Lord's word in thought, speech, action and appearance

15. I participate in church meetings, and I participate in seminary where possible

16. I am learning from experience the blessing of work and the sweetness of service

17. I study and ponder the scriptures daily

We learn more about ourselves when we set goals. We learn that we are capable of much more than we at first realized. As we try, we learn and grow.

CHAPTER EIGHT

Teaching

"AND THOU SHALT TEACH THEM ORDINANCES AND LAWS, AND SHALT SHEW THEM THE WAY WHEREIN THEY MUST WALK, AND THE WORK THAT THEY MUST DO."[140]

"Teach me Thy way O Lord; I will walk in Thy truth: Unite my heart to fear Thy name."[141]

Teaching is discipline. It can be best accomplished through love, example, imparting values, scripture study, gentleness, long suffering, persuasion and self control on our part.

"No power or influence can or ought to be maintained... only by persuasion, by long suffering, by gentleness and meekness, and by love unfeigned;[142]

"Reproving betimes with sharpness, when moved upon by the Holy Ghost; and then showing forth afterwards an increase of love toward him whom thou has reproved, lest he esteem thee to be his enemy."[143]

"To teach self-discipline, the emphasis should be on self respect and esteem rather than the use of ridicule, embarrassment and tears." [144]

As we grow and become old enough, we attend school, we learn how to get along with other children our own age. We learn how to read and write and how to do arithmetic. As we grow and become accomplished in the basics, we go on to learn about other people in other lands, and geography. We learn how they live and what their country is like. As we learn the teachings of school we become prepared to meet the challenges of life. When we

---

140　*Exodus 18:20*
141　*Psalm 86:11*
142　*D&C 121:41*
143　*D&C 121:43*
144　*Marvin J. Ashton*

graduate, we are adults. It has taken many years of dedicated teachers, both at school and at home to bring us to the point where we are ready to be on our own in the world. At the conclusion of high school, we have new choices to make. We can continue our schooling by entering college, university or a vocation. For each of these there are certain requirements needed to gain admission. If we do not have them, we will not be entitled to enter.

Along with learning in the earlier grades and years, we needed to have an idea of what we wanted to be when we grew up and were ready to go out on our own. We needed to have goals so that when the day arrived, we would be ready.

We were sent to the earth, to gain a body and then to worthily return home to our Heavenly Father. We need to set short-term goals to help us achieves our desire of eternal life. Goals set along the way show us how to achieve eternal life.

We have the scriptures and living prophets to teach and guide us. We are given trials and tribulations to teach us. These teach us things that can be learned in no other way. When we have the same trial over and over again, we need to sit down and prayerfully ask what it is that we are to learn from that trial. Sometimes we need to have the same one over and over again before we learn the lesson to be taught. When we do, we can then go on to the next one. We need to be grateful for each of them. They are not easy to go through. Some are much more difficult than others. What are some of the lessons to be learned? Patience, long-suffering, temperance, brotherly kindness, compassion, and charity are but a few.

Heavenly Father knew what each of us needed for us to succeed. He knows us individually. Just as we know each of our children and what their individual needs are, so too, does our Heavenly Father know us. We are His children. He knows what we need to reach our potential. Therefore He gives us trials and tribulations, not to discourage and depress us, or to punish us, but to help and uplift us. He is teaching us the things we need to know to be able to come back home to where our Heavenly Parents and Jesus Christ dwell.

TEACHING

As we study and learn, we can teach our children those qualities that will help them to reach their potential.

TEACH ME TO WALK IN THE LIGHT
Teach me to walk in the light of his love
Teach me to pray to my Father above;
Teach me to know of the things that are right;
Teach me, teach me, to walk in the light.

Come, little child, and together we'll learn
Of his commandments, that we may return
Home to his presence, to live in his sight
Always, always to walk in the light.

Father in Heaven, we thank thee this day
For loving guidance to show us the way.
Grateful, we praise thee with songs of delight!
Gladly, gladly we'll walk in the light.[145]

---

145 *Words and music: Clara W. McMaster, b. 1904; Isaiah 2:5; Ephesians 5:8*

CHAPTER NINE

Obedience

'WHEREFORE, IF YE SHALL BE OBEDIENT TO THE COMMANDMENTS, AND ENDURE TO THE END, YE SHALL BE SAVED AT THE LAST DAY.'[146]

'THERE IS A LAW...UPON WHICH ALL BLESSINGS ARE PREDICATED--AND WHEN WE OBTAIN ANY BLESSING FROM GOD, IT IS BY OBEDIENCE TO THAT LAW UPON WHICH IT IS PREDICATED.'[147]

'I, the Lord, am bound when ye do what I say; but when ye do not what I say, ye have no promise.'[148]

'And my people must needs be chastened until they learn obedience, if it must needs be, by the things which they suffer.'[149]

'**Obedience** is the first law of heaven, the cornerstone upon which all righteousness and progression rest. It consists in compliance with divine law, in conformity to the mind and will of Deity, in complete subjection to God and his commands. To obey gospel law is to yield obedience to the Lord, to execute the commands of and be ruled by him whose we are.

'Obedience is possible because of two things: 1. Laws were ordained by Deity so that his spirit children by conformity to them, might progress and become like him; and 2. The children of God were endowed with agency, the power and ability to either obey or disobey the divine will. Obedience and disobedience thus had their beginnings in pre-existence, the obedient spirits

---

146 *1 Nephi 22:31*
147 *D&C 130:20-21*
148 *D&C 82:10*
149 *D&C 105:6*

being the ones who kept their first estate and the disobedient the ones who were cast out with Lucifer and his hosts. The perfect formula for obedience was stated by our Lord in the pre-existent council when he volunteered to follow the Father's plan and be the Redeemer of the world: "Father, thy will be done, and the glory be Thine forever."[150]

'The very purpose of the creation of this earth was to provide a place where the spirit children of the Father, having received their mortal bodies, could be tried and tested. "We will prove them herewith," the divine decree reads, "to see if they will do all things whatsoever the Lord their God shall command them."[151] The Lord created men, placed them on earth, "And gave unto them commandments that they should love and serve him, the only living and true God, and that he should be the only being whom they should worship."[152] The whole system of creation and existence is thus centred around the eternal principle of obedience to law.

'One of Adam's great religious acts has become the classical illustration of perfect obedience. This first man of all men was commanded by the Lord to offer the firstlings of his flocks as a sacrifice, which he did. Thereupon an angel appeared to him and asked: "Why dost thou offer sacrifices unto the Lord? And Adam said unto him: I know not, save the Lord commanded me." Then the angel told him the purpose and significance of sacrifice.[153] It should be noted that obedience preceded receipt of the new revelation.

'It is also interesting that it was in connection with the law of sacrifice that another of the great classical illustrations of obedience was given. Saul, having disobeyed counsel by not destroying the cattle of the Amalekites, choosing rather to offer them in sacrifice to the Lord, received this rebuke from the Prophet Samuel: "Hath the Lord as great delight in burnt offerings and sacrifices, as in obeying the voice of the Lord? Behold, **to obey is better**

---

150 *Moses 4:2*
151 *Abraham 3:25*
152 *D&C 20:19*
153 *Moses 5:5-8*

OBEDIENCE

than sacrifice, and to hearken than the fat of rams. For rebellion is as the sin of witchcraft, and stubbornness is as iniquity and idolatry."[154]

Obedience is required in every level of life; from the laws of the land, the rules of the road, to obedience in our families. If everyone could do whatever they wanted regardless of the consequences, there would be havoc. There would be no peace, no harmony, and no order. When the laws of the land are disobeyed, there are crimes of every nature. The result of which is unhappiness, despair, and discouragement. This is not why we were sent to earth.

'Adam fell that men might be and men are that they might have joy.'[155]

'Blessed be the name of God, for because of my transgression my eyes are opened, and in this life I shall have joy, and again in the flesh I shall see God.

'Were it not for our transgression we never should have had seed, and never should have known good and evil, and the joy of our redemption, and the eternal life which God giveth unto all the obedient.'[156]

The Lord has given us commandments, not to imprison us but to free us. He is teaching us what it is that will give us happiness and peace.

Our Saviour Jesus Christ tells us 'Peace I leave with you, my peace I give unto you: not as the world giveth, give I unto you. Let not your heart be troubled, neither let it be afraid.'[157]

'But learn that he who doeth the works of righteousness shall receive his reward, even peace in this world, and eternal life in the world to come.'[158]

---

154 *1 Samuel 15:22-23*
155 *2 Nephi 2:25*
156 *Moses 5:10-11*
157 *John 14:27*
158 *D&C 59:23*

CHAPTER TEN

Education

'IF A PERSON GAINS MORE KNOWLEDGE AND INTELLIGENCE IN THIS LIFE THROUGH HIS DILIGENCE AND OBEDIENCE THAN ANOTHER, HE WILL HAVE SO MUCH THE ADVANTAGE IN THE WORLD TO COME.'[159]

The Lord places high expectations on us. We are here on this earth to learn. This life is a school. Everything we do and experience is for our good. Even the trials are a blessing to us. We need to pray for understanding of what it is the Lord would have us learn from each of the experiences we pass through.

'My son, peace be unto thy soul; thine adversity and thine afflictions shall be but a small moment; and then, if thou endure it well, God shall exalt thee on high.'[160]

We need to learn different languages, all about the world around us, politics, and peoples.

'...STUDY AND LEARN, AND BECOME ACQUAINTED WITH ALL GOOD BOOKS, AND WITH LANGUAGES, TONGUES AND PEOPLE.'[161]

Knowledge, light and truth are some of the attributes of God. In order for us to become like Him, we too need to 'study and learn.' We have the capabilities. We need to believe and trust in our Heavenly Father and know that the commandments he gives us are for our benefit.

They are not restricting as some would believe, but they give us freedom. As we follow them, someday we may become as God is. He desires for

---

159 D&C 130:19
160 D&C 121:7-8
161 D&C 90:15

us to return home. He has given us many abilities and talents. We need to learn and develop those talents.

'WHATEVER PRINCIPLE OF INTELLIGENCE WE ATTAIN UNTO IN THIS LIFE, IT WILL RISE WITH US IN THE RESURRECTION.' [162]

'O that cunning plan of the evil one! O the vainness, and the frailties, and the foolishness of men! When they are learned they think they are wise, and they hearken not unto the counsel of God, for they set it aside, supposing they know of themselves, wherefore, their wisdom is foolishness and it profiteth them not. And they shall perish.

'But to be learned is good if they hearken unto the counsels of God.'[163]

'Seek ye diligently and teach one another words of wisdom: yea, seek ye out of the best books words of wisdom; seek learning even by study and also by faith.'[164]

'For wisdom is better than rubies; and all the things that may be desired are not to be compared to it.'[165]

'Give instruction to a wise man, and he will be yet wiser: teach a just man, and he will increase in learning'[166]

Learning is ongoing. We can still learn when we have finished school. By reading good books, studying the scriptures, learning new ways of doing things for our families and those around us, we are increasing our capacity to learn.

We are being 'stretched'. We find that we have more capacity to give when we reach out to others. This life is a school. Everything is here for us to learn. The more we learn, the more we discover that we do not know. This is good because we then have the desire to continue our growth. As we teach

---

162 *D&C 130:18*
163 *2 Nephi 9:28-29*
164 *D&C 88:118*
165 *Proverbs 8:11*
166 *Proverbs 9:9*

others what we have learned, we will continue learning new ideas. Everyone has something that they can teach to another. Everyone is important. As we help others, we help ourselves.

> **I**
> I AM the Lord thy God.
> Thou shalt have no other gods before me.
>
> **II**
> Thou shalt not make unto thee any graven image.
>
> **III**
> Thou shalt not take the name of the Lord thy God in vain.
>
> **IV**
> Remember the sabbath day, to keep it holy.
>
> **V**
> Honour thy father and thy mother.
>
> **VI**
> Thou shalt not kill.
>
> **VII**
> Thou shalt not commit adultery.
>
> **VIII**
> Thou shalt not steal.
>
> **IX**
> Thou shalt not bear false witness against thy neighbour.
>
> **X**
> Thou shalt not covet.

CHAPTER ELEVEN

Ten Commandments

After Moses freed the children of Israel from bondage and led them out of Egypt, they crossed the Red Sea. The Lord called Moses up onto Mount Sinai. Moses left Aaron in charge of the people. Moses was gone for such a long time that the people thought that Moses had been consumed in the fire on top of the mountain. They built an idol calf molten from the gold and precious ores that they carried with them from their Egyptian taskmasters. Aaron bowed down to the pressure and helped them build the golden calf.

As Moses came down from the mountain from speaking with God, he saw the revelry and the golden calf which the people had made. He was very angry. He smashed the tablets of stone. The Lord wrote upon another tablet, giving only the lesser or basic laws which are known to us as the Ten Commandments. The people were not ready for the higher law of God.

1. THOU SHALT HAVE NO OTHER GODS BEFORE ME
2. THOU SHALT NOT MAKE UNTO THEE ANY GRAVEN IMAGE
3. THOU SHALT NOT TAKE THE NAME OF THE LORD THY GOD IN VAIN
4. REMEMBER THE SABBATH DAY TO KEEP IT HOLY
5. HONOUR THY FATHER AND THY MOTHER
6. THOU SHALT NOT KILL
7. THOU SHALT NOT COMMIT ADULTERY
8. THOU SHALT NOT STEAL
9. THOU SHALT NOT BEAR FALSE WITNESS
10. THOU SHALT NOT COVET

THOU SHALT HAVE NO OTHER GODS BEFORE ME
'Thou shalt have no other Gods before me.'[167]

God created this world for us, his children. He has provided for us all that we needed to be happy. This earth was created for our benefit. Here we would come to continue our schooling. We could not progress any further in the pre-existence. We desired to be like our Heavenly Parents. They have a body of flesh and bones. We didn't. In order for us be like them, we had to come to this earth to gain a body. We would be tested and tried in all things that our Father commanded to see if we would obey. However, the veil would be drawn over our eyes so that we would rely on faith. In this way, our Father would prepare us to return home to dwell with Him in the Heavenly courts on high. From the oceans and seas to the forests and mountains, there is nothing that was left undone for our happiness. Trees to shade us from the heat of the sun, flowers and plants, and animals of all varieties were created for us. We would be leaving a beautiful home to come to school. Our Father wanted everything to be perfect. We would not remember where we had been before we came to earth, but He wanted us to come to a place where we would be surrounded by beauty.

Everything belongs to the Lord. He created the earth and everything that is in it.

O MY FATHER
O my Father, thou that dwellest in the high and glorious place,
When shall I regain thy presence and again behold thy face?
In thy holy habitation, did my spirit once reside?
In my first primeval childhood, was I nurtured near thy side?

For a wise and glorious purpose Thou has placed my here on earth
And withheld the recollection of my former friends and birth;
Yet oft-times a secret something whispered "You're a stranger here,"

And I felt that I had wandered from a more exalted sphere.
I had learned to call thee Father, thru thy Spirit from on high,

---
167 Mosiah 12:35; Exodus 20:3

But, until the key of knowledge was restored, I knew not why.
In the heav'ns are parents single? No, the thought makes reason stare!
Truth is reason; truth eternal tells me I've a mother there.

When I leave this frail existence, when I lay this mortal by,
Father, Mother, may I meet you in your royal courts on high?
Then, at length, when I've completed all you sent me forth to do,
With your mutual approbation let me come and dwell with you.[168]

THOU SHALT NOT MAKE UNTO THEE ANY GRAVEN IMAGE

'Thou shalt not make unto thee any graven image, or any likeness of any thing in heaven above, or things which are in the earth beneath, or that is in the water under the earth.

'And again: Thou shalt not bow down thyself unto them, nor serve them; for I the Lord thy God am a jealous God, visiting the iniquities of the fathers upon the children unto the third and fourth generations of them that hate me.'[169]

As we think about the meaning of graven image, the first thought which enters our mind is that of idol worship, objects which were made to represent various gods for various seasons and activities. When Moses led the people of Israel out of bondage from Egypt, they took with them all manner of spoil; gold, silver, precious metals and material. When Moses left the children of Israel to go up into the mountain to speak with the Lord, they became restless.

Having been exposed to the wickedness of their Egyptian taskmasters, they demanded that Aaron allow them to build an idol. After much pressure, Aaron relented and helped them. They then gathered all their treasures into a vast melting pot. After much labour, they finally had their idol, a golden calf. They danced around the idol, with merriment and drunkenness. It was to this revelry that Moses came as he made his way down from the mountain.

---

168 *Hymns of the Church of Jesus Christ of Latter-day Saints*, 1985 Edition, p. 292; Romans 8:16-17; Acts 17:28-29 (22-31)
169 *Mosiah 12:36; Mosiah 13:12-13; Exodus 20:4-5*

Are we like the children of Israel? Do we worship golden idols? Definitely not, you say. But are you sure?

Do we pay an honest tithe, or do we make light of our obligations to the Lord? Do we say that we can't afford to pay our tithing? Do we reason that we need the money to purchase a new car, or house? Do we plan and fret about new furniture or other material items. Do we make excuses that the money is needed for schooling, bills, or perhaps a boat or other recreational item? Do we use recreation on Sundays as an excuse for not attending to our church duties and attending our meetings? Wait a minute, you say! That is not idol worship. When we put our own wants and desires before that of the Lord's, it is indeed idol worship. The Lord has promised that if we put the Lord first and fulfil our obligations, He will bless us. How then can we not have faith to do those things that the Lord has commanded? He will always bless us as we do as we are asked.

THOU SHALT NOT TAKE THE NAME OF THE LORD THY GOD IN VAIN

'Thou shalt not take the name of the Lord thy God in vain; for the Lord will not hold him guiltless that taketh his name in vain.'[170]

'Wherefore, let all men beware how they take my name in their lips-
'For behold, verily I say, that many there be who are under this condemnation, who use the name of the Lord, and use it in vain, having not authority.

'Remember that, that which cometh from above is sacred, and must be spoken with care, and by constraint of the Spirit; and in this there is no condemnation, and ye receive the Spirit through prayer; wherefore, without this there remaineth condemnation.

'These things remain to overcome through patience, that such may receive a more exceeding and eternal weight of glory, otherwise, a greater condemnation. Amen.'[171]

How do we take the name of the Lord in vain? To be profane is to use not sacred language or language devoted to sacred purposes; language not possessing any peculiar sanctity; secular; it is to be irreverent toward God or

---

170 *Mosiah 13:15; Exodus 20:7*
171 *D&C 63:61-62, 64, 65*

holy things; it is speaking or spoken, acting or acted in contempt of sacred things or implying it; blasphemous; polluted; to desecrate the name of God, or the Sabbath; to put to a wrong use; to employ basely or unworthily.[172]

When one uses contemptuous speech towards God or something that stands in a sacred relation toward God, such as his temple, his law, or his prophet, one is being blasphemous. On several occasions, the Lord was charged by the Jews as being blasphemous because he claimed that he was the Son of God and that he had the right to forgive sins. He said that they would see him 'sitting at the right hand of power, and coming in the clouds of heaven.' Had Jesus not been who he actually said he was, then these charges would have been true. One of the charges brought against Jesus was one of blasphemy against the temple. The charge was brought by false witnesses.

During the time of Jesus, the penalty for wilful and intentional blasphemy was death by stoning.

Blasphemy against the Holy Ghost is wilfully denying the Christ after having received a perfect knowledge of him from the Holy Ghost. There is no forgiveness from this sin, either in this life or the life to come.

REMEMBER THE SABBATH DAY TO KEEP IT HOLY

'Remember the Sabbath day, to keep it holy.

'Six days shalt thou labor, and do all thy work;

'But the seventh day, the Sabbath of the Lord thy God, thou shalt not do any work, thou, nor thy son, nor thy daughter, thy man-servant, nor thy maid-servant, nor thy cattle, nor thy stranger that is within thy gates.

'For in six days the Lord made heaven and earth, and the sea, and all that in them is; wherefore the Lord blessed the Sabbath day, and hallowed it.'[173]

> 'AND THAT THOU MAYEST MORE FULLY KEEP THYSELF UNSPOTTED FROM THE WORLD, THOU SHALT GO TO THE HOUSE OF PRAYER AND OFFER UP THY SACRAMENTS UPON MY HOLY DAY.

---

172 *The New Webster Encyclopedic Dictionary, 1980 Edition, Avenel Books, New York, p. 663*
173 *Mosiah 13:16-19; Exodus 20:9-11*

'FOR VERILY THIS IS A DAY APPOINTED UNTO YOU TO REST FROM YOUR LABOURS AND TO PAY THY DEVOTIONS UNTO THE MOST HIGH;

'NEVERTHELESS THY VOWS SHALL BE OFFERED UP IN RIGHTEOUSNESS ON ALL DAYS AND AT ALL TIMES;

'BUT REMEMBER THAT ON THIS, THE LORD'S DAY, THOU SHALT OFFER THINE OBLATIONS AND THY SACRAMENTS UNTO THE MOST HIGH, CONFESSING THY SINS UNTO THY BRETHREN, AND BEFORE THE LORD.[174]

Why is the Sabbath day so important to the Lord? The Lord created the earth in six days. On the seventh day, the Lord rested, and saw that everything which he had made was good. He blessed and sanctified the seventh day.[175]

'And I, God, blessed the seventh day, and sanctified it; because that in it I had rested from all my work which I, God, had created and made.'[176]

The Sabbath day provides us with rest for mind and body, with opportunities for worship. It also gives us time to give loving service to our fellowman. By using the Sabbath wisely to rest, worship and serve, we can receive temporal blessings and receive great spiritual strength.

From the beginning, the Sabbath day has been holy. From Adam and Eve to now, we are commanded to keep the Sabbath day holy. Is it only because it is the Lord's Day? Or is it for us as well? In keeping the commandment of keeping the Sabbath day holy we are bringing blessings upon ourselves. The Lord loves us and wishes to bless us. But we can only receive those blessings if we obey the laws upon which they are predicated.[177]

---

174 D&C 59:9-12
175 Moses 3:2-3
176 Moses 3:3
177 D&C 130:20-21

TEN COMMANDMENTS

Just as the Lord laboured six days to create this earth and everything that is upon it, so do we labour in earning a livelihood. For six days we think about what **we** want and need. We plan and work. For the most part, our hearts and minds are not focused on the Lord. Therefore, the Lord has set aside one day where we may rest from our labours. On that day, we are to worship him with singleness of heart and purpose. Is that too much to ask? I think not. When we obey the commandments, we are blessed. There is no way we can ever give back as much as we are given.

When we fast, we are to do so with thanksgiving and cheerful hearts. Our countenances are to be cheerful.[178]

Our meals should be simple, so as not to detract from the spirit of hungering and thirsting after righteousness. We are to confess our sins to the Lord and when appropriate, to the Bishop so as to become in tune with the Lord.

As we do these things, we are promised that the 'fullness of the earth' will be ours; 'the beasts of the field and the fowls of the air, and that which climbeth upon the trees and walketh upon the earth.

'Yea, and the herb, and the good things which come of the earth, whether for food or for raiment, or for houses, or for barns, or for orchards, or for gardens, or for vineyards. . . .

'And it pleaseth God that he hath given all these things unto man; for unto this end were they made to be used, with judgment, not to excess, neither by extortion.

> 'AND IN NOTHING DOTH MAN OFFEND GOD,
> OR AGAINST NONE IS HIS WRATH KINDLED, SAVE THOSE
> WHO CONFESS NOT HIS HAND IN ALL THINGS, AND OBEY
> HIS COMMANDMENTS.
>
> 'BUT LEARN THAT HE WHO DOETH THE WORKS OF RIGHTEOUSNESS SHALL RECEIVE HIS REWARD, EVEN PEACE IN THIS WORLD, AND ETERNAL LIFE IN THE WORLD TO COME.

---

178 *Matthew 6:16-18*

'I, THE LORD HAVE SPOKEN IT, AND THE SPIRIT BEARETH RECORD. AMEN.'[179]

Jesus was resurrected on Sunday, the first day of the week. This is another reason to keep the Sabbath holy; to help us to remember the atonement that Jesus Christ wrought for us.

The Sabbath was made to benefit man. How was this to be accomplished? What is the purpose of the Sabbath? We are not only to rest from our daily labours, but we are to direct our thoughts and actions towards God. It is a sacred day to be spent in worship and reverence and in doing the Lord's work. As our minds are freed from everyday activities, we are able to ponder spiritual matters. We can renew our covenants with the Lord and feed our souls upon things of the Spirit. Thus, just to 'sleep away the day', is not the purpose of the Sabbath.

President Spencer W. Kimball said: "The Sabbath is a holy day in which to do worthy and holy things. Abstinence from work and recreation is important but insufficient. The Sabbath calls for constructive thoughts and acts, and if one merely lounges about doing nothing on the Sabbath, he is breaking it."

We first need to sanctify the Sabbath. The Lord has commanded the Saints to go to the house of prayer and offer up their sacraments, rest from their labours, and pay their devotions to the most High. We need to attend to all of our church meetings. To keep the Sabbath holy, we need a balance of rest, worship and service.

To observe the Sabbath, one will be on his knees in prayer, preparing lessons, studying the gospel, meditating, visiting the ill, and distressed, writing letters to missionaries, taking a nap, reading wholesome material and attending all the meetings of that day at which he is expected.

How do we know if activities are appropriate on the Sabbath? First of all, we need to ask ourselves if the activity will bring us closer to our Heavenly Father.

---

179 D&C 59:9-24

TEN COMMANDMENTS

Following is a list of some appropriate activities for the Sabbath:
1. Attending church meetings
2. Reading the scriptures and the words of our church leaders
3. Visiting the sick, aged and our loved ones
4. Listening to uplifting music and singing hymns
5. Praying to our Heavenly Father with praise and thanksgiving
6. Performing church services that we have been assigned to do
7. Preparing genealogical records and personal and family histories
8. Telling faith promoting stories and bearing our testimony to family members, and sharing spiritual experiences with them
9. Writing letters to loved ones
10. Writing letters to missionaries
11. Fasting with a purpose
12. Sharing time with children and others in the home

There are many activities which are appropriate for honouring the Sabbath and keeping it holy. If we have any doubts or questions about an activity, we should ask ourselves, "Will it uplift and inspire me? Will it be something that the Saviour would do?" If we can honestly say yes to these questions, then it probably would be safe to assume that the activity is appropriate.

Following are some more appropriate things to do on the Sabbath:
1. Memorize an Article of Faith or other scriptures
2. Correlate the week's activities so that you may be able to support your family in their important events
3. Write in your journal
4. Make a tape for a friend or family member who is away
5. If you have younger children, have a puppet show telling the stories from the scriptures
6. Listen to an opera and study its history and story
7. Prepare a talk
8. Write an old school chum and renew that acquaintance
9. Take a walk and admire God's creations
10. Thank your Heavenly Father for all His blessings in your life

11. Set new goals for yourself and adapt a plan for working on them daily
12. Help each of your children start their own personal journals
13. Complete your four generation sheets
14. Read a conference talk and apply it to your life
15. Write a story
16. Teach your family a new song

As you can see, from the above lists, there are many things that we can do on Sunday to keep it a holy day. I'm sure that you will be able to add many more thoughts and ideas to the lists.

In our work or livelihood, it is sometimes necessary to work on the Sabbath. If it is at all possible, we should try to avoid it. When it is absolutely necessary, we can still maintain the spirit of Sabbath worship in our hearts to some extent. By keeping a prayer in our hearts, we are helping to maintain the spirit of the Sabbath.

As we honour the Sabbath day in a righteous manner, we will receive great spiritual and temporal blessings. The Lord has said that, **"if we keep the Sabbath day with thanksgiving and cheerful hearts, we will be full of joy."** He has promised that **"the fullness of the earth is yours...Whether for food or for raiment, or for houses or for barns, or for orchards, or for gardens, or for vineyards; yea, all things which come of the earth, in the season thereof, are made for the benefit and use of man, both to please the eye and to gladden the heart; yea for food and for raiment, for taste and for smell, to strengthen the body and enliven the soul."**

HONOUR THY FATHER AND THY MOTHER

'Honour thy father and thy mother, that thy days may be long upon the land which the Lord thy God giveth thee.'[180]

The fifth commandment establishes very clearly the importance of the family in the sight of the Lord. Proper family relationships constitute one of the ten fundamental principles of law, both in this world and in the world to come. In obedience to this law, the family unit and all other parts of society remain stable and healthy. In this day, which was prophesied to be an age

---
180 *Mosiah 13:20; Exodus 20:12*

when people are "disobedient to parents" and "without natural affection", one needs to contemplate seriously the implications of the commandment to honour father and mother and the promise included with it.

When parents are righteous, God-fearing people, children have little problem understanding the commandment to honour them, although they may have difficulty doing it. When parents are not righteous, however, two questions about this commandment are often raised. First, is one still required to honour unrighteous parents and second, does honour imply obedience if the parents ask for unrighteous behaviour?

First of all, though in most cases honour includes obedience, the two are not the same. To **honour** means "to regard or treat with honour; to revere; to respect; to reverence; to bestow honour upon; to elevate in rank or station; to exalt; Esteem paid to worth; high estimation; reverence; veneration; any mark of respect or estimation by words or actions; dignity; exalted rank or place; distinction; reputation; good name; a nice sense of what is right, just and true;..."[181] bring honour to or to have an attitude of honouring."

Obedience means "to follow direction or example." Paul, in the New Testament, said, "Children, obey your parents **in the Lord:** for this is right."[182] Immediately afterward he adds, "Honour thy father and thy mother."[183] He added no qualifying statement, describing it only as the "first commandment with promise."[184] To obey one's parents in the Lord means to obey them in righteousness. Anytime a child lives righteously he brings honour to his parents, whether those parents are themselves righteous or wicked. The opposite is also true. Anytime a child lives wickedly he brings shame to his parents, whether or not the parents are righteous. Honouring parents may not always imply obeying them. In those cases where parents may ask for or encourage unrighteous behaviour in their children, the individual brings dishonour to his parents if he obeys them.

---

181 *The New Webster Encyclopedic Dictionary, 1980 Edition, Avenel Books, New York, p. 408*
182 *Ephesians 6:10*
183 *Ephesians 6:2*
184 *Ephesians 6:2*

There is no qualification added to the commandment to honour one's father and mother. To understand why, the ultimate model of the parent-child relationship must be examined. Only in the relationship of man's heavenly parents to their children is the perfect model of parenting. The Gods, of course are perfect models, deserving honour. If they were the only parents with whom one had to deal, it would be an easy matter to honour them.

In their infinite wisdom, they have chosen to have mortal parents stand as their representatives in the bringing forth and rearing of children. In other words, parents stand as direct representatives of God in mortality, and therefore, like priesthood offices, the office of parent requires honour. Parents are obligated to strive to be as much like God as possible. Serious consequences will follow those parents who fail to teach their children what He would teach them if He were here.[185]

No one is perfect, and the Lord knows this. Those who do not fulfil their office and calling as parents, become accountable to the Lord. This does not mean that the child is not obligated to honour his parents.

To help us understand why this is so, let us use the priesthood as an example. While no priesthood holder can perfectly perform his duties and obligations, his calling and office are to be honoured in spite of the individual's imperfections. A righteous and capable man also brings honour to himself, but even if an individual were to be released because of unworthiness, one does not stop honouring the office which he held.

A parent may fail miserably in his office and calling, even to the point where a child cannot follow his example any longer, but the child always has the obligation to honour the parent because of the parent's standing as a representative of God.

"Children come into mortality with the inborn requirement, planted in their souls by that very Being who gave them birth as spirits, to honour their parents and to obey their counsel in righteousness."[186]

---

185 *D&C 68:25-31; D&C 93:39-44*
186 *Elder Bruce R. McConkie, Doctrinal New Testament Commentary, 2:521*

THOU SHALT NOT KILL

'Thou shalt not kill.'[187]

'...he that kills shall not have forgiveness in this world, nor in the world to come.

'And again, I say, thou shalt not kill; but he that killeth shall die.'[188]

'The blasphemy against the Holy Ghost, which shall not be forgiven in the world nor out of the world, is in that ye commit murder wherein ye shed innocent blood, and assent unto my death, after ye have received my new and everlasting covenant, saith the Lord God; and he that abideth not this law can in nowise enter into my glory, but shall be damned, saith the Lord.'[189]

Why is the penalty so great when someone takes another's life? The individual that is killed cannot work out their own salvation. They cannot repent of sins they have committed. They will not have the opportunity to accept the gospel in this life and by so doing, repent of their iniquities, and turn with full purpose of heart to the Lord. They will have the opportunity in the spirit world to hear the gospel, but they will not enjoy the attending blessings when they accept. They will have to wait for someone else to do their work for them in the temple before they can continue their progression.

Generations that would have been born to that individual will no longer have come through that particular lineage can no longer be. They will need to be assigned to a different line.

'...If ye deny the Holy Ghost when it once has had place in you, and ye know that ye deny it, behold, this is a sin which is unpardonable; yea, and whosoever murdereth against the light and knowledge of God, it is not easy for him to obtain forgiveness; yea, I say unto you,... that it is not easy for him to obtain forgiveness.'[190]

---

187 *Mosiah 13:21; Exodus 20:13*
188 *D&C 42:18-19*
189 *D&C 132:27*
190 *Alma 39:6*

THOU SHALT NOT COMMIT ADULTERY

'Thou shalt not commit adultery.'[191]

'Know ye not that these things are an abomination in the sight of the Lord; yea, most abominable above all sins save it be the shedding of innocent blood or denying the Holy Ghost?'[192]

'...Whosoever looketh on a woman, to lust after her, hath committed adultery already in his heart.'[193]

What constitutes adultery? As defined in the dictionary, adultery is when a man and a woman have unlawful association intimately; that is, outside the bonds of marriage. The individuals can be unmarried or they can be with persons who are not his or her husband or wife.

Marriage to those who are closely related is also forbidden by the Lord. What are those relationships? Fathers and mothers, sisters, brothers, aunts, uncles, daughter-in-laws, son-in-laws, mothers and daughters, a wife's sister. (If a man divorces his wife to be with her sister while she is living is also forbidden.) As we can see, these are close relationships. The majority of today's society sees nothing wrong with committing these abominations. However, we need to hold fast to the iron rod which the Lord has given us to lead us back into the presence of the Lord.[194]

'Thou shalt not lie carnally with thy neighbour's wife, to defile thyself with her.

'Thou shalt not lie with mankind, as with womankind: it is an abomination.

'Neither shalt thou lie with any beast to defile thyself therewith: neither shall any woman stand before a beast to lie down thereto...

'Therefore, ye shall keep mine ordinance, that ye commit not any one of these abominable customs...and that ye defile not yourselves therein: I am the Lord your God.'[195]

---

191 *Mosiah 13:22; Exodus 20:14*
192 *Alma 39:5*
193 *3 Nephi 12:28*
194 *1 Nephi 8*
195 *Leviticus 18:20-23, 30*

Sexual immorality of any type, whether it is adultery, fornication, homosexuality, petting or marriage to close kin, is an abomination in the sight of the Lord. It is iniquity. It is wickedness. It will not help us to achieve the crown of glory with which the Lord desires to give us. It will only bring heartache and sorrow. If these sins are not repented of, we will lose the opportunity to dwell with the Lord. Wickedness was never happiness. We can choose the path we will follow.

'Therefore, cheer up your hearts, and remember that ye are free to act for yourselves - to choose the way of everlasting death or the way of eternal life.'[196]

Why is petting so wrong? It can arouse appetites and passions which are to be used within the sacred bonds of marriage. Once these passions are aroused, it is very difficult to subdue them. Thoughts of propriety are left behind.

Petting can lead to other more serious acts of immorality such as adultery or fornication. We must shun the very appearance of evil. We must not let Satan get even a toehold upon our resolve to live and obey the commandments. Our Heavenly Father gives us the commandments, not to bind us down, but to free us. The commandments are the path towards eternal life and exaltation.

"Do not be misled by Satan's lies," President Benson has warned. "There is no lasting happiness in immorality. There is no joy to be found in breaking the law of chastity. Just the opposite is true. There may be momentary pleasure. For a time it may seem like everything is wonderful. But quickly the relationship will sour. Guilt and shame set in. We become fearful that our sins will be discovered. We must sneak and hide, lie and cheat. Love begins to die. Bitterness, jealousy, anger, and even hate begin to grow. All of these are the natural results of sin and transgression.

"On the other hand, when we obey the law of chastity and keep ourselves morally clean, we will experience the blessings of increased love and peace, greater trust and respect for our marital partners, deeper commitment to each other, and therefore a deep and significant sense of joy and happiness.

---

196 *2 Nephi* 10:23

"We must not be misled into thinking these sins are minor or that consequences are not that serious."[197]

It is better to prepare and prevent rather than to repair and repent. As the following steps to preparation for prevention are followed, heartache and unhappiness can be avoided.

1. Decide now is the time to be chaste. Once you are faced with the situation, it may be very difficult to make the decision.

2. Control your thoughts. What you think about is what you will do. Therefore, put all unrighteous thoughts out of your mind. Think of the words to a hymn and hum or sing it, and command Satan to leave in the name of Jesus Christ.

3. Pray for the power to be able to resist temptation.

4. Avoid flirtations of any kind if you are married. It is dangerous. Satan will use the act of flirtatiousness to slowly tear down the defence of each. The other person may become more desirous than your partner. You will not see the flaws of the other individual but only that he or she seems to be everything that your partner is not.

5. Avoid being alone with members of the opposite sex if you are married, whenever possible. This will not give Satan the opening he desires to weaken and break your resolves to do what is right. He is very deceitful. Satan often lures people into immorality by playing upon their basic needs. He promises pleasure, happiness and fulfilment. However, it is a deception. It brings only pain, guilt, shame and unhappiness.

6. For single and dating individuals, plan activities which are positive and constructive. These activities should be such that you are not put into a position that there is nothing to do but share physical affection.

If you have strayed and violated from the Law of Chastity, is there a road back? Indeed there is. The Lord has provided that road through the principle of repentance. To return to moral purity, the following guidelines will help.

1. Once you have made the decision to repent, flee from any situation which you are in that is causing you to sin or that you may sin.

---

197 *The Law of Chastity*, p.5

2. Pray to the Lord for the power to overcome the temptations.

3. For serious sins such as adultery, go to your Bishop. He will not condemn you. He will help you on your pathway back into full fellowship with the Lord.

4. Study the scriptures that you will more fully know of the promises of the Lord. He will fill you with the power of the Holy Ghost to help you overcome.

5. Through proper repentance, you may once again become clean and pure before the Lord and worthy of all the blessings which He desires to bestow upon you.

For those who pay the price required by true repentance, the promise is sure. You can be clean again. The despair can be lifted. The sweet peace of forgiveness will flow once again into your lives.[198]

"Our Heavenly Father desires nothing for us but to be happy. He tells us only those things that will bring us joy. And one of the surest principles given by God to help us find that joy is the law of chastity. I pray with all my heart that you will consider most solemnly the joyful consequences of keeping this law, and the tragic consequences of violating it."[199]

THOU SHALT NOT STEAL

'Thou shalt not steal.'[200]

In the Webster's dictionary, stealing is defined as: to take and carry away feloniously; to take clandestinely without right or leave; to gain or win by address or gradual and imperceptible means; to perform secretly; to try to accomplish clandestinely; to gain an advantage over stealthily. To practice or be guilty of theft; to withdraw or pass privily; to slip unperceived; to go or come furtively, the act of one who steals.[201]

There are many areas other than taking something which does not belong to them, which come under the definition of stealing. When a family or group of individuals attends an event where pricing is divided amongst

---

198 Isaiah 1:18; D&C 58:42
199 The Law of Chastity, p. 7
200 Mosiah 13:22; Exodus 20:15
201 The New Webster Encyclopedic Dictionary, 1980 Edition, Avenel Books, New York, p. 820

different age groups, and certain individuals are passed off as being younger than they actually are to obtain entrance, is considered not only to be dishonest, but to steal. '...Satan did stir up the hearts of the more part of the Nephites, insomuch that they did unite with those bands of robbers, and did enter into their covenants and their oaths, that they would protect and preserve one another in whatsoever difficult circumstances they should be placed, that they should not suffer for their murders, and their plunderings, and their stealings.

'And thus they might murder, and plunder, and steal, and commit whoredoms and all manner of wickedness, contrary to the laws of their country and also the laws of their God.

'Yea, it is that same being who put it into the heart to still carry on the work of darkness, and of secret murder; and he has brought it forth from the beginning of man even down to this time.

'And behold, it is he who is the author of all sin. And behold, he doth carry on his works of darkness and secret murder, and doth hand down their plots, and their oaths and their covenants, and their plans of awful wickedness, from generation to generation according as he can get hold upon the hearts of the children of men.'[202]

As people harden their hearts to the promptings of the Holy Ghost, the Spirit of the Lord withdraws because of the wickedness of the people. They are then left alone.

THOU SHALT NOT BEAR FALSE WITNESS

'Thou shalt not bear false witness.'[203]

What does 'false witness' mean? Simply put, it means to lie. What then is a lie? It is to utter a falsehood with an intention to deceive; to knowingly utter untruth. A falsehood uttered for the purpose of deception; an intentional violation of truth also constitutes a lie.

'And it shall come to pass that all lyings, and deceivings, and envyings, and strifes, and priestcrafts, and whoredoms, shall be done away.

---

202 *Helaman 6:21, 23, 29, 30*
203 *Mosiah 13:23; Exodus 20:16*

'For it shall come to pass, saith the Father, that at that day whosoever will not repent and come unto my Beloved Son, them will I cut off from among my people...'[204]

'...there shall be murders, and robbing, and lying and deceivings, and whoredoms, and all manner of abominations; when there shall be many who will say, Do this, or do that, and it mattereth not, for the Lord will uphold such at the last day. But wo unto such, for they are in the gall of bitterness and in the bonds of iniquity.'[205]

'Satan stirreth them up, that he may lead their souls to destruction.

'And thus he has laid a cunning plan, thinking to destroy the work of God; but I will require this at their hands, and it shall turn to their shame and condemnation in the Day of Judgment.

'Yea, he stirreth up their hearts to anger against this work. Yea, he saith unto them: Deceive and lie in wait to catch, that ye may destroy; behold, this is no harm. And thus he flattereth them, and telleth them that it is no sin to lie that they may catch a man in a lie, that they may destroy him.

'And thus he flattereth them, and leadeth them along until he draggeth their souls down to hell; and thus he causeth them to catch themselves in their own snare.

'And thus he goeth up and down, to and fro in the earth, seeking to destroy the souls of men.'[206]

Gossiping and spreading idle and false rumours about a person is another form of bearing false witness. Those who testify wilfully and falsely are liars and perjurers. When the Jews were seeking the life of Jesus Christ, many false witnesses came forward to testify falsely against him.[207]

To claim as truth a false system for salvation, to testify falsely about the truths of salvation, are also bearing false witness. The Lord has always had witnesses as he has established his kingdom here upon the earth. For example, Apostles and Seventies are called as special witnesses of the name

---

204   *3 Nephi 21:19-20*
205   *Mormon 8:31*
206   *D&C 10:22-27*
207   *Mark 14:53-65*

of Christ. At baptism, every member of the Church has taken upon them the sacred obligation to be a witness of Jesus Christ and the restoration of the gospel.

However, those who teach false doctrines are bearing false witness, as well as those who profess that salvation is found in some system other than the one which was ordained by the Lord from the beginning for the salvation and exaltation of mankind. All those who bear false witnesses will be rewarded according to their deeds.

THOU SHALT NOT COVET

'Thou shalt not covet thy neighbor's house; thou shalt not covet thy neighbor's wife, nor his man-servant, nor his maid-servant, nor his ox, nor his ass, nor anything that is thy neighbour's.'[208]

'See that ye love one another; cease to be covetous; learn to impart one to another as the gospel requires.'[209]

What does it mean to covet? The dictionary defines covet as; 'to desire inordinately; to desire with a greedy or envious longing; to long for; to hanker after; to have or indulge inordinate desire.'[210]

If we covet, we plan to steal, to lie, to cheat. By coveting, we are planning on breaking other commandments as well. By coveting another person's spouse, we are also planning on committing adultery.

To covet is more serious than most people are aware. It is the spring point from which many more commandments can be broken. To repent of coveting is to also repent of lying, stealing, cheating, adultery, and other sins which come from the 'simple' act of desiring to covet.

---

208 *Mosiah 13:24; Exodus 20:17*
209 *D&C 88:123*
210 *The New Webster Encyclopedic Dictionary, 1980 Edition, Avenel Books, New York, p. 198*

CHAPTER TWELVE

Compassion

"BEAR YE ONE ANOTHER'S BURDENS, AND SO FULFILL THE LAW OF CHRIST."[211]

"...REMEMBER THEM WHICH SUFFER ADVERSITY..."[212]

"BUT THOU, O LORD. ART A GOD FULL OF COMPASSION, AND GRACIOUS, LONG-SUFFERING, AND PLENTEOUS IN MERCY AND TRUTH."[213]

In the dictionary, compassion is defined as suffering with another; sympathy; pity; commiseration; an act of mercy.[214]

Mercy is defined as that benevolence, mildness, or tenderness of heart which disposes a person to overlook injuries; the disposition that tempers justice and leads to the infliction of a lighter punishment than law or justice will warrant; clemency; an act or exercise of mercy or favour; a blessing; compassion; pity; unrestrained exercise of will or authority; often in the phrase 'at one's mercy' that is, completely in one's power.[215]

The mercy seat was the golden covering of the Ark of the Covenant in the Holy of Holies.[216] It was the place of the manifestation of God's glory and his meeting place with his people[217] and was regarded as the Throne of

---

211 *Galations 6:2*
212 *Hebrews 13:3*
213 *Psalms 86:15*
214 *The New Webster Encyclopedic Dictionary, 1980 Edition, Avenel Books, New York, p. 168*
215 *The New Webster Encyclopedic Dictionary, 1980 Edition, Avenel Books, New York, p. 529*
216 *Bible Dictionary, King James Version, 1988 Edition, The Church of Jesus Christ of Latter-day Saints, p. 731*
217 *Exodus 25:22; Leviticus 16:2; Numbers 7:89*

God.[218] The mercy seat is also described as the place of mercy or forgiveness; the covering of the Ark of the Covenant among the Jews.[219]

To be merciful is to be full of mercy; unwilling to punish others for injuries done to us; to be compassionate; tender and not cruel.[220]

Charity is the good affection, love or tenderness which men should feel toward their fellow beings and which should induce them to do good to and think favourably of others; benevolence; liberality in thinking or judging; liberality in giving to the poor; any act of kindness or benevolence.[221] This is charity as defined in the dictionary. The Lord expounds on this, making it clear to us what exactly it is.

'BUT CHARITY IS THE PURE LOVE OF CHRIST AND IT ENDURETH FOREVER; AND WHOSO IS FOUND POSSESSED OF IT AT THE LAST DAY, IT SHALL BE WELL WITH HIM.'[222]

As we can see, compassion, mercy and charity overlap. We cannot accomplish one without the others. In this world, there are opportunities all around for giving compassion and service. There are the destitute and the poor. There are the sick and the hungry. There are those who are in hospitals and in prisons. We can feed the poor, visit the sick and comfort the weary.

'...Inasmuch as ye have done it unto one of the least of these my brethren, ye have done it unto me.'[223]

'And behold, I tell you these things that ye may learn wisdom; that ye may learn that when ye are in the service of your fellow beings ye are only in the service of your God.' [224]

---

218 *Exodus 30:6; Numbers 7:89*
219 *The New Webster Encyclopedic Dictionary, 1980 Edition, Avenel Books, New York, p. 529*
220 *The New Webster Encyclopedic Dictionary, 1980 Edition, Avenel Books, New York, p. 529*
221 *The New Webster Encyclopedic Dictionary, 1980 Edition, Avenel Books, New York, p. 138*
222 *Moroni 7:47*
223 *Matthew 25:40*
224 *Mosiah 2:17*

COMPASSION

'And remember in all things the poor and the needy, the sick and the afflicted, for he that doeth not these things, the same is not my disciple.'[225]

As we look around us, in our families and in our communities, we will find many areas in which we can be of service to our fellowman. The world is filled with people who have many needs. From taking a plate of cookies or homemade bread to an elderly person, shovelling sidewalks in the winter, mowing lawns in the summer, helping with small children, visiting the sick in the hospital or their homes, all are children of our Heavenly Father. He loves them just as He loves us. He wants them too, to return home. Oftentimes they do not know what their potential can be. They feel discouragement, fear and loneliness.

When we help them in their needs, we are serving and we are growing in our understanding. We are becoming what God wants us to be. We are learning the attributes to reach our potential. We are becoming better individuals and our families are becoming closer. As we reach out to those around us, we learn compassion, charity and mercy. We understand the feelings that they have and we empathize with them. We feel of their joys and their sorrows. We help them in their activities. As we do so, we are growing and learning and becoming better individuals.

A POOR WAYFARING MAN OF GRIEF

A poor wayfaring man of grief
Hath often crossed me on my way
Who sued so humbly for relief
That I could never answer nay.
I had not pow'r to ask his name,
Where-to he went, or whence he came;
Yet there was something in his eye
That won my love; I knew not why.

Once, when my scanty meal was spread,
He entered; not a word he spake,
Just perishing for want of bread.

---
225 D&C 52:40

BEYOND THE SUNSET

I gave him all; He blessed it brake,
And ate, but gave me part again.
Mine was an angel's portion then,
For while I fed with eager haste,
The crust was manna to my taste.

I spied him where a fountain burst
Clear from the rock; his strength was gone.
The heedless water mocked his thirst;
He heard it, saw it hurrying on.
I ran and raised the suffer'rer up;
Thrice from the stream he drained my cup,
Dipped and returned it running o'er;
I drank and never thirsted more.

Twas night; the floods were out; it blew
A winter hurricane aloof.
I heard his voice abroad and flew
To bid him welcome to my roof.
I warmed and clothed and cheered my guest
And laid him on my couch to rest;
Then made the earth my bed, and seemed
In Eden's garden while I dreamed.

Stripped, wounded, beaten, nigh to death,
I found him by the highway side.
I roused his pulse, brought back his breath,
Revived his spirit, and supplied
Wine, oil, refreshment—he was healed.
I had myself a wound concealed,
But from that hour forgot the smart,
And peace bound up my broken heart.

COMPASSION

In prison I saw him next, condemned
To meet a traitor's doom at morn.
The tide of lying tongues I stemmed,
And honoured him mid shame and scorn.
My friendship's utmost zeal to try,
He asked if I for him would die.
The flesh was weak; my blood ran chill,
But my free spirit cried, "I will!"

Then in a moment to my view
The stranger started from disguise.
The tokens in his hands I knew;
The Saviour stood before my eyes.
He spake, and my poor name he named,
"Of me thou has not been ashamed.
Theses deeds shall thy memorial be;
Fear not, thou didst them unto me."[226]

"Then shall the King say unto them on his right hand, Come ye blessed of my Father, inherit the kingdom prepared for you from the foundation of the world."[227]

"Verily I say unto you, Inasmuch as ye have done it unto one of the least of these my brethren, ye have done it unto me."[228]

---

226 *Hymns of the Church of Jesus Christ of Latter-Day Saints, Text James Montgomery, 1771-1854, Music: George Coles, 1792-1858, p.29; Matthew 25:31-40; Mosiah 2:17 (Hymn beloved of the Prophet Joseph Smith)*
227 *Matthew 25:34*
228 *Matthew 25:40*

CHAPTER THIRTEEN

Contention

'FOR VERILY, VERILY I SAY UNTO YOU, HE THAT HATH THE SPIRIT OF CONTENTION IS NOT OF ME, BUT IS OF THE DEVIL, WHO IS THE FATHER OF CONTENTION, AND HE STIRRETH UP THE HEARTS OF MEN TO CONTEND WITH ANGER, ONE WITH ANOTHER.'[229]

This is Satan's domain, this earth. He thinks that he is god. Because he was kicked out of heaven, and has no chance for happiness, he does not want us to be happy either. He wants us to be miserable like himself.

He tells us lies to do things that we know are wrong. He makes us think that 'just a little' won't do any harm. He leads us quietly down the path to destruction. Each thread of wrong choice we make, binds us ever tighter until we are fully in the clutches of Satan.

Contention, as defined in the dictionary is to 'struggle, or strife; strife in words; debate; angry contest; quarrel; controversy; competition; emulation.[230] When we argue, we cannot have the Spirit of the Lord. Where there is contention, the spirit of the Lord flees. This is what Satan desires. There can be no peace and harmony with Satan. He does not want us to return home. He does not want us to become everything that God has planned for us to be and become.

Satan uses contention to make us believe that what we want is acceptable and no one else is. He wants us to argue and fight, to be selfish and demanding.

---

229 *3 Nephi 11:29*
230 *The New Webster Encyclopedic Dictionary*, 1980 Edition, Avenel Books, New York, p. 184

Contention creates pressure and tension which may erupt, like a volcanic explosion, damaging relationships because of hurt and angry feelings.

If uncontrolled, it can lead to spouse and child abuse and other serious consequences. Contention brings unhappiness into our homes and into our lives. Satan is the father of lies and contention and all the misery that it brings.[231]

If Satan can succeed in creating in us habits of arguing, quarrelling and contention, it is easier for him to bind us with the heavier sins which can destroy our eternal lives. A contentious spirit can affect almost any phase of our lives.

One of Satan's most effective tools is a destroyer of happiness, peace, contentment and family solidarity. Because of its crippling effect, families are stumbling and falling. What is this dangerous tool? It is **contention.**

What are some specific things which cause Satan to be so successful in creating contention?

Some basic causes are selfishness, jealousy, pride, stress, having to do as one is told, not listening...

Pressures of various kinds, both in and out of the home, frustrations, and disappointments can create a high level of tension in family members. This with a guilty conscience and anger will cause contention. As we can see, we need to be aware of Satan's tools and not let him succeed.

Contention breeds contention, causing a chain reaction in a family. For example, a brother becomes angry with his sister; his sister then quarrels with a parent who then takes out hurt feelings by shouting at his or her spouse. Soon the disease has spread throughout the family. It also works in reverse order from parent to child. When we are tired, hungry or ill, we are more likely to be susceptible to becoming angry and contentious.

By setting our own desires and opinions above the needs of others, we are cultivating selfishness and pride. "Selfishness is the canker that drives out peace and love. Selfishness is the root on which grow argument, anger, and disrespect." **'Only by pride cometh contention.'**[232]

---

231 *Moses 4:4*
232 *Proverbs 13:10*

CONTENTION

There will always be differences in families. When those differences become the cause of contention, there are ways in which the Lord would have us handle them in a Christlike manner.

1. Keep the commandments
2. Fasting and prayer
3. Keeping the Sabbath Day Holy
4. Attending our church meetings
5. Marry in the temple for time and all eternity
6. We need to work out differences in a manner that our Heavenly Father would expect.
7. By answering softly even though someone is talking to you in anger will turn that anger away.
8. We cannot bring back angry words once they have been spoken. Think twice before you say something degrading to the other person.
9. When your heart is full of anger, go into another room where you can be alone. Pray to your Heavenly Father to remove the angry feelings from your heart. Ask him to help you have love for this person with whom you are angry and to bring peace and love back into your home. Ask for patience and to be able to understand the other person as you sit down and discuss what it is that has made each of you so angry.

By honouring the commitments we have made with the Lord and striving to do all that we are commanded to do, we will have the spirit of the Holy Ghost with us. As the Spirit of the Holy Ghost is with us, we will not have the desire to be contentious because the Spirit of the Lord gives us peace and happiness whereas the spirit of the devil gives us the spirit of contention. Wickedness never was happiness.[233]

As we seek the Lord's help in controlling our bad feelings toward others, we will have more love in our homes. The Lord will help us make our weaknesses into strengths as we seek his help. As we gradually make changes and strive to improve our bad ways to stop contention, we will have peace, love and harmony in our homes.

---

[233] *Alma 41:10*

It will take a lifetime to completely avoid contention, in or out of our homes. As we try, we will build more loving relationships with our family members and friends. We are then becoming more as Christ would have us be when he said, "Be ye therefore perfect, even as your Father in Heaven is perfect."[234] We can attain perfection, not in this life time, but eventually, in the eternities. The process is day by day, where we strive to do as our Father has asked. He has not given us any commandment whereby he has not prepared a way for us to achieve.[235]

---

234 *Matthew 5:48*
235 *1 Nephi 3:7*

CHAPTER FOURTEEN

Honesty

'AND THEY WERE ALSO DISTINGUISHED FOR THEIR ZEAL TOWARDS GOD...FOR THEY WERE PERFECTLY HONEST AND UPRIGHT IN ALL THINGS; AND THEY WERE FIRM IN THE FAITH OF CHRIST, EVEN UNTO THE END.'[236]

What does it mean to be honest? The Webster dictionary defines honesty as: 'Fair in dealing with others; free from trickishness, fraud, or theft; upright; just; equitable; sincere, candid, or unreserved; honourable; reputable; chaste or virtuous; pleasant-looking in features. To regard or treat with honour; to revere; to respect; to reverence; to bestow honour upon; to elevate in rank or station, to exalt.'[237]

As we can see, being honest can and does help pave the way towards exaltation. As we strive to be honest in all of our actions, we are keeping each of the commandments. Our Father, when he says to 'Be ye therefore perfect, even as I am,'[238] is guiding and directing us towards eternal life. We should have this goal in mind as we strive to obey him.

To be worthy to enter the Holy Temples of God, we must be honest. When we pay a full tithing, when we deal honestly and justly with our families and our fellowman, we are keeping the commandments. When we make the decision to obey the commandments, we will not be swayed when choices are placed before us. We will have already made the decision to be honest, thereby enabling us to better keep each of the other commandments.

---

236   Alma 27:27
237   *The New Webster Encyclopedic Dictionary*, 1980 Edition, Avenel Books, New York, p. 408
238   Matthew 5:48

CHAPTER FIFTEEN

Principle of Work (Idleness)

'CEASE TO BE IDLE; CEASE TO BE UNCLEAN; CEASE TO FIND FAULT ONE WITH ANOTHER; CEASE TO SLEEP LONGER THAN IS NEEDFUL; RETIRE TO THY BED EARLY, THAT YE MAY NOT BE WEARY; ARISE EARLY, THAT YOUR BODIES AND YOUR MINDS MAY BE INVIGORATED.'[239]

'Thou shalt not be idle; for he that is idle shall not eat the bread nor wear the garments of the labourer.'[240]

'...Thou shalt not idle away thy time, neither shalt thou bury thy talent that it may not be known.'[241]

'And the inhabitants of Zion also shall remember their labours, inasmuch as they are appointed to labour, in all faithfulness; for the idler shall be had in remembrance before the Lord.'[242]

'Now I, the Lord am not well pleased with the inhabitants of Zion, for there are idlers among them; and their children are also growing up in wickedness; they also seek not earnestly the riches of eternity, but their eyes are full of greediness.'[243]

'Let every man be diligent in all things. And the idler shall not have place in the church, except he repent and mend his ways.'[244]

---

239 D&C 88:124
240 D&C 42:42
241 D&C 60:13
242 D&C 68:30
243 D&C 68:31
244 D&C 75:29

'...cast away your idle thoughts and excessive laughter far from you.'[245]

The Lord places great value on the principle of work. He is greatly displeased with those who are idle. Idlers waste their time and energy. The adversary can more easily reach them and encourage them to do mischief, thereby gradually binding them until they can no longer escape. Once that happens, we are his. No longer can we qualify for exaltation, but only for endless torment. We can choose. By not doing anything, we are choosing to follow the adversary.

We have to work out our own salvation. No one can do it for us. It takes time, work and effort on our part. It will not happen overnight. We cannot sit idly by and wait for it to happen. The Lord knows that we have only so long upon this earth to work out our probation.[246]

When Adam and Eve were cast out of the Garden of Eden, the Lord commanded them to work.

'Cursed shall be the ground for thy sake; in sorrow shalt thou eat of it all the days of thy life.

'Thorns also, and thistles shall it bring forth to thee, and thou shalt eat the herb of the field.

'By the sweat of thy face shalt thou eat bread, until thou shalt return unto the ground - for thou shalt surely die - for out of it wast thou taken: for dust thou wast, and unto dust shalt thou return.

'Therefore I, the Lord God, will send him forth from the Garden of Eden, to till the ground from whence he was taken.'[247]

As people work for their livelihood, not relying on others but living the commandments, they will find peace and happiness. They do not covet their neighbours' property.

On the other hand, the Lord has a great work to do. '**FOR BEHOLD, THIS IS MY WORK AND GLORY, TO BRING TO PASS THE IMMORTALITY AND ETERNAL LIFE OF MAN.**'[248] He could do it

---

245 *D&C 88:69*
246 *Alma 12:24*
247 *Moses 4: 23-25, 29*
248 *Moses 1:39*

PRINCIPLE OF WORK (IDLENESS)

himself, but that would deprive us of our free agency. We must work out our own salvation.

'For the time cometh, saith the Lamb of God, that I will work a great and a marvellous work among the children of men; a work which shall be everlasting, either on the one hand or on the other - either to the convincing of them unto peace and life eternal or unto the deliverance of them to the hardness of their hearts and the blindness of the minds unto their being brought down into captivity, and also unto destruction, both temporally and spiritually, according to the captivity of the devil, of which I have spoken.'[249]

The marvellous work spoken of is the restoration of the gospel of Jesus Christ of Latter-day Saints. The baptismal, priesthood, and marriage covenants in the temple are everlasting. The restoration of the gospel of Jesus Christ is a great divider, bringing either great blessings or terrible punishments to each individual. When one has hardened his heart and blinded their minds they have rejected the gospel and it's attending blessings. He is brought into captivity and destruction, both temporally and spiritually. It is in direct contrast to the blessings of peace in this life and eternal life in the world to come for those who have chosen to follow the Saviour.

'And the Lord God doth work by means to bring about his great and eternal purposes; and by very small means the Lord doth confound the wise and bringeth about the salvation of many souls.'[250]

'And when the day cometh that the wrath of God is poured out upon the mother of harlots, which is the great and abominable church of all the earth, whose founder is the devil, then, at that day, the work of the Father shall commence, in preparing the way for the fulfilling of his covenants, which he hath made to his people who are of the house of Israel.'[251]

'For behold, the Lord saw that his people began to work in darkness, yea, work secret murders and abominations; therefore the Lord said, if they did not repent they should be destroyed from off the face of the earth.'[252]

---

249 1 Nephi 14:7
250 Alma 37:7
251 1 Nephi 14:17
252 Alma 37:22

'Therefore, when ye shall receive this record ye may know that the work of the Father has commenced upon all the face of the land.

'Therefore, repent all ye ends of the earth, and come unto me, and believe in my gospel, and be baptized in my name; for he that believeth and is baptized shall be saved; but he that believeth not shall be damned; and signs shall follow them that believe in my name.

'And blessed is he that is found faithful unto my name at the last day, for he shall be lifted up to dwell in the kingdom prepared for him from the foundation of the world. And behold it is I that hath spoken it. Amen.'[253]

The Book of Mormon, the Lord's instrument in finding those seeking the truth, would come forth in a time of wars and all manner of wickedness.

'And no one need say they shall not come, for they surely shall, for the Lord hath spoken it; for out of the earth shall they come, by the hand of the Lord, and none can stay it; and it shall come in a day when it shall be said that miracles are done away; and it shall come even as if one should speak from the dead.

'And it shall come in a day when the blood of saints shall cry unto the Lord, because of secret combinations and the works of darkness.

'Yea, it shall come in a day when the power of God shall be denied, and churches become defiled and be lifted up in the pride of their hearts; yea, even in a day when leaders of churches and teachers shall rise in the pride of their hearts, even to the envying of them who belong to their churches.

'Yea, it shall come in a day when there shall be heard of fires, and tempests, and vapours of smoke in foreign lands;

'And there shall also be heard of wars, rumours of wars, and earthquakes in divers places.

'Yea, it shall come in a day when there shall be great pollutions upon the face of the earth; there shall be murders, and robbing, and lying and deceivings, and whoredoms, and all manner of abominations; when there shall be many who will say, Do this, or do that, and it mattereth not, for the Lord will uphold such at the last day. But wo unto such, for they are in the gall of bitterness and in the bonds of iniquity.

---

253 *Ether 4:17-19*

'Yea, it shall come in a day when there shall be churches built up that shall say: Come unto me, and for your money you shall be forgiven of your sins.'[254]

'And then shall the work of the Father commence at that day, even when this gospel shall be preached among the remnant of this people. Verily I say unto you, at that day shall the work of the Father commence among all the dispersed of my people, yea, even the tribes which have been lost, which the Father hath led away out of Jerusalem.

'Yea, the work shall commence among all the dispersed of my people, with the Father to prepare the way whereby they may come unto me, that they may call on the Father in my name.'[255]

From the beginning, Satan put into the heart of men secret combinations, and murder. There must be opposition in all things[256] for us to be able to choose correctly and gain eternal life.[257]

'Yea, it is that same being who put it into the heart of Gadianton to still carry on the work of darkness, and of secret murder; and he has brought it forth from the beginning of man even down to this time.

'And behold, it is he who is the author of all sin. And behold, he doth carry on his works of darkness and secret murder, and doth hand down their plots, and their oaths, and their covenants, and their plans of awful wickedness, from generation to generation according as he can get hold upon the hearts of the children of men.

'And now behold, he had got great hold upon the hearts..., yea insomuch that they had become exceedingly wicked; yea, the more part of them had turned out of the way of righteousness, and did trample under their feet the commandments of God, and did turn unto their own ways, and did build up unto themselves idols of their gold and their silver.

'And thus we see that they did dwindle in unbelief, and grow in wickedness and abominations,

---

254 *Mormon 8: 26-31*
255 *3 Nephi 21:26-27*
256 *2 Nephi 2:11*
257 *2 Nephi 2:27*

'And thus we see that the Spirit of the Lord began to withdraw because of the wickedness and the hardness of their hearts.

'...they were in an awful state, and ripening for an everlasting destruction.'[258]

'THIS IS MY WORK AND GLORY TO BRING TO PASS THE IMMORTALITY AND ETERNAL LIFE OF MAN.'[259]

In the end, the Lord will succeed. However, there is much work to do. There is no room for the idler. The Lord desires for each of his children to return home to a glorious crown of eternal life. However, he knows that the choice is up to us. We can choose eternal life or damnation, depending upon our works. We cannot afford to be idle. There is too much work to do, not only for ourselves, but for others who have not had the opportunity to hear the gospel and the blessings it will bring.

---

258   *Helaman 6: 29-31, 34-35, 40*
259   *Moses 1: 39*

CHAPTER SIXTEEN

Patience

'BE PATIENT IN AFFLICTIONS, REVILE NOT AGAINST THOSE THAT REVILE. GOVERN YOUR HOUSE IN MEEKNESS, AND BE STEADFAST.'[260]

Our time here on earth is a probation. We will have many trials and tribulations to face. There will be many choices to make; some will be easy, others not. There will be times when every thing seems dark with no escape. We need to trust in the Lord; to know that He knows each of us individually. He will not ask us to endure anything that we are not capable of. We will go through the refiner's fire. The Lord will prepare us for a crown of eternal glory. We must be patient with the process. He knows what we need and what it is that we must endure. He has told us that all things which we experience, whether good or bad, will be for our benefit.

'...Peace be unto thy soul; thine adversity and thine afflictions shall be but a small moment;

'And then, if thou endure it well, God shall exalt thee on high; thou shalt triumph over all thy foes.

'Thy friends do stand by thee, and they shall hail thee again with warm hearts and friendly hands.

'Thou art not yet as Job; thy friends do not contend against thee, neither charge thee with transgression, as they did Job.

'And they who do charge thee with transgression, their hope shall be blasted, and their prospects shall melt away as the hoar frost melteth before the burning rays of the rising sun;

---

260 D&C 31:9

'Cursed are all those that shall lift up the heel against mine anointed, saith the Lord, and cry they have sinned when they have not sinned before me, saith the Lord, but have done that which was meet in mine eyes, and which I commanded them.

'Behold, mine eyes see and know all their works, and I have in reserve a swift judgment in the season thereof, for them all;

'God shall give unto you knowledge by his Holy Spirit, yea, by the unspeakable gift of the Holy Ghost, that has not been revealed since the world was until now;

'All thrones and dominions, principalities and powers, shall be revealed and set forth upon all who have endured valiantly for the gospel of Jesus Christ.'[261]

To fill the full measure and purpose of our mortal probation, we must have patience. This mortal existence is the Lord's sifting sphere, the time when we are subject to trials, testing, and tribulations. Future rewards will be based on our patient endurance of all things.

'"The patience of the Saints" consists in bearing or enduring pains, trials, and persecutions (even unto death), without complaint and with equanimity.[262] It was the Master himself who said: "In your patience possess ye your souls"[263] and anyone who yields his whole soul and being to the Lord "becometh as a child, submissive, meek, humble, **patient**, full of love, willing to submit to all things which the Lord seeth fit to inflict upon him, even as a child doth submit to his father."[264]

'Patience, also, involves an exercise of forbearance under provocation as illustrated in the celestial principle, "whosoever shall smite thee on thy right cheek, turn to him the other also."[265] Patience in righteousness leads to perfection and eternal life. Thus Paul wrote that "by patient continuance in well doing" the saints "seek for glory and honour and immortality, and eternal

---

261 D&C 121:7-11,16, 24, 26, 29
262 Revelations 13:10; Revelations 14:2
263 Luke 21:19
264 Mosiah 3:19
265 Matthew 5:38-42; 3 Nephi 12:38-42

life."[266] And by revelation in our day the Lord commanded: "**Continue in patience until ye are perfected**";[267]

"And seek the face of the Lord always, that in patience ye may possess your souls, and ye shall have eternal life."[268,269]

---

266 *Romans 2:7*
267 *D&C 67:13*
268 *D&C 101:38*
269 *Mormon Doctrine, Bruce R. McConkie, p. 557-558*

CHAPTER SEVENTEEN

Sermon On The Mount

THE GOSPEL OF JESUS CHRIST HAS AS ITS GOAL THE PERFECTION OF ALL WHO WILL FOLLOW IN ITS WAY.

'BE YE THEREFORE PERFECT, EVEN AS YOUR FATHER IN HEAVEN IS PERFECT.'[270]

'Blessed are the poor in spirit, for theirs is the kingdom of heaven.'[271]

'Blessed are they that mourn, for they shall be comforted.'[272]

'Blessed are the meek: for they shall inherit the earth.'[273]

'Blessed are they which do hunger and thirst after righteousness for they shall be filled.'[274]

'Blessed are the merciful: for they shall obtain mercy.'[275]

'Blessed are the pure in heart, for they shall see God.'[276]

'Blessed are the peacemakers, for they shall be called the children of God.'[277]

'Blessed are they which are persecuted for righteousness' sake: for theirs is the kingdom of heaven.'[278] [279]

---

270 *Matthew 5:48; 3 Nephi 12:48*
271 *Matthew 5:3; 3 Nephi 12:3*
272 *Matthew 5:4; 3 Nephi 12:4*
273 *Matthew 5:5; 3 Nephi 12:5*
274 *Matthew 5:6; 3 Nephi 12:6*
275 *Matthew 5:7; 3 Nephi 12:7*
276 *Matthew 5:8; 3 Nephi 12:8*
277 *Matthew 5:9; 3 Nephi 12:9*
278 *Matthew 5:10*
279 *3 Nephi 12:10*

'Blessed are ye, when men shall revile you, and persecute you, and shall say all manner of evil against you falsely, for my sake.'[280] [281]

We receive that which we desire with all of our hearts.[282]

The rock of perfection is doing what the Lord commands.[283]

The trials of life will refine us toward perfection.[284] We are here to be tested. As we put our faith in our Saviour Jesus Christ, he will lead us and strengthen us. With the knowledge that we will not be given more than we can endure,[285] we can cope with anything that the Lord gives to us. After all, He is preparing us to return home to a crown of glory. It is up to us whether or not we will succeed.

Matthew 5:11:12; James 1:12 (The Inspired Version of these verses makes it clear that the Saviour is speaking of the removal of all sin.)

'Whosoever, therefore, shall break one of these least commandments, and shall teach men so to do, he shall in no wise be saved in the kingdom of heaven; but whosoever shall do and teach these commandments of the law until it be fulfilled, the same shall be called great, and shall be saved in the kingdom of heaven.'[286]

'Then came some of the Scribes and said unto him, Master, it is written that, Every sin shall be forgiven; but ye say, Whosoever speaketh against the Holy Ghost shall not be forgiven; And they asked him, saying, How can these things be?

'And he said unto them, When the unclean spirit is gone out of a man, he walketh through dry places, seeking rest and findeth none; but when a man speaketh against the Holy Ghost, then he saith, I will return into my house from whence I came out; and when he is come, he findeth him empty, swept and garnished; for the good spirit leaveth him unto himself.'[287]

---

280 *Matthew 5:11*
281 *3 Nephi 12:11*
282 *Matthew 7:7-11; James 1:4-7*
283 *Matthew 7:21, 24-27; James 1:22-25*
284 *Matthew 5:11-12; James 1:12*
285 *1 Nephi 3:7*
286 *Matthew 5:21*
287 *Matthew 12:37-38*

SERMON ON THE MOUNT

When we have repented of a sin or a transgression, we need to replace it with something that is uplifting and beneficial to us. We must provide actions with repentance. When we don't, we still have the desire to do that which we had been doing. There is an empty feeling inside of us that needs to be filled. It continues to gnaw at us, trying to break down our resolve to do better. As we introduce new ideas and behaviour, we fill that space so that old habits no longer have any hold over us.

All sin must be shunned or there can be no hope for perfection.[288]
Lust is destructive to the soul and must be overcome.[289]
Control of the tongue is basic in the process of perfection.[290]
The riches of life may cause us to be poor toward God.[291]
Prayer is a vital avenue to perfection.[292]
The ordinances of the gospel are essential to perfection.[293]
Matthew 5:4; James 5:14, 15 (This beatitude is included in the Inspired Version but not in other versions of the Bible; see also 3 Nephi 12:2)
True prophets help move us toward perfection by example and precept.
Matthew 5:10, 11; James 5:10 (In the account of the Sermon on the Mount given to the Nephites the Saviour specifically commands the people to follow the prophets. See 3 Nephi 12:1)
Service is a hallmark of perfection.[294]
Charity, the pure love of Christ, is essential to perfection.[295]
'And above all these things, put on charity, which is the bond of perfectness.'[296]

---

[288] *Matthew 5:27-30; James 1:22-25*
[289] *Matthew 5:27-30; James 4:2-4*
[290] *Matthew 5:33-37; James 3:2*
[291] *Matthew 6:19-21; James 5:1-5*
[292] *Matthew 6:5-15; James 5:16*
[293] *Matthew 5:4; James 5:14,15; (This Beatitude is included in the Inspired Version but not in other versions of the Bible; see also 3 Nephi 12:2)*
[294] *Matthew 5:38-47; James 1:27*
[295] *Matthew 5:38-47; James 2:8*
[296] *Colossians 3:14*

Perfection is, after all we can do, a gift of God.[297] 'Blessed is the man that endureth temptation: for when he is tried, he shall receive the crown of life, which the Lord hath promised to them that love Him.'[298]

---

297 *Matthew 5:48; Matthew 6:33; Matthew 7:11; James 1:4, 17*
298 *James 1:12*

CHAPTER EIGHTEEN

Beatitudes

Beatitudes is a name given to certain declarations of blessedness in the Sermon on the Mount[299]. They describe certain elements that go to form the refined and spiritual character, and all of which will be present whenever that character exists in its perfection. Rather than being isolated statements, the Beatitudes are interrelated and progressive in their arrangement. A more comprehensive and accurate listing is found in 3 Nephi 12 and JST Matthew 5, where a greater spiritual emphasis is given.

BLESSED ARE THE POOR IN SPIRIT FOR THEIRS IS THE KINGDOM OF HEAVEN.

BLESSED ARE THEY THAT MOURN: FOR THEY SHALL BE COMFORTED.

BLESSED ARE THE MEEK: FOR THEY SHALL INHERIT THE EARTH.

BLESSED ARE THEY WHICH DO HUNGER AND THIRST AFTER RIGHTEOUSNESS: FOR THEY SHALL BE FILLED.

BLESSED ARE THE MERCIFUL: FOR THEY SHALL OBTAIN MERCY.

BLESSED ARE THE PURE IN HEART: FOR THEY SHALL SEE GOD.

---

299 *Matthew 5:3-11; Luke 6:20-22*

BLESSED ARE THE PEACEMAKERS: FOR THEY SHALL BE
CALLED THE CHILDREN OF GOD.

BLESSED ARE THEY WHICH ARE PERSECUTED FOR
RIGHTEOUSNESS SAKE: FOR THEIRS IS THE KINGDOM
OF HEAVEN.

BLESSED ARE YE, WHEN MEN SHALL REVILE YOU, AND
PERSECUTE YOU, AND SHALL SAY ALL MANNER OF EVIL
AGAINST YOU FALSELY, FOR MY SAKE.

TO BE POOR IN SPIRIT
"To be poor in spirit is to feel yourselves as the spiritually needy, ever dependent upon the Lord for your clothes, your food and the air you breathe, you health, your life; realizing that no day should pass without fervent prayer of thanksgiving, for guidance and forgiveness and strength sufficient for each day's need." [300]

TO MOURN
"To mourn, as the Master's lesson here would teach, one must show that 'godly sorrow that worketh repentance' and wins for the penitent a forgiveness of sins and forbids a return to the deeds of which he mourns."[301]

TO HUNGER AND THIRST
"Did you ever hunger for food or thirst for water when just a crust of stale bread or a sip of tepid water to ease the pangs that distressed you would seem to be the most prized of all possessions? If you have so hungered then you may begin to understand how the Master meant we should hunger and thirst after righteousness."[302]

TO BE PURE IN HEART
"Only if you are the pure in heart will you see God, and also in a lesser degree will you be able to see the 'God' or good in man and love him because

---

300 *Harold B. Lee, Decisions for Successful Living, p. 57-58*
301 *Harold B. Lee, Decisions for Successful Living, p. 58*
302 *Harold B. Lee, Decisions for Successful Living, p. 58*

of the goodness you see in him. Mark well that person who criticizes and maligns the man of God or the Lord's anointed leaders in his Church. Such a one speaks from an impure heart."[303]

TO BE MEEK

"A meek man is defined as one who is not easily provoked or irritated and forbearing under injury or annoyance. Meekness is not synonymous with weakness. The meek man is the strong, the mighty, the man of complete self-mastery. He is the one who has the courage of his moral convictions, despite the pressure of the gang or the club."[304]

TO BE MERCIFUL

"Our salvation rests upon the mercy we show to others. Unkind and cruel words, or wanton acts of cruelty toward man or beast, even though in seeming retaliation, disqualify the perpetrator in his claims for mercy when he has need of mercy in the day of judgment before earthly or heavenly tribunals."

TO BE A PEACEMAKER

"Peacemakers shall be called the children of God. The trouble-maker, the striker against law and order, the leader of the mob, the law-breaker are prompted by motives of evil and unless they desist will be known as the children of Satan rather than God."[305]

TO ENDURE PERSECUTION

"To be persecuted for righteousness sake in a great cause where truth and virtue and honour are at stake is god-like."[306]

---

303 Harold B. Lee, *Decisions for Successful Living*, p. 59
304 Harold B. Lee, *Decisions for Successful Living*, p. 60
305 Harold B. Lee, *Decisions for Successful Living*, p. 61
306 Harold B. Lee, *Decisions for Successful Living*, p. 61

CHAPTER NINETEEN

Virtue

'THUS SAITH THE LORD YOUR GOD, EVEN JESUS CHRIST, THE GREAT I AM, ALPHA AND OMEGA, THE BEGINNING AND THE END, THE SAME WHICH LOOKED UPON THE WIDE EXPANSE OF ETERNITY, AND ALL THE SERAPHIC HOSTS OF HEAVEN, BEFORE THE WORLD WAS MADE;

'THE SAME WHICH KNOWETH ALL THINGS, FOR ALL THINGS ARE PRESENT BEFORE MINE EYES;

'I AM THE SAME WHICH SPAKE, AND THE WORLD WAS MADE, AND ALL THINGS CAME BY ME,

'I AM THE SAME WHICH HAVE TAKEN THE ZION OF ENOCH INTO MINE OWN BOSOM; AND VERILY, I SAY, EVEN AS MANY AS HAVE BELIEVED IN MY NAME, FOR I AM CHRIST, AND IN MINE OWN NAME, BY THE VIRTUE OF THE BLOOD WHICH I HAVE SPILT, HAVE I PLEADED BEFORE THE FATHER FOR THEM.'[307]

Virtue is spoken of many times in the scriptures. What does it mean? In the dictionary, virtue is defined as goodness, power, worth, excellence, moral goodness, uprightness; morality; female purity, chastity; any good quality, merit, or accomplishment; an inherent power or property; efficacy, (by or through the efficacy or authority of); Theological virtues, the three virtues, Faith, Hope and Charity.[308]

---

[307] D&C 38:1-4
[308] *The New Webster Encyclopedic Dictionary*, 1980 Edition, Avenel Books, New York, p. 938

'We believe in being honest, true, chaste, benevolent, virtuous, and in doing good to all men; indeed, we may say that we follow the admonition of Paul---We believe all things, we hope all things, we have endured many things, and hope to be able to endure all things. If there is anything virtuous, lovely, or of good report or praiseworthy, we seek after these things.'[309]

As we strive for honesty, integrity, chastity, benevolence, good works, hope, perseverance, steadfastness, modesty, virtue and beauty we are becoming as God would have us be. We are reaching toward our potential. He is leading us. As we listen to Him and obey the commandments, we will attain our crown of eternal life.

'Who can find a virtuous woman? For her price is far above rubies.

'The heart of her husband doth safely trust in her, so that he shall have no need of spoil.

'She will do him good and not evil all the days of her life.

'She seeketh wool, and flax, and worketh willingly with her hands.

'She is like the merchants' ships; she bringeth her food from afar.

'She riseth also while it is yet night, and giveth meat to her household, and a portion to her maidens.

'She considereth a field, and buyeth it: with the fruit of her hands she planteth a vineyard.

'She girdeth her loins with strength, and strenghtheneth her arms.

'She perceiveth that her merchandise is good: her candle goeth not out by night.

'She layeth her hands to the spindle, and her hands hold the distaff.

'She stretcheth out her hand to the poor; yea, she reacheth forth her hands to the needy.

'She is not afraid of the snow for her household; for all her household are clothed with scarlet.

'She maketh herself coverings of tapestry; her clothing is silk and purple.

'Her husband is known in the gates, when he sitteth among the elders of the land.

---

309   13th *Article of Faith, Joseph Smith; Philippians 4:8*

VIRTUE

'She maketh fine linen, and selleth it; and delivereth girdles unto the merchant.

'Strength and honour are her clothing; and she shall rejoice in time to come.

'She openeth her mouth with wisdom; and in her tongue is the law of kindness.

'She looketh well to the ways of her household, and eateth not the bread of idleness.

'Her children arise up, and call her blessed; her husband also, and he praiseth her.

'Many daughters have done virtuously, but thou excellest them all.

'Favour is deceitful, and beauty is vain; but a woman that feareth the Lord, she shall be praised.

'Give her of the fruit of her hands; and let her own works praise her in the gate.'[310]

'He that hath clean hands and a pure heart; who hath not lifted up his soul unto vanity, nor sworn deceitfully.

'He shall receive the blessings from the Lord, and righteousness from the God of his salvation.'[311]

'According as his divine power hath given unto us all things that pertain unto life and godliness, through the knowledge of him that hath called us to glory and virtue:

'Whereby are given unto us exceeding great and precious promises; that by these ye might be partakers of the divine nature, having escaped the corruption that is in the world through lust.

'And beside this, giving all diligence, add to your faith virtue; and to virtue knowledge;

'And to knowledge temperance; and to temperance patience; and to patience godliness;

'And to godliness brotherly kindness; and to brotherly kindness charity.

---

310 *Proverbs 10:10-31*
311 *Psalms 24:4-5*

For if these things be in you, and abound, they make you that ye shall neither be barren nor unfruitful in the knowledge of our Lord Jesus Christ.'[312]

'Remember faith, virtue, knowledge, temperance, patience, brotherly kindness, godliness, charity, humility, diligence.

'Ask, and ye shall receive; knock, and it shall be opened unto you. Amen.'[313]

---

312   2 Peter 1:3-8
313   D&C 4:6-7

CHAPTER TWENTY

Unselfishness

As we strive to live the gospel truths, we purify ourselves. No longer do we strive to do that which will benefit only ourselves. Our prime concern is with others; their happiness, to help them to achieve the blessings of our Father in Heaven. As we strive to help others, we reach outside of ourselves. We forget about the problems we have as we strive to help and encourage others. Our capacity to learn and love grows.

Learning to serve others helps us to lift another's burdens. As we do so, we learn to love. We begin to understand that each is a child of God and is precious in his sight.

'When ye are in the service of your fellow-beings, ye are only in the service of your God.'[314]

Many lessons can be learned in the school of service. Some of which are patience, humility, long-suffering, endurance, faith and love. Each of these qualities must be learned for us to become as God is, for these are just a few of his attributes.

Our Father knows how best to teach us the lessons we need to become perfected. He knows each one of us individually by name. It is up to us how often the lessons need to be repeated for us to learn that particular lesson.

As we do things for others, we are learning to be unselfish. Many times when we serve, it is not convenient; but when we put others needs ahead of our own, we learn the art of unselfishness.

---

[314] Mosiah 2:17

CHAPTER TWENTY ONE

Prepare

'IF YE ARE PREPARED, YE SHALL NOT FEAR.'[315]

'Peace I leave with you, my peace I give unto you: not as the world giveth, give I unto you. Let not your heart be troubled, neither let it be afraid.'[316]

As we travel throughout the course of our lives, there are many areas in which we can prepare.

When we are young, we learn to crawl, to walk and to talk. As we enter school, we learn the basics of reading, writing and arithmetic. If we study and listen, we will learn our lessons well. However, if we choose to 'play', then we reap the 'rewards' of not being able to do our work well with understanding. As we progress to higher grades, the results of our attitude in those early years will follow us relentlessly. If we have the desire to overcome these difficulties, we can by extra study and effort.

---

315 D&C 38:30
316 John 14:27

Throughout our school years there are many opportunities for new and exciting projects. If we are willing to expend the time and effort required to succeed, we have no fear after all preparation has been done. We know that we have done our best.

As one comes to the crossroads of life as high school is finished, diplomas are awarded to those who have expended the effort to complete their schooling. It will not have been easy, but the feeling that one has, is well worth all of the hard work when their diploma is handed to them. It represents twelve years of struggle. It completes a phase of life.

Choices are made whether to continue their schooling by attending college or university, or entering into the work force. In each instance, preparations need to have been made to take these steps. Entrance exams are administered by colleges and universities to test for eligibility. Different jobs require different requirements.

In the gospel, we are encouraged to prepare for the celestial kingdom by obeying the commandments. As we struggle with each of our individual weaknesses, the Lord will bless us as we strive to live the commandments.

As we keep the law of tithing, diligently study the scriptures, have daily personal and family prayer, attend our church meetings, magnify our callings, among all the other commandments, we are preparing for entrance into the celestial kingdom and exaltation.

The Lord has told us that he will give us further light and knowledge, line upon line, precept upon precept.[317] As we do those things with which we have been commanded, the Lord will reveal further things for us until we are encompassed about with his glory.

However if we choose to disregard the Lord's council, and follow the precepts of men, we are unwittingly preparing for a far different life in the hereafter. We are choosing to follow Satan.

If we do not strive to keep the commandments, the Lord will take away that light and knowledge that we currently have.[318] Our minds will then become darkened with the spirit of evil.

---

317 *D&C 98:12; D&C 128:21*
318 *Matthew 25:29*

To be able to choose wisely and to prepare for the choices which we make, we need to know what we are choosing.

Wickedness never was happiness![319]

What is the difference between Heavenly Father's Plan and Satan's Plan? We know that Heavenly Father wants us to be happy. We also know that the opposite is true for Satan. He desires nothing more than that we are as miserable as he.

Let's define the difference in the two plans. Their knowledge is essential for our salvation. We have to know that the choices we make lead to either one plan or the other. There is no in between.

HEAVENLY FATHER'S PLAN – The Plan of Salvation

'And there stood one among them that was like unto God, and he said unto those who were with him: We will go down, for there is space there, and we will take of these materials, and we will make an earth whereon these may dwell;

'And we will prove them herewith, to see if they will do all things whatsoever the Lord their God shall command them;

'And they who keep their first estate shall be added upon; and they who keep not their first estate shall not have glory in the same kingdom with those who keep their first estate; and they who keep their second estate shall have glory added upon their heads for ever and ever.

'And the Lord said: Whom shall I send? And one answered like unto the Son of Man: Here am I, send me. And another answered and said: Here am I, send me. And the Lord said: I will send the first.

'And the second was angry, and kept not his first estate; and, at that day, many followed after him.'

Jesus Christ came into the world, the Only Begotten Son, the only perfect being, to atone for the sins of all mankind. When the Plans were presented, Jesus Christ said "Thy will be done, and the glory be Thine." It is only through Jesus Christ that we can be saved in the Kingdom of God. We have our free agency, to choose good, the way to eternal life; or evil, the way to captivity and the devil. The choice is up to us. As much as Heavenly

---

319 Alma 41:10

Father wants each of us to return home, He also knew that it would have to be our choice. We would need to have the opportunity to choose good over evil. Free agency was extremely important in the Plan of Salvation. To briefly sum up our Heavenly Fathers plan, it is one of happiness: As we learn the gospel and the commandments, striving to do our best, being honest with our fellow-man in everything by not cheating, lying or stealing, we gain self-confidence within ourselves. Working hard on our goals of keeping the commandments and earning a living gives us the blessing of good jobs and the honour of knowing that you are trusted. The Lord desires to bless us with good health. As we prove ourselves worthy to attend the temples of our God by staying morally clean and pure, we gain perfect freedom and earn the privilege of eventual Godhood in the Celestial Kingdom, thus bringing about eternal happiness.

SATAN'S PLAN

Lucifer, also known as Satan, the devil, would make sure all mankind returned home to Heavenly Father. For that, he wanted all the glory for himself. When Lucifer was cast out of heaven, a third of the hosts were cast out as well because they followed Lucifer. We would not be able to make choices. Satan was angry. He could not obtain a body of flesh and bones. That would be forever denied him and all who followed him. As a result, they try to get the children of men to choose opposite that which God wants for His children. He does not want us to have happiness and eternal life.

Briefly summing up Satan's plan is one of misery. When we lie, cheat and steal, we lose the trust of our fellowman. We will not have good jobs because we cannot be trusted. We have no true friends; relationships suffer because of the mistrust and abuse. Relationships also suffer because of the selfishness and laziness of individuals. To fill the void, we turn to smoking and drinking, among other things displeasing to God. Low self-confidence makes one be unkind to those around them in the hopes that they will feel important. Because of impure things being taken into the body, bad health ensues. Jail often follows as freedom is lost. We enjoy no temple blessings. We have become a slave to Satan and sin, thus ensuring our everlasting unhappiness.

CHAPTER TWENTY TWO

Humility

As we live the gospel, praying always, we gain true joy and humility. Humility makes it possible for our Father in Heaven to answer our prayers. "Be thou humble; and the Lord thy God shall lead thee by the hand, and give thee answer to thy prayers."[320]

'I GIVE UNTO MEN WEAKNESS THAT THEY MAY BE HUMBLE... FOR IF THEY HUMBLE THEMSELVES BEFORE ME, AND HAVE FAITH IN ME, THEN WILL I MAKE WEAK THINGS BECOME STRONG UNTO THEM.'[321]

'And now I would that ye should be humble, and be submissive and gentle; easy to be entreated; full of patience and long-suffering; being temperate in all things; being diligent in keeping the commandments of God at all times.'[322]

What does it mean to be humble or to have humility? The dictionary defines humble as being modest, meek, and submissive; low self-esteem in that we are not be proud or arrogant or assuming.[323]

Beware of pride. When we are full of pride, we are not humble. We are not teachable. We cannot and will not learn. We feel that what we know and do is right. A wise man has said that pride goeth before destruction and a haughty spirit before a fall.

By his words and deeds are a man judged, not by the outward appearance. However, his lips will betray those things which he thinks about. His

---

320 D&C 112:10
321 Ether 12:27
322 Alma 7:23
323 *The New Webster Encyclopedic Dictionary*, 1980 Edition, Avenel Books, New York, p. 413

actions and words betray his innermost thoughts. Flattery is also a deadly poison, as it causes us to become self-centred and full of self-importance.

The things of God can only be discovered through prayer, scripture study and pondering upon those sacred truths. As we seek to learn more and become closer to the Lord, we will have the continual guidance of the Holy Ghost. The Lord will bless us and reveal those truths to us which we earnestly ask and seek for.

'All progress in spiritual things is conditioned upon the prior attainment of **humility**. Pride, conceit, haughtiness, and vainglory are of the world and stand as a bar to the receipt of spiritual gifts. We are commanded to be humble.'[324]

"Always retain in remembrance, the greatness of God, and your own nothingness, and his goodness and long-suffering towards you, unworthy creatures," King Benjamin taught, "and **humble yourselves even in the depths of humility,** calling on the name of the Lord daily, and standing steadfastly in the faith."[325]

"Humility must accompany repentance to qualify a person for baptism;[326] it is required of all engaged in gospel service;[327] it is an essential attribute for all who embark in the service of God;[328] it precedes the acquiring of wisdom from the Spirit;[329] it is needed to qualify the righteous to see God;[330] and without it no one can gain entrance to the kingdom of God hereafter."[331] [332]

---

324 *D&C 105:23; D&C 112:10; D&C 124:97, 103; James 4:6, 10*
325 *Mosiah 4:11*
326 *D&C 20:37*
327 *D&C 12:8*
328 *D&C 4:6*
329 *D&C 136:32-33*
330 *D&C 67:10*
331 *2 Nephi 9:42*
332 *Mormon Doctrine, Bruce R. McConkie, p. 370*

CHAPTER TWENTY THREE

Prayer

'PRAY ALWAYS, LEST YOU ENTER INTO TEMPTATION AND LOSE YOUR REWARD.'[333]

'WHEREFORE, MY BELOVED BRETHREN, PRAY UNTO THE FATHER WITH ALL THE ENERGY OF HEART, THAT YE MAY BE FILLED WITH THIS LOVE, WHICH HE HATH BESTOWED UPON ALL WHO ARE TRUE FOLLOWERS OF HIS SON, JESUS CHRIST.'[334]

We need our Heavenly Fathers help. To access that help is through prayer. What is the importance of prayer? Do we need to pray often or only when we are having difficulties? What is this love that is referred to in the above scripture? It is charity, or the pure love of Christ.

'Watch and pray, that ye enter not into temptation: the spirit indeed is willing, but the flesh is weak.'[335]

'Watch ye and pray, lest ye enter into temptation. The spirit truly is ready, but the flesh is weak.'[336]

'...Pray always lest that wicked one have power in you, and remove you out of you place.'[337]

'Pray always, lest you enter into temptation and lose your reward.'[338]

---

333 *D&C 31:12*
334 *Moroni 7:48*
335 *Matthew 26:41*
336 *Mark 14:38*
337 *D&C 93:49*
338 *D&C 31:12*

'And whatsoever ye shall ask the Father in my name, which is right, believing that ye shall receive, behold it shall be given unto you.'[339]

'Yea, he that repenteth and exerciseth faith, and bringeth forth good works, and prayeth continually without ceasing---unto such it is given to know the mysteries of God; yea, unto such it shall be given to reveal things which never have been revealed.'[340]

'But this much I can tell you, that if ye do not watch yourselves, and your thoughts, and your words, and your deeds, and observe the commandments of God...even unto the end of your lives, ye must perish.'[341]

Family home evenings and family prayer are a part of our defence system against the adversary in these trying times.

President Joseph Fielding Smith said, "Every effort we can make to foster meaningful and close family relationships will help the home serve as a sanctuary from evil and become a source of strength to each family member. In our home evenings and other positive family experiences, we can fill our souls with the things of God, thus leaving no room for evil to find a place in our hearts or minds."

Through family prayers our families can feel of our Heavenly Father's spirit and strength in overcoming trials and tribulations, and the joy in thanking him for His help.

President David O. McKay said, "A family that prays together stays together." What a great promise this is to us in a world where Satan is trying to destroy the divine and eternal institution of the family. In this day of deteriorating moral standards in the world, families need the strength that comes from the Lord's words and the courage that comes from being a part of a strong, active L.D.S. family that loves and exercises faith in Jesus Christ. Family home evenings and family prayer help to unify the family and teach gospel principles.

Through prayer, we can also develop a companionship with God. We can develop a closeness to God that will bring pure joy and peace. These special feelings can later be recalled or re-experienced through meditation.

---

339 *3 Nephi 18:20*
340 *Alma 26:22*
341 *Mosiah 4:30*

A deficiency in love supplies can be filled by developing a relationship with God. Spend 15 - 20 minutes every day pondering on these special traits before or after you read the scriptures. Sit and meditate. You may experience tears of gratitude for your heavenly being. That is **NOT** an ego trip. It is self respect, self-love and self-appreciation. It is a sacred experience. You would not want to tell everybody about it; it is too private, too precious. It is a love supply from yourself and God. He loves you **UNCONDITIONALLY**. You should too.

Dependency upon God can lead to total independence from other human beings. We then only need others so that **we** may GIVE from our fullness-to share kindness, service, companionship, firmness, compassion, etc.

Dependency on God can overcome all the inadequate treatment we have received in the growing years and help the real self to achieve full expression.

God loves us unconditionally. We do not have to earn His love. Can we then love in ourselves the same things He loves in us? Yes, we can.

Following are five ways in which we can improve communication with our Heavenly Father.

1. Pray frequently
2. Find an appropriate place to meditate or pray
3. Prepare yourself for prayer. Often times if we have had a stressful day, we do not feel like praying. At times like this, we need to stay on our knees and pray until we feel the spirit. When we feel the spirit, we then feel like praying.
4. Prayer should be meaningful. Do not ramble on about just anything. Be specific and pertinent.
5. After making a request from our Father, stay on your knees. Listen to the still small voice. Do not be in a hurry.

PRAYER IS THE SOUL'S SINCERE DESIRE

Prayer is the soul's sincere desire,
Uttered or unexpressed
The motion of a hidden fire
That trembles in the breast.

Prayer is the burden of a sigh,
The falling of a tear,

BEYOND THE SUNSET

The upward glancing of an eye
When none but God is near.

Prayer is the simplest form of speech
That infant lips can try;
Prayer, the sublimest strains that reach
The Majesty on high.

Prayer is the Chrisian's vital breath,
The Chrisian's native air,
His watchword at the gates of death,
He enters heav'n with prayer.

Prayer is the contrite sinner's voice,
Returning from his ways,
While angels in their songs rejoice
And cry, "Behold, he prays!"
The Saints in prayer appear as one
In word and deed and mind,
While with the Father and the Son
Their fellowship they find.

Nor prayer is made on earth alone:
The Holy Spirit pleads,
And Jesus at the Father's throne
For sinners intercedes.

O thou by whom we come to God,
The Life, the Truth, the Way!
The path of prayer thyself has trod;
Lord, teach us how to pray.[342]

---

[342] *Hymns of the Church of Jesus Christ of Latter-Day Saints, page 145 (written by James Montgomery, 1771-1854)*; Nephi 13:5-13; 18:15-20; James 5:16

PRAYER

Enjoy your time spent in prayer. It is a refuge from the cares of the world. Heavenly Father enjoys hearing from you. He also enjoys speaking with you, whether directly or through the Holy Ghost. It is important to be in tune so as to hear him.

<u>DID YOU THINK TO PRAY?</u>
Ere you left your room this morning,
Did you think to pray?
In the name of Christ, our Saviour,
Did you sue for loving favour
As a shield today?

When your heart was filled with anger,
Did you think to pray?
Did you plead for grace, my brother,
That you might forgive another
Who had crossed your way?

When sore trials came upon you,
Did you think to pray?
When your soul was full of sorrow,
Balm of Gilead did you borrow
At the gates of day?

<u>Chorus</u>
Oh, how praying rests the weary!
Prayer will change the night to day.
So, when life gets dark and dreary,
Don't forget to pray.[343]

---

343 *Hymns of the Church of Jesus Christ of Latter-Day Saints*, page 140 (written by Mary A. Pepper Kidder, 1820-1905) Psalm 5:3; 12; Mark 11:24-25

"I long have been impressed with the truth that meaningful prayer requires both holy communication and consecrated work. Blessings require some effort on our part before we can obtain them, and prayer, as 'a form of work...is an appointed means for obtaining the highest of all blessings' (Bible dictionary, "Prayer," 753). We press forward and persevere in the consecrated work of prayer, after we say 'amen,' by acting upon the things we have expressed to Heavenly Father. Asking in faith requires honesty, effort, commitment, and persistence."[344]

---

[344] *David A. Bednar*

CHAPTER TWENTY FOUR

Word of Wisdom

'AND ALL SAINTS WHO REMEMBER TO KEEP AND DO THESE SAYINGS, WALKING IN OBEDIENCE TO THE COMMANDMENTS, SHALL RECEIVE HEALTH IN THEIR NAVEL AND MARROW TO THEIR BONES;

'AND SHALL FIND WISDOM AND GREAT TREASURES OF KNOWLEDGE, EVEN HIDDEN TREASURES;

'AND SHALL RUN AND NOT BE WEARY, AND SHALL WALK AND NOT FAINT.

'AND I, THE LORD, GIVE UNTO THEM A PROMISE, THAT THE DESTROYING ANGEL SHALL PASS BY THEM, AS THE CHILDREN OF ISRAEL, AND NOT SLAY THEM. AMEN.'[345]

'Behold, verily, thus saith the Lord unto you: In consequence of evils and designs which do and will exist in the hearts of conspiring men in the last days, I have warned you, and forewarn you, by giving unto you this word of wisdom by revelation—'[346]

The Lord loves us. He wants us to be happy and healthy. He knows the thoughts of men and what they will do to entice us to disobey the commandments. He knows that in order for our bodies and minds to be healthy, there are certain things that we need to do. Therefore the Lord has given us the word of wisdom. As we follow it, we will be healthy and strong, able to more fully follow our Saviour and the commandments that we have been given.

---

345 D&C 89:18-21
346 D&C 89:4

CHAPTER TWENTY FIVE

Temptation

'BLESSED IS THE MAN THAT ENDURETH TEMPTATION: FOR WHEN HE IS TRIED, HE SHALL RECEIVE THE CROWN OF LIFE, WHICH THE LORD HATH PROMISED TO THEM THAT LOVE HIM.'[347]

'PREACH UNTO THEM REPENTANCE, AND FAITH ON THE LORD JESUS CHRIST; TEACH THEM TO HUMBLE THEMSELVES AND TO BE MEEK AND LOWLY IN HEART; TEACH THEM TO WITHSTAND EVERY TEMPTATION OF THE DEVIL, WITH THEIR FAITH ON THE LORD JESUS CHRIST.'[348]

'...BUT GOD IS FAITHFUL, WHO WILL NOT SUFFER YOU TO BE TEMPTED ABOVE THAT YE ARE ABLE; BUT WILL WITH THE TEMPTATION ALSO MAKE A WAY TO ESCAPE, THAT YE MAY BE ABLE TO BEAR IT.'[349]

'FOR AFTER MUCH TRIBULATION COME THE BLESSINGS. WHEREFORE THE DAY COMETH THAT YE SHALL BE CROWNED WITH MUCH GLORY; THE HOUR IS NOT YET, BUT IS NIGH AT HAND.'[350]

---

347 *James 1:12*
348 *Alma 37:33*
349 *Corinthians 10:13*
350 *D&C 58:4*

This life is a school. We are here to be tested and tried. We can take comfort that the Lord knows each of us individually. He knows our strengths and weaknesses. He will not try us more than we are able to cope. Sometimes it seems that we are being stretched beyond our ability and that we will break. However, if we put our faith and trust in the Lord, we will be able to endure. In this way, we are being refined in the refiner's fire.

Satan and his followers are out in all their strength. Not only has he one third of the hosts of heaven who failed to pass their first estate, but he has also enlisted men on earth who have failed to recognize the voice of the Saviour, and they have chosen to follow Satan.

We must be strong. We must remember who we are and our potential. We need to keep our eyes upon the goal of the Celestial kingdom. We have been saved to come forth in these last days. We are the chosen and Royal Generation. We were the most valiant in the spirit world. We were chosen to prepare the earth and its people to meet the Saviour at his Second Coming. We were taught well in the Holy Courts on High and we were prepared to come to earth now.

"My dear friends, you are a royal generation. You were preserved to come to the earth in this time for a special purpose. Not just a few of you, but all of you. There are things for each of you to do that no one else can do as well as you. If you do not prepare to do them, they will not be done. Your mission is unique and distinctive for you. Please don't make another have to take your place. He or she can't do it as well as you can. If you will let Him, I testify that our Father in Heaven will walk with you through the journey of life and inspire you to know your special purpose here."[351]

'Wherefore, beware lest ye are deceived; and that ye may not be deceived seek ye earnestly the best gifts, always remembering for what they are given.'[352]

We need to put on the whole armour of God to help protect us from the adversary. What is this armour?

---

351 *H. Burke Peterson*
352 *D&C 46:8*

TEMPTATION

'Put on the whole armour of God that ye may be able to stand against the wiles of the devil.

'For we wrestle not against flesh and blood, but against principalities, against powers, against the rulers of the darkness of this world, against spiritual wickedness in high places.

'Wherefore take unto you the whole armour of God that ye may be able to withstand in the evil day, and having done all, to stand.

'Stand therefore, having your loins girt about with truth, and having on the breastplate of righteousness;

'And your feet shod with the preparation of the gospel of peace;

'Above all, taking the shield of faith, wherewith ye shall be able to quench all the fiery darts of the wicked

'And take the helmet of salvation, and the sword of the Spirit, which is the word of God:

'Praying always with all prayer and supplication in the Spirit, and watching therunto with all perseverance and supplication for all saints;

'And for me, that utterance may be given unto me, that I may open my mouth boldly, to make known the mystery of the gospel.'[353]

Satan has many ways to deceive us. How can we hope to overcome? By knowing his strategy and his ways, we can conquer anything that he may throw in our pathway. He knows that he will never attain the glory that our Heavenly Father has planned for those who are faithful. Because he cannot have that glory, he does not want any of us to succeed and have it either.

What are the different tactics that Satan uses?

Many times we experience discouragement, anger, envy and greed. We encounter flattery, selfishness, lying, deceit, pride, wealth, class distinction, murder and fear of what others will think (where men love men more than they fear God).

How do we know if something is of God or if it is Satan trying to deceive us?

---

353 *Ephesians 6:11-19*

The Lord has told us, 'And again, I will give unto you a pattern in all things, that ye may not be deceived; for Satan is abroad in the land, and he goeth forth deceiving the nations,

'Wherefore, he that prayeth, whose spirit is contrite, the same is accepted of me if he obey mine ordinances.

'He that speaketh, whose spirit is contrite, whose language is meek and edifieth, the same is of God if he obey mine ordinances.

'And again, he that trembleth under my power shall be made strong, and shall bring forth fruits of praise and wisdom, according to the revelations and truths which I have given you.

'And again he that is overcome and bringeth not forth fruits, even according to this pattern, is not of me.

'Wherefore, by this pattern ye shall know the spirits in all cases under the whole heavens.'[354]

Throughout life we will be faced with trials and adversity. That is part of this life. We will be tried and tested. By accepting the challenges of adversity will allow us to grow closer to our Saviour. Tragedy is not adversity. The tragedy is when we don't deal with it in a positive manner. If we keep God's commandments, He will not let us fail. He wants us to succeed. Each time we are faced with a temptation, trial or tragedy, ask yourself what it is you are to learn. There is always something positive in every situation, no matter how bleak it seems at the time. Sometimes we need to step back and look at it objectively, as if it were happening to someone else. Each time we overcome, we become closer to our Saviour and to what our potential is. We can only see straight ahead, whereas He sees what we may become. If we are not faced with situations that require us to look at things from a new perspective, we will never gain the insight and discover the talents that we never knew that we possessed because we would have not had need for them.

'...Peace be unto thy soul; thine adversity and thine afflictions shall be but a small moment; and then, if thou endure it well, God shall exalt thee on high.'[355]

---
354 *D&C 52:14-19*
355 *D&C 121:7-8*

'For verily I say unto you, blessed is he that keepeth my commandment, whether in life or in death; and he that is faithful in tribulation, the reward of the same is greater in the kingdom of heaven.' [356]

'And ye cannot bear all things now; nevertheless, be of good cheer, for I will lead you along.'[357]

Let me relate a story that will illustrate how Satan plans and works to deceive.

CHOCOLATE CHIP COOKIE
(Unknown author)

Once upon a time there was a little kingdom called Rayad. The tiny people who inhabited this kingdom were called Rayadites. They lived happily, sharing and caring about each other. Life was good to them. There were only a few things they needed to watch out for; for instance, chocolate cake or wearing the colour red. If any Rayadite ever ate chocolate cake or wore red, his spirit would become weakened and he would care less and less about himself and the rules of the kingdom.

Also living in this tiny kingdom was Zynock, an evil person who wanted to destroy the kingdom and all of the people in it. He hated for them to be happy and loving, for that made it harder for him to influence them. He knew what weakened their spirits and made them easier to capture. But Zynock also knew that he could not just offer the Rayadites chocolate cake and have them devour it - they were not that foolish! Nor could he make the most wonderful garment in bright red and expect them to wear it immediately. The Rayadites wanted to be good and strong. They had promised each other that they would help and strengthen each other in times of need. So how could Zynock weaken this people? How could he get them to succumb to him so that he could destroy them and thus the whole kingdom?

"Let's see," he said, "I can't get them to eat chocolate cake right off, but maybe I can get them to develop a taste for chocolate."

---

356 D&C 58:2
357 D&C 78:18

That's when chocolate chip cookies were introduced to the kingdom of Rayad. At first the cookies were ignored and scoffed at. Then some commercials and billboards were produced that showed handsome, wonderful-looking Rayadites eating chocolate chip cookies. And nothing happened to them, except they became more popular and sophisticated - at least that's what the message conveyed on the screens and billboards.

It wasn't long before a few Rayadites could be seen eating a chocolate chip cookie every now and then, and they seemed to be doing fine. They were still loving and caring and hadn't changed at all - so it seemed. So more and more Rayadites began eating the cookies. What they didn't realize was that the portion of chocolate chips in each cookie had been doubled. They were getting a double dose of chocolate, disguised in the cookie. You'd hear phrases like these: "That cookie is really good except for a couple of places where it tastes pretty chocolaty. But don't miss the cookie just for those two places. It's too good a cookie, and you can overlook the taste." "I heard that one of our friends has eaten a chocolate chip cookie and she says it's nothing to be afraid of. It won't ruin your life if you eat it!"

That was true: lives didn't seem to be ruined by chocolate chip cookies. Things were pretty much the same as usual. However, some of the teachers and leaders and parents in Rayad suggested avoiding the cookies because tastes for chocolate were being developed.

"Avoid the cookies?" came the cries of surprise. "What for?" "What's wrong with them? They're not chocolate cake!" "How stuffy can you get?"

Some who refused to eat the cookies were even laughed at and made fun of. Zynock himself started chuckling. He had no idea his plan would work so well. And Zynock was patient. He didn't care how long it took to destroy Rayad, just so it was destroyed.

Chocolate chip cookies seemed to be moving pretty well. Zynock didn't worry about the words of caution and counsel from the leaders, because his commercials and billboards were so exciting and enticing. He had to make them that way, or the truth of the leaders would have swayed the Rayadites away from the cookies.

TEMPTATION

Now it came time to introduce a new product of destruction. No, not chocolate cake, not quite yet. Rather Zynock began advertising spice cake, white cake, yellow cake, carrot cake, any kind of cake but chocolate - but all with chocolate frosting, rich chocolate frosting. More commercials, more billboards, a few songs to hum and sing all day about how wonderful chocolate cake would be, although they're not eating it - yet! Get them thinking about it before they will actually succumb. Then in the kingdom of Rayad, you could hear:

"Have you tried that yellow cake with chocolate frosting?"

"Well, no. Is it good?"

"Oh, yes! Granted, it is chocolaty, but it's not chocolate cake. And it really doesn't have much more chocolate than those cookies we've been eating!"

"But the cake doesn't seem right. I mean, cookies are one thing, but cake?"

"Ah, come on! The important thing is the chocolate, and this is no more than you've already been eating. Everybody's eating it. You can't pass it up and be the only one left out."

In the meantime, the songs were subtly strumming away in the background, singing the praises of chocolate cake. Right, the words were not good, but the beat and the rhythm were so cool that many Rayads listened just for the music. After all, what can music do?

Zynock began thinking again: "One thing that strengthens those Rayadites is when they are together talking to each other. What can I do about that?" Then he reasoned, "Well, it's all right for them to be together. In fact, maybe there is some way I could use their gatherings and parties for my purposes. Aha! I've got it!"

So parties in Rayad began changing. Instead of the Rayadites talking to each other and playing games so they could get to know one another and share their strengths and talents, a new trend began. Everyone who was anyone had the new kinds of parties.

"Have you been to a party over at our Rayad friend's place yet?"

"No, I haven't."

"You should go. It's really cool!"

"Oh? What do you do?"

"Well, it isn't like any other party you've been to. It's pretty cool. All you do is go and sit down and watch stuff on the screen."

"Stuff on the screen? Like what?"

"Oh, exciting, scary stuff that's pretty good. There are a few scenes showing people eating chocolate cake, but no 'biggie'."

"People eating chocolate cake? But..."

"Oh, it's not bad, and besides, there's nothing any more without a little bit of that. It's just fun to get together with your friends."

So Zynock stood back and watched the plot unfold. "Let's see now. They're eating chocolate and they're eating cake. They're listening to songs and watching movies about chocolate cake. They're becoming weaker and weaker, although they're not even aware of it yet because they haven't actually eaten chocolate cake. They talk about it, make jokes about it, but they haven't eaten it - yet! They are falling into my trap! They think their leaders and parents are square and stuffy. It's very helpful when their friends tell them what I want them to hear. Friends are my greatest asset!"

"Hey!" says a friend Rayadite, "haven't you seen the latest movie?"

"No," comes the response. "I thought it was C-rated, for chocolate."

"No, it isn't. It's R-rated for Red. There's no chocolate in it."

And so Zynock continues his plotting - this time, a gorgeous garment, but not in red...yet. It's a luscious pink colour.

And so Satan's tactics never cease. He is constantly trying to tempt us, little by little, making us think that it won't hurt anything; that nothing is wrong with 'just a little'. Once he has us doing 'little' things which are not right, he gradually gets us to do more which are not right until we have finally done that which we had vowed in the beginning never to do or indulge in.

When we have the Spirit of the Lord with us, it is much easier to be able to withstand the temptation. How can we discern whether or not we have the Spirit?

When we have the Spirit, we feel happy and calm. We feel full of light and our minds are clear. Our bosom burns within us. Nobody offends us. We feel generous towards everyone we come in contact with. We are confident in everything we do; we are excited for everyone to see what we do. People give us pleasure and we are happy when they succeed. When we have the spirit, we want to make others happy. We say the best and bring out the best of others. Church duties are happily and willingly performed. It is an honour to serve the Lord and magnify your calling. Temple service is where you would like to be every day. Your desire is to pray and keep all the Lord's commandments. You feel in control of your life; your appetites, emotions, food and sleep in moderation, sexual restraint, and diversion of things which are wholesome and moderate. Your speech is calm and controlled; neither do you feel anger toward anyone. You are glad to be alive!

When Satan is prompting you and you do not have the spirit, you have feelings of unhappiness, depression, confusion and frustration. Your soul and mind are heavy and full of darkness. Your mind is muddled. You feel cold, empty and hollow inside. Selfishness, possessiveness and self-centredness control your life. Everything people do bothers you. You are always on your guard as your defences are up. Discouragement comes easily. You want to be alone. You become secretive, sneaky and evasive. Other family members are avoided.

You are critical and envious of others, of what they do and have. You feel hesitant and unworthy to perform church ordinances. Temple service has no place in your life. Your church calling is distasteful and you wish you had another calling or no calling at all. Prayer has no place in your life. The commandments have become bothersome, restricting and senseless. You have become a slave to your appetites; your emotions become passionate; over-indulgence in food, sleep, sex, stimulating entertainment, strong anger and out-spokenness. You wonder why you are alive. You wonder if live is worth living.

Yes, life **is** worth living! It is worth all the trials and struggles we will face. One day we will face our Saviour, Jesus Christ, and He will welcome us home with open arms.

'Well done thou good and faithful servant.'[358]

Yes, it will have been worth it. We will look back upon this life with all of its attending heartache and sadness. But we will also see the goodness and joy we experienced. If we were asked if we would experience the joy and

---

358 Matthew 25:21

sorrow, the heartache and happiness, knowing what we now know, we would accept gladly. All things suffered will be worth it to prove ourselves worthy of exaltation in the Celestial kingdom.

CHAPTER TWENTY SIX

Repentance

'WHEREFORE TEACH IT UNTO YOUR CHILDREN, THAT ALL MEN, EVERYWHERE, MUST REPENT, OR THEY CAN IN NOWISE INHERIT THE KINGDOM OF GOD, FOR NO UNCLEAN THING CAN DWELL THERE.'[359]

'BEHOLD, HE WHO HAS REPENTED OF HIS SINS, THE SAME IS FORGIVEN, AND I, THE LORD, REMEMBER THEM NO MORE.'[360]

'Behold, this life is the time for men to prepare to meet God,'[361] What is repentance? The Greek word of which this is the translation denotes a change of mind, i.e., a fresh view about God, about oneself, and about the world. It is to feel pain, sorrow, or regret for something done or left undone by one's self; to experience such sorrow for sin as produces amendment of life. It is contrition for sin; such sorrow for past conduct as to produce new life.[362] Since we are born into conditions of mortality, repentance comes to mean a turning of the heart and will to God, and a renunciation of sin to which we are naturally inclined. Without this there can be no progress in the things of the soul's salvation, for all accountable persons are stained by sin, and must be cleansed in order to enter the kingdom of heaven. Repentance is not optional for salvation; it is a commandment o God.[363] The

---

359 *Moses 6:57*
360 *D&C 58:42*
361 *Alma 34:32*
362 *The New Webster Encyclopedic Dictionary, 1980 Edition, Avenel Books, New York, p. 712*
363 *D&C 18:9-22; D&C 20:29; D&C 133:16*

preaching of repentance by John the Baptist formed the preparation for the ministry of our Lord.[364]

'For it must needs be, that there is an opposition in all things.'[365]

In the pre-existence, the war in heaven was about taking away our free agency. Therefore, in order for us to be able to choose good over evil, there must be opposition.

'I give unto men weakness that they may be humble...for if they humble themselves before me, and have faith in me, then will I make weak things become strong unto them.'[366]

'For I the Lord thy God will hold thy right hand, saying unto thee, Fear not; I will help thee.'[367]

'Therefore, cheer up your hearts, and remember that ye are free to act for yourselves--to choose the way of everlasting death or the way of eternal life.'[368]

'And again, believe that ye must repent of your sins and forsake them, and humble yourselves before God; and ask in sincerity of heart that he would forgive you; and now, if you believe all these things, see that ye do them.'[369]

Let me use the following analogy.

It is night-time in the winter. You are driving home not paying much attention to the road. There are twists and turns along with the straight patches. Some of the hills are not as steep as others. You automatically slow down where you have encountered black ice in the past. You are confident that you know the road very well as you have travelled the road many times back and forth on a daily basis. You feel that you could drive blindfolded. Suddenly a blizzard blows in catching you off guard. All of a sudden, visibility is almost nil.

All that you can see in the headlights of your vehicle is a yellow line down the middle of the highway. The headlights have to be on low as visibility

---

364 *Bible Dictionary, Holy Bible, King James Version, 1988 Edition, The Church of Jesus Christ of Latter-Day Saints, p. 760-761*
365 *2 Nephi 2:11*
366 *Ether 12:27*
367 *Isaiah 41:13*
368 *2 Nephi 10:23*
369 *Mosiah 4:10*

REPENTANCE

is nil when they are on high. The wind is whipping the snow against the window. The wipers cannot keep the windows clear. The loose snow on the ground is brutally swept across your pathway making the right side of the road by the ditch impossible to see. All that you can do is follow the yellow line to help you stay in the middle of the road. Suddenly the yellow line disappears as well. Now all you have to go on is your memory.

You are travelling too fast for the changed road conditions. Misjudging a turn, you hit a patch of black ice and veer off the road and overturn in the ditch.

You have hit your head against the windshield and lose consciousness. You did not buckle your seat belt as you felt that you would not need it. When you come to, you awake in pain and agony. You have concussion, a broken leg, collar bone and cracked ribs, along with numerous cuts and bruises.

Before you can drive a vehicle again, you must be healed.

Repentance is similar to the above analogy. The yellow line represents the Gospel of Jesus Christ. The twists and turns and hills represent temptations Satan sets in our way. The storm represents giving into those temptations. The accident represents losing our way and becoming lost.

In order to get back on the right path again, we must heal. That healing process is repentance. Once repentance is started, we can begin our progression again along the path towards eternal life.

'Yea, he that repenteth and exerciseth faith, and bringeth forth good works, and prayeth continually without ceasing--unto such it is given to know the mysteries of God; yea, unto such it shall be given to reveal things which never have been revealed.'[370]

This life is the time for men to repent and prepare to meet God. This life is the time given to us to prepare for eternity. We cannot improve ourselves after we die. No work can be performed. We cannot say that we will change and repent because that same Spirit that possesses our bodies when we die will have power to possess them in the eternal world.[371]

When we know we are about to meet our maker, we cannot repent upon our death bed. If we procrastinate our repentance until death, we have

---

370 Alma 26:22
371 Alma 34:33-34

become subjected to the spirit of the devil and we are sealed as his. The Spirit of the Lord has withdrawn from us and the devil has all power over us. This is the final state of the wicked.[372]

'And again, believe that ye must repent of your sins and forsake them, and humble yourselves before God; and ask in sincerity of heart that he would forgive you; and now, if you believe all these things see that ye do them.'[373]

When we have truly repented of our sins, we strive to keep the commandments of the Lord. As we do so, the Lord has promised us that our sins shall be forgiven.[374]

We must show that we have forsaken our sins by doing works of righteousness.

True repentance cannot be accomplished by anyone other than each individual. You cannot repent for someone else.

You cannot rationalize to cover and hide your sins. You must humble yourselves with a consciousness of guilt. Rationalizing is an enemy to repentance. There must be remorse and deep sorrow. True repentance comes before one is apprehended or imprisoned. Even though his sins may never be known, he is very sorry and feels anguish of soul. There are many sleepless nights and tear-stained eyes. Do not be ashamed of the tears.

Expressing sorrow or regret for what they have done is not true repentance. There must be a transformation in their lives, changes in their habits, and new thoughts to their minds. Being sorry is only a beginning. Once the path to repentance has begun, there must be no turning back. To do so only allows the former sins to return.[375]

True repentance is timeless. It is ongoing. Forgiveness is conditional. If the original sin is committed again, then the original sins return. It is much more difficult to repent. It can be done, but it takes much more work and dedication.

---

372 *Alma 34:35*
373 *Mosiah 4:10*
374 *D&C 1:32*
375 *D&C 82:7*

REPENTANCE

True repentance incorporates a changing of attitudes, a strengthening toward self-mastery. It must include restitution where possible. Though one may have abandoned a particular sin, even confessing to the Bishop when necessary, if he has not developed a life of service and righteousness, he is not repentant. The Lord said "...**He that repents and does the commandments of the Lord shall be forgiven.**"[376]

'Conscience is a celestial spark that God has put into every man for the purpose of saving his soul.' (Author unknown) It awakens the soul to consciousness of sin; it stimulates him to want to do better, to make adjustments, accept the sin in its full size and be willing to face facts, meet issues and pay penalties.

True repentance is to forgive all others. You cannot be forgiven if you hold grudges against others. A temporary or momentary change of like is not sufficient. Repentance must be consistent and continuous.

---

[376] D&C 1:32

CHAPTER TWENTY SEVEN

Forgiveness

'I, THE LORD, WILL FORGIVE WHOM I WILL FORGIVE, BUT OF YOU IT IS REQUIRED TO FORGIVE ALL MEN.'[377]

We are required to forgive and forget. That is very difficult. It is in our natures to hold a grudge and remember every wrong that someone has done to us. However, if we are to become as the Lord would have us be, then we must learn to forgive. We are forgiven our sins as we forgive others. How important it is then to forgive!

None of us are perfect. All of us have need for forgiveness.

'For if ye forgive men their trespasses your heavenly Father will also forgive you.'[378]

'Ye have heard that it hath been said, An eye for an eye, and a tooth for a tooth: But I say unto you...whosoever shall smite thee on thy right cheek, turn to him the other also.'[379]

'And we talk of Christ, we rejoice in Christ, we preach of Christ, we prophesy of Christ, and we write according to our prophecies, that our children may know to what source they may look for a remission of their sins.'[380]

'But as oft as they repented and sought forgiveness, with real intent, they were forgiven.'[381]

As we forgive others, we open the way for ourselves to continue striving toward our potential of one day returning to our heavenly home. Often the other person who has offended us does not know that he has done so. When

---

377 *D&C 64:10*
378 *3 Nephi 13:14*
379 *Matthew 5:38-39*
380 *2 Nephi 25:26*
381 *Moroni 6:8*

we hold onto a grudge and refuse to forgive him, we are no longer able to focus on what we want to do. All of our energy is focused on the thing that we are refusing to let go of. The Lord tells us that we must forgive all men and that He will forgive whom He will forgive.

No one on the face of the earth is perfect. We are bound to make mistakes. People are bound to be offended. However it is up to us to forgive them. When we forgive others we are forgiven of our sins and mistakes. How important it is then for us to forgive! We are not to judge others for how we judge them; the Lord will also judge us. If we don't forgive them, then the Lord will not forgive us.

We will all make mistakes along the way. How we handle those mistakes and how we live will determine where we will be. Our actions speak louder than words. We may say that we desire to return to live in the Celestial kingdom, but if our actions do not follow suit, we will not be able to go there. We will be assigned another place. It is up to us where we will go. The choice is ours.

CHAPTER TWENTY EIGHT

Jesus Christ

'BEHOLD, I AM JESUS CHRIST, THE SON OF THE LIVING GOD, WHO CREATED THE HEAVENS AND THE EARTH, A LIGHT WHICH CANNOT BE HID IN DARKNESS.'[382]

'BEHOLD, I AM THE LAW, AND THE LIGHT. LOOK UNTO ME, AND ENDURE TO THE END, AND YE SHALL LIVE; FOR UNTO HIM THAT ENDURETH TO THE END WILL I GIVE ETERNAL LIFE.'[383]

'THEREFORE I WOULD THAT YE SHOULD BE PERFECT EVEN AS I, OR YOUR FATHER WHO IS IN HEAVEN IS PERFECT.'[384]

'He that is baptized in my name, to him will the Father give the Holy Ghost, like unto me; wherefore, follow me, and do the things which ye have seen me do.'[385]

'Jesus saith unto him, I am the way, the truth, and the life: no man cometh unto the Father, but by me.'[386]

Who is Jesus Christ? He is the Son of the Living God, even God the Father. He is our Saviour and Redeemer. He is our Elder Brother. He is our mediator with the Father.

---

[382] *D&C 14:9*
[383] *3 Nephi 15:9*
[384] *3 Nephi 12:48*
[385] *2 Nephi 31:12*
[386] *John 14:6*

In the Greek language, Christ means the **anointed**. In Hebrew, Christ means the **Messiah**. Jesus, who is called Christ, is the firstborn of the Father in the spirit and the Only Begotten of the Father in the flesh. He is Jehovah, and was foreordained to his great calling in the Grand Councils before the world was. He was born of Mary at Bethlehem, lived a sinless life, and wrought out a perfect atonement for all mankind by the shedding of his blood and his death on the cross. He rose from the grave and brought to pass the bodily resurrection of every living thing and the salvation and exaltation of the faithful.

He is the greatest Being to be born on this earth - the perfect example - and all religious things should be done in his name. He is the Lord of lords, King of kings, the Creator, the Saviour, the God of the whole earth, the Captain of our salvation, the Bright and Morning Star. He is in all things, above all things, through all things, and round about all things; he is Alpha and Omega, the first and the last; his name is above every name, and is the only name under heaven by which we can be saved.

He will come again in power and glory to dwell on the earth, and will stand as Judge of all mankind at the last day.

Jesus is spoken of as the Christ and the Messiah, which means he is the one anointed of the Father to be his personal representative in all things pertaining to the salvation of mankind. The English word **Christ** is from a Greek word meaning **anointed**, and is the equivalent of **Messiah**, which is from a Hebrew and Aramaic term meaning **anointed**.[387]

Jesus Christ appeared to many worthy individuals before he was born. Among others, He appeared to Moses, Esaias, Isaiah and the brother of Jared.

'Wherefore, ye must press forward with a steadfastness in Christ, having a perfect brightness of hope, and a love of God and of all men.'[388]

'Behold, I am the law, and the light. Look unto me, and endure to the end, and ye shall live; for unto him that endureth to the end will I give eternal life.'[389]

---

387 *Psalms 2:2; Isaiah 61:1-3; Luke 4:16-32; Acts 4:23-30;Acts 10:38*
388 *2 Nephi 31:20*
389 *3 Nephi 15:9*

'Therefore, whatsoever ye shall do, ye shall do it in my name; therefore ye shall call the church in my name; and ye shall call upon the Father in my name that he will bless the church for my sake.'[390]

'For thus shall my church be called in the last days, even The Church of Jesus Christ of Latter-day Saints.'[391]

Jesus Christ came into the world to redeem his people. He took upon Him the sins and transgressions of all those who would believe on his name and be baptized. These are the ones who shall inherit eternal life and salvation. No one else can lay claim to this unless they come unto Christ and repent of their sins.[392]

Every person who comes to earth depends on Jesus Christ to fulfil the promise He made in Heaven to be our Saviour. Without Him, the whole plan of salvation would have failed.

Because His mission was necessary, all of the prophets from Adam to Jesus Christ testified that He would come. All the prophets since Jesus Christ have testified that He did come. Each of us needs to study the life of the Saviour and strive to keep His commandments throughout our lives in order to develop a personal relationship with Him. Jesus wants us to follow him.

The Life of Christ was predicted long before his birth

Adam was told by an angel, "The Saviour's name would be Jesus Christ."[393] Enoch saw that Jesus would die upon the cross and take up His body again.[394]

Noah and Moses also testified of Him.[395] About 800 years before the Saviour was born on the earth, Isaiah foresaw His life. When he saw the grief and sorrow that the Saviour would suffer in order to pay the price for our sins, he exclaimed: "He is despised and rejected of men; a man of sorrows and acquainted with grief...Surely He hath borne our griefs, and carried our

---

390 *3 Nephi 27:7*
391 *D&C 115:4*
392 *Alma 11:40*
393 *Moses 6:51-52*
394 *Moses 7:55-56*
395 *Moses 8:23-24*

sorrows...He was wounded for our transgressions, He was afflicted, yet He opened not His mouth: He is brought as a lamb to the slaughter."[396]

Nephi also saw a vision of the Saviour's future birth and mission. He saw a beautiful virgin, and an angel explained: "Behold, the virgin whom thou seest is the mother of the Son of God, after the manner of the flesh."[397] Then he saw the virgin holding a child in her arms. The angel declared: "Behold the lamb of God, yea, even the Son of the Eternal Father!"[398] About 124 years before Jesus was born, King Benjamin, another Nephite prophet and king, also foresaw the Saviour's life:

"For behold, the time cometh, and is not far distant, that with power, the Lord Omnipotent who reigneth, who was, and is from all eternity to all eternity, shall come down from heaven among the children of men, and shall dwell in a tabernacle of clay, and shall go forth amongst men, working mighty miracles, such as healing the sick, raising the dead, causing the lame to walk, the blind to receive their sight, and the deaf to hear, and curing all manner of diseases.

"And He shall cast out devils, or the evil spirits which dwell in the hearts of the children of men.

"And lo, He shall suffer temptations, and pain of body, hunger, thirst, and fatigue, even more than man can suffer, except it be unto death; for behold, blood cometh from every pore, so great shall be his anguish for the wickedness and the abominations of his people.

"And He shall be called Jesus Christ, Son of God, the Father of Heaven and Earth, the Creator of all things from the beginning; and his mother shall be called Mary."[399]

He was the Only Begotten of the Father

The birth of the Saviour Jesus Christ was foretold in the Book of Mormon[400] and the Pearl of Great Price. 'For according to the words of the prophets, the Messiah cometh in six hundred years from the time that my

---

396 *Isaiah 53:3-7*
397 *1 Nephi 11:18*
398 *1 Nephi 11:21*
399 *Mosiah 3:5-8*
400 *1 Nephi 10:4; 2 Nephi 25:19; 2 Nephi 17: 14*

JESUS CHRIST

father left Jerusalem; and according to the words of the prophets, and also the word of the angel of God, his name shall be Jesus Christ, the Son of God.'[401]

'For they would not hearken unto his voice, nor believe on his Only Begotten Son, even him whom he declared should come in the meridian of time, who was prepared from before the foundation of the world.

'And thus the Gospel began to be preached, from the beginning, being declared by holy angels sent forth from the presence of God, and by his own voice, and by the gift of the Holy Ghost.'[402]

The story of the birth and life of the Saviour is found in the New Testament in the books of Matthew, Mark, Luke and John. From their accounts, we learn that Jesus was born of a virgin[403] named Mary. She was engaged to marry Joseph when an angel of the Lord appeared to her. The angel told her that she was to be the mother of the Son of God. She asked him how this was possible.[404]

He told her: "The Holy Ghost shall come upon thee, and the power of the Highest shall overshadow thee: therefore also the Holy thing which shall be born of thee shall be called the Son of God."[405]

Thus, God the Father became the literal father of Jesus Christ. Jesus was born of a mortal mother and an immortal father. He is the only one to be born in this way on the earth. That is why He is called the Only Begotten Son. He inherited divine powers from his Father. No man could take the Saviour's life from him unless he willed it. He had power to lay it down and the power to take up his body again after dying.[406] From his mother, he inherited mortality and was subject to hunger, thirst, pain and death.

He led a Perfect Life

From his youth, Jesus obeyed all that was required of him by our Heavenly Father. Under the guidance of Mary and Joseph, Jesus grew much as other children grow.[407]

---

401 *2 Nephi 25:19*
402 *Moses 5:57, 58*
403 *2 Nephi 17: 14*
404 *Luke 1:34*
405 *Luke 1:35*
406 *John 10:17-18*
407 *Luke 2:40*

By the time he was twelve years old, he knew that he had been sent to do the will of his Father. He went with his parents to Jerusalem. When his parents were returning home, they discovered that he was not with their group. They went back to Jerusalem to look for him. "After three days, they found him in the temple, sitting in the midst of the doctors both hearing them, and asking them questions. And all that heard him were astonished at his understanding and answers."[408]

Joseph and Mary were relieved to find him but unhappy that he had treated them so. Mary said: "Son, why hast thou thus dealt with us? Behold thy father Joseph and I have sought thee sorrowing." Jesus answered her gently, reminding her that Joseph was only a stepfather.[409] In order to fulfil his mission, he was to do the will of his Father in Heaven. Later he declared; "I do nothing of myself; but as my Father hath taught me, I speak these things..."[410]

When Jesus was thirty years old, he went to his cousin John, to be baptized in the Jordan River.[411] John was reluctant to baptize Jesus because he knew that Jesus had never sinned. Jesus asked John to baptize him in order "to fulfil all righteousness."[412] John did baptize the Saviour, immersing him completely in the water. When Jesus was baptized, his Father spoke from Heaven saying, "This is my beloved Son, in whom I am well pleased."[413]

The Holy Ghost descended, as shown by the sign of the dove.[414]

Soon after Jesus baptism, Satan came to him to tempt him.[415] He wanted Jesus to fail his mission. If he could just get him to commit one sin, then Jesus would not be worthy to be our Saviour and the plan would fail. In this way, Satan could make us just as miserable as he is. We would never be able to return to our Heavenly Father. The temptations of Satan came after Jesus

---

408 *Luke 2:46-47*
409 *Luke 2:48-49*
410 *John 8:28-29*
411 *Matthew 3:13-17*
412 *Matthew 3:15*
413 *Matthew 3:17*
414 *Matthew 3:16*
415 *Matthew 4:3-9*

JESUS CHRIST

had been fasting for forty days.[416] Jesus firmly resisted all of Satan's temptations, and then commanded Satan to leave.[417] When Satan was gone, angels came and ministered to Jesus.[418]

HE TAUGHT US HOW TO LOVE AND SERVE ONE ANOTHER

After being tempted by Satan, Jesus began his public ministry. He had not only come to earth to die for us, but he also came to teach us how to live. He taught that there were two great commandments - first, to love God with all our heart, mind, and strength; and second, to love our fellowmen as we love ourselves.[419] Jesus life is an example of how we should obey these two commandments. If we love God, we will trust and obey Him. Jesus was obedient in all things. If we love our fellowmen, we will help them to meet their physical and spiritual needs.

Jesus life was spent in service to others. He cured them of diseases, made the deaf to hear, the blind to see and the lame to walk. Once it became late. The crowd was hungry. Jesus did not want to see the people suffer, so he took five loaves of bread and two fish and blessed them. From these loaves and fish, he fed the multitude of five thousand people.[420]

Jesus loved every one; little children, the elderly and those who had sinned. He taught them to repent and be baptized. Often He wept because his heart was so full of compassion. He taught them, "**I am the Way, the Truth and the Light.**"[421]

When Jesus hung on the cross, He prayed for the soldiers, who had crucified Him saying, "**Father, forgive them, for they know not what they do.**"[422] He even loved and had compassion for those who were unrepentant.

Jesus wanted everyone to be taught His gospel. He chose twelve apostles to testify of Him. They received their authority from Him. Because of their authority, they were able to teach, baptize and perform other ordinances

---

416 *Matthew 4:2*
417 *Matthew 4:10*
418 *Matthew 4:11*
419 *Matthew 22:36-39*
420 *Matthew 14:14-21*
421 *John 14:6*
422 *Luke 23:34*

in the name of Jesus. After the death of Jesus Christ, the apostles continued to preach repentance and baptism to the people. Eventually the people became so wicked that they killed the apostles.

At the conclusion of his life, when His work was finished of teaching the people, he prepared himself for the final and ultimate sacrifice, that of atoning for the sins of all mankind.

In the garden of Gethsemane, He knelt and prayed, asking, "**O my Father, if it is possible, let this cup pass from me; nevertheless, not as I will, but as thou wilt.**"[423]

The Saviour wept as He was weighted down with deep sorrow. Blood oozed from every pore, so great was His pain and agony. Only Jesus Christ, chosen from the beginning, could perform so great a sacrifice. He was the only perfect being who could satisfy the demands of justice, and unlock the gates of death.

In the Garden, Jesus suffered every horror that Satan could inflict. Even the crucifixion could not surpass the bitter anguish that He suffered for each of us.

The following day Jesus was beaten, humiliated and spat upon. He had to carry his own cross up the hill, where He was nailed to it. Crucifixion was one of the cruellest ways that man had devised. After nine hours of excruciating pain, **He cried out in agony, "My God, my God, why has thou forsaken me?"**[424]

In order for Jesus to have all the glory and victory over death, the Father had withdrawn His spirit from him. Never before had Jesus felt so alone.

Once Jesus knew that his suffering was complete and that the Father had accepted His sacrifice, He exclaimed in a loud voice, "**It is finished. Father, into thy hands I commend my spirit.**"[425]

During the three days that Jesus body lay in the tomb, His spirit preached to other spirits in the spirit world who needed to receive the gospel. On the third day, He returned to his body and took it up again. He was the

---

423 *Matthew 26:39*
424 *Mark 15:34*
425 *John 19:30*

JESUS CHRIST

first to overcome death. The prophecy had been fulfilled that He would rise again from the dead.[426]

Jesus appeared to the Nephites shortly after his resurrection. There He established His church where He taught and blessed the people.[427]

Jesus willingly suffered and paid the price for our sins. If we do not repent and obey Him, He will have suffered in vain. We then, will have to suffer, even as did He.

> 'FOR BEHOLD, I, GOD, HAVE SUFFERED THESE THINGS FOR ALL, THAT THEY MIGHT NOT SUFFER IF THEY WOULD REPENT;
>
> 'BUT IF THEY WOULD NOT REPENT THEY MUST SUFFER EVEN AS I; 'WHICH SUFFERING CAUSED MYSELF, EVEN GOD, THE GREATEST OF ALL, TO TREMBLE BECAUSE OF PAIN, AND TO BLEED AT EVERY PORE, AND TO SUFFER BOTH BODY AND SPIRIT—AND WOULD THAT I MIGHT NOT DRINK THE BITTER CUP, AND SHRINK—
>
> 'NEVERTHELESS, GLORY BE TO THE FATHER, AND I PARTOOK AND FINISHED MY PREPARATIONS UNTO THE CHILDREN OF MEN,
>
> 'WHEREFORE, I COMMAND YOU AGAIN TO REPENT, LEST I HUMBLE YOU WITH MY ALMIGHTY POWER; AND THEN YOU CONFESS YOUR SINS, LEST YOU SUFFER THESE PUNISHMENTS OF WHICH I HAVE SPOKEN, OF WHICH IN THE SMALLEST, YEA, EVEN IN THE LEAST DEGREE YOU HAVE TASTED AT THE TIME I WITHDREW MY SPIRIT.

---

426 *John 20:9*
427 *3 Nephi 11-28*

'LEARN OF ME, AND LISTEN TO MY WORDS; WALK IN THE MEEKNESS OF MY SPIRIT, AND YOU SHALL HAVE PEACE IN ME.

'I AM JESUS CHRIST; I CAME BY THE WILL OF THE FATHER, AND I DO HIS WILL.'[428]

All He asks is that we repent, come unto Him and love Him with all our hearts. He has said, "And this is the gospel which I have given unto you-that I came into the world to do the will of my Father, because my Father sent me. And my Father sent me that I might be lifted up upon the cross; and after that I had been lifted up upon the cross, that I might draw all men unto me...that they may be judged according to their works...for the work which ye have seen me do, that shall ye also do...Therefore, what manner of men ought ye to be? Verily, verily I say unto you, even as I am"

Alma the younger, who was the son of Alma, (the first being the chief judge among the people of Nephi, as well as being the high priest in the Church), gives us additional information as to the mission of Jesus Christ.

'But behold the Spirit hath said this much unto me, saying: Cry unto this people, saying - Repent ye, and prepare the way of the Lord, and walk in his paths, which are straight; for behold, the kingdom of heaven is at hand, and the Son of God cometh upon the face of the earth.

'And behold, he shall be born of Mary, at Jerusalem which is the land of our forefathers, she being a virgin, a precious and chosen vessel, who shall be overshadowed and conceive by the power of the Holy Ghost, and bring forth a son, yea, even the Son of God.

'And he shall go forth, suffering pains and afflictions and temptations of every kind; and this that the word might be fulfilled which saith he will take upon him the pains and the sicknesses of his people.

---

428 D&C 19:16-20

'And he will take upon him death, that he may loose the bands of death which bind his people; and he will take upon him their infirmities, that his bowels may be filled with mercy, according to the flesh, that he may know according to the flesh how to succour his people according to their infirmities.

'Now the Spirit knoweth all things; nevertheless the Son of God suffereth according to the flesh that he might take upon him the sins of his people, that he might blot out their transgressions according to the power of his deliverance; and now behold, this is the testimony which is in me.'[429]

All prophets, beginning with Adam, have been commanded to call the people to repentance. It is no different in this dispensation, The Dispensation of the Fullness of Time. As we prepare for the Second Coming of our Saviour, Jesus Christ, it is more vital than ever for the people to repent and prepare themselves for His Second Coming.

'Now I say unto you that ye must repent, and be born again; for the Spirit saith if ye are not born again ye cannot inherit the kingdom of heaven; therefore come and be baptized unto repentance that ye may be washed from you sins, that ye may have faith on the Lamb of God, who taketh away the sins of the world, who is mighty to save and to cleanse from all unrighteousness.

'Yea, I say unto you come and fear not, and lay aside every sin, which easily doth beset you, which doth bind you down to destruction, yea, come and go forth, and show unto your God that ye are willing to repent of your sins and enter into a covenant with him to keep his commandments, and witness it unto him this day by going into the waters of baptism.

'And whosoever doeth this, and keepeth the commandments of God from thenceforth, the same will remember that I say unto him, yea, he will remember that I have said unto him, he shall have eternal life, according to the testimony of the Holy Spirit, which testifieth in me.'[430]

---

429   Alma 7: 9-13
430   Alma 7: 14-16

'FEAST UPON THE WORDS OF CHRIST; FOR BEHOLD, THE WORDS OF CHRIST WILL TELL YOU ALL THINGS WHAT YE SHOULD DO.'[431]

---

431   2 Nephi 32:3

CHAPTER TWENTY NINE

Atonement

'O how great the holiness of our God! For he knoweth all things, and there is not anything save he knows it.

'And he cometh into the world that he may save all men if they will hearken unto his voice; for behold, he suffereth the pains of all men, yea, the pains of every living creature, both men, women, and children, who belong to the family of Adam.

'And he suffereth this that the resurrection might pass upon all men, that all might stand before him at the great and judgement day.

'And he commandeth all men that they must repent, and be baptized in his name, having perfect faith in the Holy One of Israel, or they cannot be saved in the kingdom of God.

'And if they will not repent and believe in his name, and be baptized in his name, and endure to the end, they must be damned; for the Lord God, the Holy One of Israel, has spoken it.

'Wherefore, he has given a law; and where there is no law given there is no punishment; and where there is no punishment there is no condemnation; and where there is no condemnation the mercies of the Holy One of Israel have claim upon them, because of the atonement; for they are delivered by the power of him.

'For the atonement satisfieth the demands of his justice upon all those who have not the law given to them, that they are delivered from that awful monster, death and hell, and the devil, and the lake of fire and brimstone, which is endless torment; and they are restored to that God who gave them breath, which is the Holy One of Israel.

'But wo unto him that has the law given, yea, that has all the commandments of God, like unto us, and that transgresseth them, and that wasteth the days of his probation, for awful is his state!'[432]

In the Bible dictionary, the word atonement describes the setting "at one" of those who have been estranged, and denotes the reconciliation of man to God.[433] Sin is the cause of the estrangement, and therefore the purpose of the atonement is to correct or overcome the consequences of sin. From the time of Adam to the death of Jesus Christ, true believers were instructed to offer animal sacrifices to the Lord. These sacrifices were symbolic of the forthcoming death of Jesus Christ, and were done by faith in him.[434]

Jesus Christ, as the Only Begotten Son of God and the only sinless person to live on this earth, was the only one capable of making atonement for mankind. By his selection and fore-ordination in the Grand Council before the world was formed, his divine Son-ship, his sinless life, the shedding of His blood in the Garden of Gethsemane, His death on the cross and subsequent bodily resurrection from the grave, He made a perfect atonement for all mankind. All are covered unconditionally as pertaining to the fall of Adam. Hence, all shall rise from the dead with immortal bodies, because of Jesus' atonement. "For as in Adam all die, even so in Christ shall all be made alive."[435] All little children are innocent at birth.[436] 'Wherefore, they cannot sin, for power is not given unto Satan to tempt little children, until they begin to become accountable before me.'[437]

The atonement is conditional, however, so far as each person's individual sins are concerned, and touches every one to the degree that he has faith in Jesus Christ, repents of his sins, and obeys the gospel. The services of the Day of Atonement foreshadowed the atoning work of Christ.[438]

---

432 *2 Nephi 9:20-27*
433 *Bible Dictionary, Holy Bible, King James Version, 1988 Edition, The Church of Jesus Christ of Latter-Day Saints, p. 617*
434 *Moses 5:5-8*
435 *1 Corinthians 15:22*
436 *D&C 29:46*
437 *D&C 29:47*
438 *Leviticus 4; Leviticus 23:26-32; Hebrews 9*

ATONEMENT

The scriptures point out that no law, ordinance, or sacrifice would be satisfactory if it were not for the atonement of Jesus Christ.[439]

Sin is lawlessness.[440] It is a refusal on men's part to submit to the law of God.[441] By transgression man loses control over his own will and becomes the slave of sin,[442] and so incurs the penalty of spiritual death, which is alienation from God.[443] The atonement of Jesus Christ redeems all mankind from the fall of Adam and causes all to be answerable for their own manner of life. This means of atonement is provided by the Father,[444] and is offered in the life and person of his Son, Jesus Christ.[445]

No matter how perfect a life one lives, no one can atone for their individual sins and be reunited into our Heavenly Fathers presence. We need a mediator, or a person to represent us, to our Father. Jesus Christ is that person. He is our Saviour.

The following story illustrates this point.

There was once a man who owed a large sum of money to his creditors. Since he had no way to repay the money, his creditors were going to put him in jail until he could repay the money. In jail, he would have no opportunity to be able to find the way to pay his debts so he would be there forever.

A kind man upon hearing of the predicament of this fellow stepped forward and offered to pay the debt for him. The creditors were satisfied in that their debt was paid. The man was happy because he did not have to go to prison.

We are the individuals who owe. What we owe are our sins. Of ourselves, we cannot rid ourselves of them and become pure. Our creditor is the law of justice. The demands of justice must be satisfied. The kind man is our Saviour, Jesus Christ. By taking upon himself all the sins of the world, suffering in the Garden of Gethsemane, dying upon the cross, and in three

---

439   *Hebrews 10:1-9; 2 Nephi 9:5-24; Mosiah 13:27-32*
440   *1 John 3:4*
441   *Romans 8:7*
442   *Romans 7:14*
443   *Romans 6:23*
444   *John 3:16-17*
445   *2 Corinthians 5:19*

days being resurrected, He satisfied the demands of the laws of justice and the laws of mercy.

What the Saviour asks of us is to repent and obey the commandments. By doing so, we are preparing ourselves for entrance into the Celestial kingdom to be reunited with our Heavenly Parents and Jesus Christ.

Jesus Christ opened the way for us to return. He unlocked the keys of death and the grave. He has taken away our sins. All we need to do is repent and strive to do all that we are asked to. If we do, we will not have to suffer as Jesus did. However if we do not, we will have to suffer for them ourselves.[446]

'Therefore, I command you to repent... For behold I, God, have suffered these things for all, that they might not suffer if they would repent;

'But if they would not repent they must suffer even as I; Which suffering caused myself, even God, the greatest of all, to tremble because of pain, and to bleed at every pore, and to suffer both body and spirit---and would that I might not drink the bitter cup, and shrink---

'Nevertheless, glory be to the Father, and I partook and finished my preparations unto the children of men,

'Wherefore, I command you again to repent, lest I humble you with my almighty power; and that you confess your sins, lest you suffer these punishments of which I have spoken, of which in the smallest, yea, even in the least degree you have tasted at the time I withdrew my Spirit.'[447]

'And now, behold, I will testify unto you of myself that these things are true. Behold, I say unto you, that I do know that Christ shall come among the children of men, to take upon him the transgressions of his people, and that he shall atone for the sins of the world; for the Lord God hath spoken it.

'For it is expedient that an atonement should be made; for according to the great plan of the Eternal God there must be an atonement made, or else all mankind must unavoidably perish; yea, all are hardened; yea, all are alien and are lost, and must perish except it be through the atonement which it is expedient should be made.

---

446 *D&C 19:16-20*
447 *D&C 19:15-20*

ATONEMENT

'For it is expedient that there should be a great and last sacrifice; yea, not a sacrifice of man, neither of beast, neither of any manner of fowl; for it shall not be a human sacrifice, but it must be an infinite and eternal sacrifice.

'Now there is not any man that can sacrifice his own blood which will atone for the sins of another. Now, if a man murdereth, behold will our law, which is just, take the life of his brother? I say unto you, nay.

'But the law requireth the life of him who hath murdered; therefore there can be nothing which is short of an infinite atonement which will suffice for the sins of the world.

'Therefore, it is expedient that there should be a great and last sacrifice, and then shall there be, or it is expedient that there should be, a stop to the shedding of blood; then shall the law of Moses be fulfilled; yea, it shall be all fulfilled, every jot and tittle, and none shall have passed away.

'And behold, this is the whole meaning of the law, every whit pointing to that great and last sacrifice which will be the Son of God, yea, infinite and eternal.

'And thus he shall bring salvation to all those who shall believe on his name; this being the intent of this last sacrifice, to bring about the bowels of mercy, which overpowereth justice, and bringeth about means unto men that they may have faith unto repentance.

'And thus mercy can satisfy the demands of justice, and encircles them in the arms of safety, while he that exercises no faith unto repentance is exposed to the whole law of the demands of justice; therefore only unto him that has faith unto repentance is brought about the great and eternal plan of redemption.'[448]

What Would Have Happened if There Had Been No Atonement?
– The Consequences if there had been no Atonement
See Appendix on page 301

---

448 *Alma 34:8-16*

CHAPTER THIRTY

Missionary Work

'AND YE SHALL GO FORTH IN THE POWER OF MY SPIRIT, PREACHING MY GOSPEL, TWO BY TWO, IN MY NAME, LIFTING UP YOUR VOICES AS WITH THE SOUND OF A TRUMP, DECLARING MY WORD LIKE UNTO ANGELS OF GOD.'[449]

'GO YE THEREFORE, AND TEACH ALL NATIONS, BAPTIZING THEM IN THE NAME OF THE FATHER, AND OF THE SON, AND OF THE HOLY GHOST.'[450]

'Therefore, O ye that embark in the service of God, see that ye serve him with all your heart, might, mind and strength, that ye may stand blameless before God at the last day.

'Therefore, if ye have desires to serve God ye are called to the work;

'For behold the field is white already to harvest; and lo, he that thrusteth in his sickle with his might, the same layeth up in store that he perisheth not, but bringeth salvation to his soul;

'And faith, hope, charity and love, with an eye single to the glory of God, qualify him for the work.

'Remember faith, virtue, knowledge, temperance, patience, brotherly kindness, godliness, charity, humility, diligence.

'Ask, and ye shall receive; knock, and it shall be opened unto you. Amen.'[451]

We do not have to be called as full time missionaries to do the Lord's work. We can love and serve our neighbours. We can invite them to church

---

449 D&C 42:6
450 Matthew 28:19
451 D&C 4:2-7

activities. We can be sensitive to their needs. We need to love them as our Father loves us. After all, they are our brothers and sisters. Do we not want them to be happy and enjoy the blessings which we have?

'And now, if your joy will be great with one soul that you have brought unto me into the kingdom of my Father, how great will be your joy if you should bring many souls unto me!' [452]

The Lord himself, revealed to Adam the gospel plan:

'And thus the gospel began to be preached from the beginning being declared by holy angels sent forth from the presence of God and by his own voice, and by the gift of the Holy Ghost.'[453]

Each prophet of the Church of Jesus Christ of Latter-day Saints has emphasized the necessity of the members of the church to help spread the gospel. President David O McKay summed it up clearly, saying, '**EVERY MEMBER A MISSIONARY.**'[454] We influence others by the way we live the gospel, our attitude toward our friends and family. It is what we are, not what we pretend to be, that will affect their decision to investigate the church and thereby enjoy the blessings which we have to offer and share.

President Spencer W. Kimball has further emphasized this message by clearly stating that the members, each and every one of us, have the basic responsibility for missionary work. "The missionaries," said President Kimball, "are to help the members do their job."

The members find, and the missionaries teach. Every member is a missionary. The Lord's commission to preach the gospel to every creature[455] applies to us just as it did to His disciples of old. "We must take missionary work more seriously," President Ezra Taft Benson says. "We have been greatly blessed with the material means, the technology, and an inspired message to bring the gospel to all men. More is expected of us than any previous generation."

---

[452] *D&C 18:16*
[453] *Moses 5:58*
[454] *'Every Member a Missionary', Improvement Era, October 1961, p. 710-711*
[455] *Mark 16:15*

MISSIONARY WORK

We must not be afraid to be missionaries. We must trust in the Lord. In D&C 38:30, the Lord has said, "**If ye are prepared, ye shall not fear.**"

What a wonderful promise! We do not need to be afraid of what others may think or say. The Lord's work **will** roll forth. Will we be part of that glorious work in preparing the earth for the Second Coming of our Saviour, Jesus Christ? Or will we be content to just sit and watch others?

The Lord will assist us in doing missionary work as we diligently prepare for and pray for opportunities to share the gospel. It is His program. He will not allow it to fail. After all, the Lord tells us, "**This is my work and my glory to bring to pass the immortality and eternal life of man.**"[456]

How can man be exalted if he has not been given opportunity to hear and accept the gospel? The work that needs to be done here on the earth are baptism, priesthood ordinations, temple endowments and temple marriage.

Elder Ballard has outlined a procedure to help us in doing missionary work:

First, prayerfully set a date by which we will have someone prepared to hear the gospel message. Second, fast and pray for guidance about whom the Lord would have us share the gospel with. It may be someone we already know, or it could be someone whom we have not yet met.

As we sincerely strive to do the Lord's work, we will have special spiritual experiences as the Lord inspires us. He will enhance your vision of this work by bringing names of non members to your mind. You will be blessed to know what you should say and how you should approach each person.

He will bring great blessings into our own lives and into the lives of others as we strive to do missionary work. Elder Ballard says, "No joy equals that of bringing the light of the gospel of Jesus Christ into the life of one of Heavenly Father's children."

There are four proven keys which will help to move the spirit of missionary work forward.

---

[456] *Moses 1:39*

First: strive to obtain the Spirit

How do you obtain the Spirit? Pray for increased faith with sincerity and real intent. You will have to search the scriptures daily. Pray for the spirit to accompany you. Fast, that you may have the spirit and that the Lord will direct your thoughts to those who are ready to hear the gospel.

Second: Acquire humility

The Lord has said, "No one can assist with this work who is not humble and full of love, having faith, hope, and charity, being temperate in all things, whatsoever shall be entrusted to his care."[457]

Third: Love people

We must develop love for all people. Our hearts must go out to them in the pure love of the gospel. Remember that every person is a child of God, and as such, is our brother or sister.

Fourth: Work diligently

If we want to keep the spirit, we must work. There is no greater exhilaration or satisfaction than to know that after a hard day of work, we have done our very best. The greatest secret of missionary work **is** work.

The gospel of Jesus Christ has been restored in its fullness, together with His Holy Priesthood, to bless our Father's children. Our message is a world message. The church is a world organization with the greatest message in the entire world. The Lord has commanded us **"to arise and shine and to be a light unto the world."**[458]

If the Lord was to ask each of you personally to do missionary work, would you? That is exactly what He is doing. The Lord says that whether it is through the voice of Himself or through the voice of his servants, it is the same.[459]

"With all my soul, I testify that this work will go forward till every land and people have had opportunity to accept our message. Barriers will come down for us to accomplish this mission and some of us will see it done.

---

457 *D&C 12:8*
458 *3 Nephi 18:24*
459 *D&C 1:38*

MISSIONARY WORK

"Our Heavenly Father will cause conditions in the world to change so that his gospel can penetrate every border. We must prove every day of our lives that we are willing to do the will of the Lord to spread the restored gospel, to bear testimony to the world, and to share the gospel with others."[460]

What can we do to help forward the missionary program? Following is a list of some common member missionary activities that will help all of us to do missionary work:

1. Talk about the church or the gospel
2. Socialize outside of church activities
3. Socialize at church activities
4. Extend an invitation to attend regular Sunday meetings
5. Extend an invitation to meet with the missionaries
6. Extend an invitation to attend a fireside
7. Give copies of the Book of Mormon
8. Extend an invitation to attend family home evening
9. Share a church video
10. Bear your testimony
11. Be aware of someone's needs (a birth, a death, a marriage). Let them know about Heavenly Father's plan for eternal families
12. Be of service. As we serve, opportunities will present themselves to talk about the gospel
13. We should all be missionaries. Every member of the church is to be a missionary even if we are not formally called and set apart. We have the responsibility to teach the gospel by word and deed to all of our Heavenly Father's children.
14. Our prophets have told us that we must love our neighbours before we warn them. They need to experience our friendship and fellowship.
15. Missionary work is part of our church. It is important to each of us; if it isn't, then it should be.

Our Heavenly Father will help us to be effective missionaries when we have the desire to share the gospel and pray for guidance. He will help us to find ways to share the gospel with those around us. As we do our part in the

---

[460] *President Ezra Taft Benson*

great missionary program of the church, the Lord will hasten his coming. He will not come until everyone has had an opportunity to hear the gospel. Let us **"lengthen our stride"** and commit ourselves to spreading the gospel. Then the glorious morn will break forth and shine as the Saviour comes to reign in the millennium. Let us do our part in hastening the work of the Lord!

CHAPTER THIRTY ONE

Baptism

'AND THEIR CHILDREN SHALL BE BAPTIZED FOR THE REMISSION OF THEIR SINS WHEN EIGHT YEARS OLD, AND RECEIVE THE LAYING ON OF THE HANDS.'[461]

Baptism is the gateway to the celestial world. Without it, we cannot gain entrance in any of the other 'gates' or ordinances. Even though Jesus Christ was perfect in every way, he too was baptised to show us the way.

'WHEREFORE, I WOULD THAT YE SHOULD REMEMBER THAT I HAVE SPOKEN UNTO YOU CONCERNING THAT PROPHET WHICH THE LORD SHOWED UNTO ME, THAT SHOULD BAPTIZE THE LAMB OF GOD, WHICH SHOULD TAKE AWAY THE SINS OF THE WORLD.

'AND NOW, IF THE LAMB OF GOD, HE BEING HOLY, SHOULD HAVE NEED TO BE BAPTIZED BY WATER, TO FULFIL ALL RIGHTEOUSNESS, O THEN, HOW MUCH MORE NEED HAVE WE, BEING UNHOLY, TO BE BAPTIZED, YEA, EVEN BY WATER!

'AND NOW, I WOULD ASK OF YOU, MY BELOVED BRETHREN, WHEREIN THE LAMB OF GOD DID FULFIL ALL RIGHTEOUSNESS IN BEING BAPTIZED BY WATER?

'KNOW YE NOT THAT HE WAS HOLY? BUT NOTWITHSTANDING HE BEING HOLY, HE SHOWETH UNTO THE CHILDREN

---

461   D&C 68:27

OF MEN THAT, ACCORDING TO THE FLESH HE HUMBLETH HIMSELF BEFORE THE FATHER, AND WITNESSETH UNTO THE FATHER THAT HE WOULD BE OBEDIENT UNTO HIM IN KEEPING HIS COMMANDMENTS.

'AND AGAIN, IT SHOWETH UNTO THE CHILDREN OF MEN THE STRAIGHTNESS OF THE PATH, AND THE NARROWNESS OF THE GATE, BY WHICH THEY SHOULD ENTER, HE HAVING SET THE EXAMPLE BEFORE THEM.'[462]

We must follow the path of Jesus Christ; be baptized, receive the Holy Ghost and endure to the end. Repentance and baptism are the gates that lead to the strait and narrow path. Eternal life will come to those who keep the commandments after they are baptized. It is not easy, but our Saviour has promised us that it will be worth the sacrifice and endurance in keeping the commandments and following Him.

Little children have no need for baptism.[463] When they die, they are received directly into the Celestial kingdom.[464] **'But little children are holy, being sanctified through the atonement of Jesus Christ; and this is what the scriptures mean.'**[465] How wonderful to be parents of children so perfect that all they needed was to gain a body of flesh and bones!

'For all men must repent and be baptized, and not only men, but women, and children who have arrived at the years of accountability.'[466]

Each of us was born into the world to fulfil a mission. The mission of Jesus was so important that John the Baptist was sent to prepare the way for Him.

Today, as in the days of Jesus, there are certain principles and ordinances of the gospel which the Lord said we must learn and obey.

---

462 *2 Nephi 31:4-9*
463 *Moroni 8:10-12*
464 *D&C 137:10*
465 *D&C 74:7*
466 *D&C 18:42*

BAPTISM

The first two beliefs of the gospel are; 1) faith in the Lord Jesus Christ and 2) repentance.

Baptism is the first ordinance of the gospel. One of the instructions the Lord gave to his apostles was "Go ye therefore and teach all nations, baptizing them in the name of the Father, and the Son and the Holy Ghost, teaching them to pay attention to all things whatsoever I have commanded you."[467]

Because none of us are perfect, we must be baptized for the remission of our sins. As we repent and are baptized, our sins are forgiven through the atonement of Jesus Christ.

All who humble themselves before God and desire to be baptized, who have truly repented of all their sins, shall be received by baptism into His church. In this way we become members of the Church of Jesus Christ of Latter-day Saints. The Lord said, **'if thou wilt turn unto me, and repent of all thy transgressions** (sins) **and be baptized, even in water, in the name of mine Only Begotten Son, ye shall receive the gift of the Holy Ghost.'**[468]

There is only one correct mode of baptism. Jesus told the Prophet Joseph Smith that a person having the proper priesthood authority to perform baptism, shall go down into the water with the person who is to be baptized, then he shall immerse (completely cover with water) that person and come forth again out of the water.

Immersion is necessary. The apostle Paul taught that being immersed and coming out again is symbolic of death and the resurrection. Our sinful life ends when we are baptized. We start a new life after baptism.

Every person who has reached the age of accountability of eight years should be baptized.[469]

'And again, inasmuch as parents have children in Zion, or in any of her stakes which are organized, that teach them not to understand the doctrine of repentance, faith in Christ the Son of the living God, and of baptism and

---

467 *Matthew 28:19*
468 *Moses 6:52*
469 *D&C 68:25, 27*

the gift of the Holy Ghost by the laying on of the hands, when eight years old, the sin be upon the heads of the parents.'

Covenants are made between the individual and God. A covenant is a promise that each party makes that they will do certain things.

The baptismal covenant is a sacred agreement between the individual and Heavenly Father. What is the baptismal covenant?

'I the Lord, am bound when ye do what I say; but when ye do not what I say, ye have no promise.'[470]

When we are baptized, we make certain promises to God. We will:
1. Repent of sins
2. Take upon me the name of Christ
3. Always remember Him
4. Serve Him and keep His commandments
5. Stand as a witness for Him at all times
6. Love my fellow men

God also makes promises to us when we are baptized. God will:
1. Take away my sins
2. My name in the Lamb's Book of Life
3. His Spirit will be with me
4. Peace of mind and joy in this life
5. Come forth in the first resurrection
6. Eternal life with God in the Celestial Glory

'Repent, and be baptized every one of you in the name of Jesus Christ for the remission of sins, and ye shall receive the gift of the Holy Ghost.'[471]

---

470 *D&C 82:10*
471 *Acts 2:38*

CHAPTER THIRTY TWO

Holy Ghost

'AND BY THE POWER OF THE HOLY GHOST YE MAY KNOW THE TRUTH OF ALL THINGS.'[472]

'CAST ALL BITTERNESS OUT OF YOUR OWN HEARTS--ALL ANGER, WRATH, STRIFE, COVETOUSNESS, AND LUST, AND SANCTIFY THE LORD GOD IN YOUR HEARTS, THAT YOU MAY ENJOY THE HOLY GHOST, AND HAVE THAT SPIRIT TO BE YOUR CONSTANT COMPANION DAY BY DAY, TO LEAD YOU INTO ALL TRUTH, AND THEN YOU WILL HAVE GOOD DOCTRINE, GOOD FEELINGS, GOOD WIVES, GOOD CHILDREN, A GOOD COMMUNITY; AND FINALLY, YOU WILL BE SAINTS IN THE FULLEST SENSE OF THE WORD...'[473]

The Holy Ghost is the third personage of the Godhead. There is God the Father, His son Jesus Christ, and the Holy Ghost. God the Father and Jesus Christ have bodies of flesh and bones, but the Holy Ghost is a personage of spirit. [474]

The Holy Ghost was first made known to Adam and has been manifest in every dispensation since the beginning.[475]

The Holy Ghost is manifested to men on the earth both as the power of the Holy Ghost and as the gift of the Holy Ghost. The power can come upon one before baptism, and is the convincing witness that the gospel is true. It gives one a testimony of Jesus Christ and of his work and the work of his

---

472 Moroni 10:5
473 Brigham Young, April 5, 1860 Journal of Discourses, 1966, Vol. 8 p. 44
474 D&C 130:21-22
475 1 Nephi 10:17-22; Moses 6:51-68

servants upon the earth. The gift can come only after proper and authorized baptism, and is conferred by the laying on of hands.[476]

Whenever one is worthy, one has the right to have the companionship of the Holy Ghost. It is more powerful than that which is available before baptism. Upon baptism, the Holy Ghost acts as a cleansing agent to purify and sanctify a person from all sin. That is the reason it is often spoken of as "fire".[477]

The manifestation on the day of Pentecost (Acts 2) was the gift of the Holy Ghost that came upon the Twelve. Without it, they were not ready for their ministries to the world.

The scriptures do not explain why the Holy Ghost did not operate in its fullness among the Jews during the years of Jesus' mortal sojourn.[478] Statements to the effect that the Holy Ghost did not come until after Jesus was resurrected must of necessity refer to that particular dispensation only, for it is abundantly clear that the Holy Ghost was operative in earlier dispensations.

Furthermore, it has reference only to the gift of the Holy Ghost not being present, since the power of the Holy Ghost was operative during the ministries of John the Baptist and Jesus; otherwise no one would have received a testimony of the truths that these men taught.[479] When a person speaks by the power of the Holy Ghost, that same power carries a conviction of the truth into the heart of the hearer.[480] The Holy Ghost knows all things,[481] and can therefore lead one to know of future events. [482]

The Holy Ghost is also known by other names in the scriptures; Holy Spirit, Spirit of God, Spirit of the Lord, Comforter, and Spirit.

---

476 *Acts 8:12; Moroni 2:1-3*
477 *Matthew 3:11; 2 Nephi 31:17; D&C 19:31*
478 *John 7:34; John 16:7*
479 *Matthew 16:16, 17; 1 Corinthians 12:3*
480 *2 Nephi 33:1*
481 *D&C 35:19*
482 *2 Peter 1:21*

HOLY GHOST

'But the fruit of the Spirit is love, joy, peace, longsuffering, gentleness, goodness, faith, meekness, temperance.'[483]

'...if ye shall ask with a sincere heart, with real intent, having faith in Christ, he will manifest the truth of it unto you, by the power of the Holy Ghost.'[484]

The Holy Ghost is an individual spiritual being in the Godhead, who does not have a body of flesh and bones as does the Father and Jesus Christ.

There are several gifts of the Holy Ghost which are bestowed upon those who are worthy. Not everyone has the same gift, so everyone may benefit thereby.

'For all have not every gift given unto them; for there are many gifts, and to every man is given a gift by the Spirit of God.'[485]

'To some it is given by the Holy Ghost to know that Jesus Christ is the Son of God, and that he was crucified for the sins of the world.

'To others it is given to believe on their words, that they also might have eternal life if they continue faithful.

'And again, to some it is given by the Holy Ghost to know the differences of administration, as it will be pleasing unto the same Lord, according as the Lord will, suiting his mercies according to the conditions of the children of men.

'And again, it is given by the Holy Ghost to some to know the diversities of operations, whether they be of God, that the manifestations of the Spirit may be given to every man to profit withal.

'And again, verily I say unto you, to some is given, by the Spirit of God, the word of wisdom.

'To another is given the word of knowledge, that all may be taught to be wise and to have knowledge.

'And again, to some it is given to have faith to be healed;

'And to others, it is given to have faith to heal.

'And again, to some is given the working of miracles;

'And to others it is given to prophesy;

---

483   *Galatians 5:22-23*
484   *Moroni 10:4*
485   *D&C 46:11*

'And to others the discerning of spirits.

'And again, it is given to some to speak with tongues;

'And to another is given the interpretation of tongues.

'And all these gifts come from God, for the benefit of the children of God.

'And unto the bishop of the church, and unto such as God shall appoint and ordain to watch over the church and to be elders unto the church, are to have it given unto them to discern all those gifts lest there shall be any among you professing and yet be not of God.

'...he that asketh in Spirit shall receive in Spirit;

'He that asketh in the Spirit asketh according to the will of God; wherefore it is done even as he asketh.

'And ye must give thanks unto God in the Spirit for whatsoever blessing ye are blessed with.

'And ye must practise virtue and holiness before me continually. Even so. Amen.'[486]

How do you know when you do or do not have the Spirit?

WHEN YOU HAVE THE SPIRIT

1. You feel happy and calm
2. You feel full of light
3. Your mind is clear
4. Your bosom burns with love for the Lord and for others
5. You feel generous
6. No one can offend you
7. You are very forgiving and kind
8. You feel confident in what you do
9. You don't mind anyone seeing what you are doing
10. You feel outgoing and anxious to be with others (especially family members)
11. You are glad when others succeed
12. You want to make others happy, even those opposed to you

---

[486] D&C 46:13-28, 30, 32, 33

13. You bring out the best and say the best about others
14. You gladly and willingly perform Church work
15. You feel like praying and reading the scriptures
16. You wish you could keep all the Lord's commandments
17. You feel you have control of your appetites and emotions: food and sleep in moderation, sexual restraint, recreation that is wholesome and moderate, controlled speech, and no anger
18. You feel a deep desire to help others---usually in a way no one else will know about
19. You speak and think only good about others
20. You feel sorrow when others have problems and sincerely desire to help them
21. You realize that your thoughts and your actions are open to God

WHEN YOU DO NOT HAVE THE SPIRIT; OR WHEN SATAN IS PROMPTING YOU

1. You feel unhappy, depressed, confused and frustrated.
2. You feel heavy and full of darkness.
3. Your mind is muddled.
4. You feel empty, hollow and cold inside.
5. You feel selfish, possessive, and self-centred.
6. Everything anyone does bothers you.
7. You are always on the defensive.
8. You are easily discouraged.
9. You become secretive and evasive.
10. You want to be alone, and you avoid others (especially family members).
11. You are envious of what others do and of what they have.
12. You want to get even and show others up.
13. You are critical of others, especially family members and those in authority.
14. You feel hesitant, unworthy, and unwilling to perform Church ordinances.
15. You don't want to pray or read the scriptures.

16. You find the commandments of God and rules of the family bothersome, restricting, or senseless.

17. You become a slave to your appetites; your emotions become passionate; overindulgence in food, sleep, sex, stimulating entertainment, loud music, strong anger, and outspokenness all become part of your character.

18. You want to make sure all the help you give others is duly noted by them and the world.

19. You look for and find evil in others and broadcast it.

20. You question others' motives and secretly delight in their problems; then you say "I'm glad I'm not that way."

21. You feel that what you do and think is only your business and no one else knows or cares.[487]

We may ask ourselves the following questions to see if we have the Spirit of the Lord with us. Alma, from the Book of Mormon, has given us this checklist for self-assessment.

1. Have ye spiritually been born of god?[488]
2. Have ye received his image in your countenances?[489]
3. Have ye experienced this mighty change in your hearts?[490]
4. Do ye exercise faith in the redemption of him who created you?[491]
5. Do you look forward...to stand before God to be judged according to the deeds which have been done in the mortal body?[492]
6. Can you imagine to yourselves that ye hear the voice of the Lord, saying unto you, in that day: Come unto me ye blessed...?[493]
7. Or do ye imagine to yourselves that ye can lie unto the Lord in the day...and that he will save you?[494]

---

487 Don Norton, *Ensign, August 1878, p. 32-33; John H. Groberg, "Investing for Eternity," in Speeches of the Year, 1981-1982 (Provo:Brigham Young University Press, 1982, p. 167-168*
488 Alma 5:14
489 Alma 5:14
490 Alma 5:14
491 Alma 5:15
492 Alma 5:15
493 Alma 5:16
494 Alma 5:17

8. Can ye imagine yourselves brought before the tribunal of God with your souls filled with guilt and remorse?[495]

9. Can ye look up to God at that day with a pure heart and clean hands?[496]

10. Can ye think of being saved when you have...become subjects to the devil?[497]

11. How will you feel to stand before God "having your garments stained with blood and all manner of filthiness?[498]

12. If ye have experienced a change of heart and have felt to sing the song of redeeming love...can ye feel so now? [499]

13. Have ye walked, keeping yourselves blameless before God? [500]

14. Have you been sufficiently humble? [501]

15. Are ye stripped of pride? [502]

16. Are you stripped of envy? [503]

17. Do you mock or persecute a brother? [504]

There are several ways to tell which side we are on. When we are on God's side, we have feelings of love, rejoicing, praise, thankfulness, gratitude, joy, faith, forgiveness, patience, longsuffering, humility, meekness, harmony, peace, temperance, goodness, gentleness, etc.

However, we can cross the line to the other side quite easily. We find fault with others, we criticise, quarrel, argue; we have feelings of contention, pride, discouragement, disbelief, doubt, fear, worry, anxiety, and hate.

Examples from the scriptures that come from God make us feel good. They lift us and help to give us self-esteem.

---

495 Alma 5:18
496 Alma 5:19
497 Alma 5:20
498 Alma 5:22
499 Alma 5:26
500 Alma 5:27
501 Alma 5:27
502 Alma 5:28
503 Alma 5:29
504 Alma 5:30

Jesus Christ told us, 'If ye love me, keep my commandments.'[505] Our Heavenly Father gave His Only Begotten Son, that whosoever believeth in Him should not perish but have everlasting life.[506] **'For behold, this is my work and my glory---to bring to pass the immortality and eternal life of man.'**[507]

LOVE

'FOR GOD SO LOVED THE WORLD, THAT HE GAVE HIS ONLY BEGOTTEN SON, THAT WHOSOEVER BELIEVETH IN HIM SHOULD NOT PERISH BUT HAVE EVERLASTING LIFE.'[508]

Before we came to this earth, we lived in heaven with our Heavenly parents. There they taught us. We learned all that we could. We yearned to be like them. In order for us to continue in our desire to become like our Heavenly Parents, we had to come to this earth and gain a body. There was a Council in Heaven. Two plans were presented before the Father.[509]

Jesus Christ presented the first plan wherein he said, "Father, thy will be done and the glory be thine forever."[510]

The other plan presented was by Satan. He said, "Behold, here am I, send me, I will be thy son, and I will redeem all mankind, that one soul shall not be lost, and surely I will do it; wherefore give me thine honour."[511]

Our Father chose the first. He replied, "But, behold, my Beloved Son, which was my Beloved and Chosen from the beginning, said unto me---'Father, thy will be done, and the glory be thine forever.'[512]

---

505 *John 14:15*
506 *John 3:16*
507 *Moses 1:39*
508 *John 3:16*
509 *Moses 4:1*
510 *Moses 4:2*
511 *Moses 4:1*
512 *Moses 4:2*

HOLY GHOST

"Wherefore, because that Satan rebelled against me, and sought to destroy the agency of man, which I, the Lord God, had given him, and also, that I should give unto him mine own power; by the power of mine Only Begotten, I caused that he should be cast down;

"And he became Satan, yea, even the devil, the father of all lies, to deceive and to blind men, and to lead them captive at his will, even as many as would not hearken unto my voice."[513]

"And there stood "one among them that was like unto God, and he said unto those who with him: We will go down, for there is space there, and we will take of these materials, and we will make an earth whereon these may dwell;[514]

"And we will prove them herewith, to see if they will do all things whatsoever the Lord their God shall command them;[515]

"And they who keep their first estate shall be added upon; and they who keep not their first estate shall not have glory in the same kingdom with those who keep their first estate; and they who keep their second estate shall have glory added upon their heads for ever and ever."[516]

What a glorious promise! We know that we kept our first estate because we are here now upon the earth. If we obey the commandments and live to be worthy, we will be able to return home.

Our Heavenly Father and Jesus Christ want each of us to return and live with them and have eternal life. They have shown us the way. The commandments that we have been given are to help us to reach our goal of someday being able to return to our Heavenly home.

Jesus Christ came to this earth to teach us and to show us what we needed to do. He was **"the way, the truth and the light. No man cometh unto the Father but by me."**[517]

---

513 *Moses 4:3, 4*
514 *Abraham 3:24*
515 *Abraham 3:25*
516 *Abraham 3:26*
517 *John 14;6*

From the very beginning, we had our free agency. As much as our Heavenly Father wanted each of his children to come home, he knew that we must have our free agency to choose good or evil. At the Council in Heaven, we had our free agency. One third of the hosts of heaven sided with Satan and chose to go with him. Therefore, they too, were cast out.[518]

We are to love our neighbours as ourselves.[519] What does this mean? The Saviour taught that, "It is written thou shalt love thy neighbour and hate thine enemy;

"But behold I say unto you, love your enemies, bless them that curse you, do good to them that hate you, and pray for them who despitefully use you and persecute you;

"That ye may be the children of your Father in heaven; for he maketh his sun to rise on the evil and on the good.

"Therefore those things which were of old time, which were under the law, in me are all fulfilled.

"Therefore I would that ye should be perfect even as I, or your Father in heaven is perfect."[520]

Love – We are to love one another. The Lord tells us, "See that ye love one another; cease to be covetous; learn to impart one to another as the gospel requires." [521]

'He that loveth his brother abideth in the light, and there is none occasion of stumbling in him. But he that hateth his brother is in darkness, and walketh in darkness, and knoweth not whither he goeth, because that darkness hath blinded his eyes.'[522] God is love. As we follow the example of Jesus Christ, we are becoming what God wants us to be. **"Love one another, as I have loved you.**

---

518 *Abraham 3: 27-28*
519 *Matthew 22:39; D&C 112:11*
520 *3 Nephi 12:43-46; 3 Nephi 12:48*
521 *D&C 88:123*
522 *1 John 2:10, 11*

HUMILITY

'BE THOU HUMBLE AND THE LORD THY GOD SHALL LEAD THEE BY THE HAND, AND GIVE THEE ANSWER TO THY PRAYERS.'[523]

'Humble yourselves in the sight of the Lord, and he shall life you up.'[524]

'Humble yourselves therefore under the mighty hand of God, that he may exalt you in due time.'[525]

'Whosoever therefore shall humble himself as this little child, the same is greatest in the kingdom of heaven.'[526]

THANKFULNESS

'And he who receiveth all things with thankfulness shall be made glorious: and the things of this earth shall be added unto him, even an hundred fold, yea, more.'[527]

'Wherefore be ye not unwise, but understanding what the will of the Lord is.'

'Giving thanks always for all things unto God and the Father in the name of our Lord Jesus Christ.'[528]

'But ye are commanded in all things to ask of God, who giveth liberally; and that which the Spirit testifies unto you even so I would that ye should do in all holiness of heart, walking uprightly before me, considering the end of your salvation, doing all things with prayer and thanksgiving, that ye may not be seduced by evil spirits, or doctrines of devils, or the commandments of men; for some are of men, and others of devils.'[529]

---

523 D&C 112:10
524 James 4:10
525 1 Peter 5:6
526 Matthew 18:4
527 D&C 78:19
528 Ephesians 5:20
529 D&C 46:7

FORGIVENESS

'For if ye forgive men their trespasses, your heavenly Father will also forgive you:

'But if ye forgive not men their trespasses, neither will your Father forgive your trespasses.'[530]

'And when ye stand praying forgive, if ye have ought against any; that your Father also which is in heaven may forgive you your trespasses.'[531]

'Yea, and as often as my people repent will I forgive them their trespasses against me. . .

'And ye shall also forgive one another your trespasses; for verily I say unto you, he that forgiveth not his neighbour's trespasses when he says that he repents, the same hath brought himself under condemnation.'[532]

'Nevertheless, he has sinned; but verily I say unto you, I, the Lord, forgive sins unto those who confess their sins before me and ask forgiveness, who have not sinned unto death.

'My disciples, in days of old, sought occasion against one another and forgave not one another in their hearts; and for this evil they were afflicted and sorely chastened.

'Wherefore, I say unto you, that ye ought to forgive one another; for he that forgiveth not his brother his trespasses standeth condemned before the Lord; for there remaineth in him the greater sin.

'I, the Lord, will forgive whom I will forgive, but of you it is required to forgive all men.

'And ye ought to say in your hearts---let God judge between me and thee, and reward thee according to thy deeds.'[533]

Conversely, the following are examples of scriptures that describe the negative feelings of Satan:

---

530 *Matthew 6:14, 15*
531 *Mark 11:25*
532 *Mosiah 26:30,31*
533 *D&C 64:7-11*

FEAR
Fear – 'Look unto me in every thought; doubt not, fear not.'[534, 535]

ANGER
Anger- 'Yea, he stirreth up their hearts to anger against this work.

'Yea, he saith unto them; Deceive and lie inwait to catch, that ye may destroy; behold, this is no harm. And thus he flattereth them, and telleth them that it is no sin to lie that they may catch a man in a lie, that thy may destroy him.

'And thus he flattereth them, and leadeth them along until he draggeth their souls down to hell; and thus he causeth them to catch themselves in their own snare.

'And thus he goeth up and down, to and fro in the earth, seeking to destroy the souls of men.

'Verily, verily, I say unto you, wo be unto him that lieth to deceive because he supposeth that another lieth to deceive, for such are not exempt from the justice of God.'[536]

'God shall give unto you knowledge by his Holy Spirit, yea, by the unspeakable gift of the Holy Ghost, that has not been revealed since the world was until now; 'Which our forefathers have awaited with anxious expectation to be revealed in the last times, which their minds were pointed to by the angels, as held in reserve for the fullness of their glory;

'A time to come in the which nothing shall be withheld, whether there be one God or many gods, they shall be manifest.

'According to that which was ordained in the midst of the Council of the Eternal God of all other gods before this world was, that should be reserved unto the finished and the end thereof, when every man shall enter into his eternal presence and into his immortal rest.'[537]

---

534 *D&C 6:36*
535 *2 Timothy 1:7; Joshua 1:9; Revelations 21:8*
536 *D&C 10:24-28; Moroni 9:3; Matthew 5:22; 2 Nephi 33:5; Psalms 37:8*
537 *D&C 121:26-28, 32*

The Holy Ghost will unlock the scriptures and the mysteries of God if we earnestly seek and are striving to be worthy. It is our choice. The Lord will not withhold anything from us if we truly desire and seek.

'Behold, I stand at the door and knock: if any man hear my voice and open the door, I will come in to him and will sup with him and he with me.'[538]

'Wherefore, now after I have spoken these words, if ye cannot understand them it will be because ye ask not, neither do ye knock; wherefore, ye are not brought into the light, but must perish in the dark.'[539]

'Ask, and it shall be given unto you; seek, and ye shall find; knock, and it shall be opened unto you.'[540]

'Behold, I say unto you, go forth as I have commanded you; repent of all your sins; ask and ye shall receive; knock and it shall be opened unto you.'[541]

'Draw near unto me and I will draw near unto you; seek me diligently and ye shall find me; ask, and ye shall receive; knock, and it shall be opened unto you.'[542]

The scriptures are abundant with the Lord pleading for us to seek him diligently. As we do so, he will give unto us that which we seek, to know the mysteries of God.

As we follow the promptings of the Holy Ghost, we strive to live more righteously; following the commandments and doing all we can to follow the teachings of Jesus Christ.

---

[538] *Revelations 3:20*
[539] *2 Nephi 32:4-5*
[540] *3 Nephi 14:7*
[541] *D&C 49:26*
[542] *D&C 88:63*

CHAPTER THIRTY THREE

Loyalty

'No man can serve two masters; for either he will hate the one, and love the other; or else he will hold to the one, and despise the other. Ye cannot serve God and mammon.'[543] As defined in the dictionary, mammon is the Syrian God of riches, mentioned in the New Testament as a personification of worldliness; hence, riches; wealth.[544] It is an Aramaic word meaning riches, personified in Matthew 6:24 and Luke 16:9, 11, 13.[545]

Faithfulness, Obedience, Steadfastness, Trustworthiness

Fidelity: faithful, trust, faith, to trust; faithfulness; careful and exact observance of duty or performance of obligations; firm adherence to a person or to a party; loyalty; honesty; veracity; adherence to truth[546]

Faithful: firm in faith; firmly adhering to religious or other duty; of true fidelity; loyal; true and constant to a person to whom one is bound; true to one's word; in conformity to the letter and spirit; conformable to truth; conformable to a prototype; true or exact; worthy of belief[547]

Faithfulness: The quality or character of being faithful; fidelity; truth; loyalty; constancy[548]

Obedience: The act or habit of obeying; compliance with a command, prohibition, or known law and rule prescribed; submission to authority[549]

---

543 Matthew 6:24
544 The New Webster Encyclopaedic Dictionary, 1980 Edition, Avenel Books, New York, p. 513
545 The Bible Dictionary, The Holy Bible, King James Version, 1988 Edition, The Church of Jesus Christ, p. 728
546 The New Webster Encyclopaedic Dictionary, 1980 Edition, Avenel Books, New York, p. 327
547 The New Webster Encyclopaedic Dictionary, 1980 Edition, Avenel Books, New York, p. 316
548 The New Webster Encyclopaedic Dictionary, 1980 Edition, Avenel Books, New York, p. 316
549 The New Webster Encyclopaedic Dictionary, 1980 Edition, Avenel Books, New York, p. 573

Obedient: Submission to authority; complying with all commands; yielding compliance; dutiful[550]

Obediently: In an obedient manner; dutifully; submissively[551]

Steadfastness: The state of being steadfast; firmness of mind or purpose; constancy; resolution; not fickle or wavering[552]

Trustworthiness: As defined in the Bible, trustworthiness is to be dependable, faithful, honest, and obedient and to trust in God[553]

'Every faithful member of the Church enjoys and cultivates the attribute of loyalty --- loyalty to the truth, to the Church itself, to the gospel of salvation, to sacred covenants made with the Lord, to the brethren of the priesthood, to the apostles and prophets whom God has sent, to family and friends, to the civil government, and to every righteous principle. Loyalty to true principles is of God, disloyalty of Lucifer. Brethren and sisters who are loyal and true to the Lord's plan and purposes are the ones chosen to administer his affairs on earth and the ones who shall be honoured by him in his eternal kingdom hereafter.'[554]

'True devotion consists in a man loving and worshiping Deity with all his heart, and with all his might, mind, and strength. It presupposes that he will keep the commandments, walk uprightly, serve in the Church with an eye single to the glory of God, and put first in his life the things of God's kingdom. True devotion to the end gives an absolute guarantee of eternal salvation.'

As we obey the commandments, we are showing that we love the Lord and we are loyal to all that He is asking of us. He has promised us eternal life if we endure to the end. As we put our trust and faith in the Lord, He will not let us down. He wants us to achieve. He will open the way for us. The Lord has told us **"Draw near unto me and I will draw near unto you; seek me diligently and ye shall find me; ask, and ye shall receive; knock, and it shall be opened unto you."**

---

550 *The New Webster Encyclopaedic Dictionary,* 1980 Edition, Avenel Books, New York, p. 573

551 *The New Webster Encyclopaedic Dictionary,* 1980 Edition, Avenel Books, New York, p. 573

552 *The New Webster Encyclopaedic Dictionary,* 1980 Edition, Avenel Books, New York, p. 820

553 *Topical Guide, The Holy Bible, King James Version,* 1988 Edition, The Church of Jesus Christ of Latter-Day Saints, p. 540

554 *Mormon Doctrine,* Bruce R. McConkie, 1966 Edition, Bookcraft Inc. p. 460-461

LOYALTY

Notes
[551] *D&C 88:63; Matthew 7:7-8; Luke 11:9-10; 3 Nephi 14:7-8*

CHAPTER THIRTY FOUR

Meekness

As given to both the Jews and the Nephites in the Sermon on the Mount, Christ promised that the **meek** shall inherit the earth.[555] 'Few virtues have such inherent worth as **meekness**, for the meek are the god-fearing and the righteous. They are the ones who willingly conform to the gospel standards, thus submitting their wills to the will of the Lord. They are not the fearful, the spiritless, and the timid. Rather, the most forceful, dynamic personality who ever lived - He who drove the money changers from the temple, and with violence threw down their merchandising equipment[556] - said of Himself, "I am meek and lowly in heart."[557]

'Meekness is a fruit of the Spirit.'[558] The Lord has said that his grace is sufficient for the meek in this life,[559] and that in eternity they shall have an inheritance in the celestial kingdom.[560] When the earth is sanctified, cleansed from all unrighteousness, and prepared for celestial glory, then the meek shall claim their promised inheritance.[561]

In the dictionary, meek is defined as follows: Mild of temper; gentle; submissive; not easily provoked or irritated; marked by meekness; in a meek manner; gently; submissively; the quality of being meek; mildness; gentleness; forbearance under injuries and provocations.[562]

'For the natural man is an enemy to God, and has been from the fall of Adam, and will be, forever and ever, unless he yields to the enticings of the

---

555 *Matthew 5:5; 3 Nephi 12:5*
556 *Matthew 21:12-13*
557 *Matthew 11:29*
558 *Galatians 5:23*
559 *Ether 12:26*
560 *D&C 88:17-20*
561 *D&C 88:16-32*
562 *The New Webster Encyclopedic Dictionary; 1980 Edition, Avenel Books, New York, p. 526*

Holy Spirit, and putteth off the natural man and becometh a saint through the atonement of Christ the Lord, and becometh as a child, submissive, meek, humble, patient, full of love, willing to submit to his father.'[563]

The Lord has many things to teach us. He tells us, "Take my yoke upon you, and learn of me; for I am meek and lowly in heart; and ye shall find rest unto your souls. For my yoke is easy, and my burden is light."[564] Jesus goes on to tell us, "Be ye therefore perfect, even as your Father which is in Heaven is perfect."[565] Jesus is our perfect example. As we obey the commandments, we are teaching our children by example.

'Preach unto them repentance, and faith on the Lord Jesus Christ; teach them to humble themselves and to be meek and lowly in heart; teach them to withstand every temptation of the devil, with their faith on the Lord Jesus Christ.'[566]

'And again, behold I say unto you that he cannot have faith and hope, save he shall be meek, and lowly of heart.

'If so, his faith and hope is vain, for none is acceptable before God, save the meek and lowly in heart; and if a man be meek and lowly in heart, and confesses by the power of the Holy Ghost that Jesus is the Christ, he must needs have charity, for if he have not charity he is nothing; wherefore he must have charity.

'And charity suffereth long, and is kind, and envieth not, and is not puffed up, seeketh not her own, is not easily provoked, thinketh no evil, and rejoiceth not in iniquity but rejoiceth in the truth, beareth all things, believeth all things, hopeth all things, endureth all things.

'Wherefore my beloved brethren, if ye have not charity, ye are nothing, for charity never faileth. Wherefore, cleave unto charity, which is the greatest of all, for all things must fail---'But charity is the pure love of Christ, and it endureth forever; and whoso is found possessed of it at the last day, it shall be well with him.

---

563 *Mosiah 3:19*
564 *Matthew 11:29-30*
565 *Matthew 5:48*
566 *Alma 37:33*

MEEKNESS

'Wherefore, my beloved brethren, pray unto the Father with all the energy of heart, that ye may be filled with this love, which he hath bestowed upon all who are true followers of his Son, Jesus Christ; that ye may become the sons of God.; that when he shall appear we shall be like him, for we shall see him as he is; that we may have this hope; that we may be purified even as he is pure. Amen.'[567]

---

567 *Moroni 7:43-48*

CHAPTER THIRTY FIVE

Priesthood

'FOR WHOSO IS FAITHFUL UNTO THE OBTAINING THESE TWO PRIESTHOODS OF WHICH I HAVE SPOKEN, AND THE MAGNIFYING THEIR CALLING, ARE SANCTIFIED BY THE SPIRIT UNTO THE RENEWING OF THEIR BODIES.

'AND ALSO ALL THEY WHO RECEIVE THIS PRIESTHOOD RECEIVE ME, SAITH THE LORD;

'FOR HE THAT RECEIVETH MY SERVANTS RECEIVETH ME;

'AND HE THAT RECEIVETH ME RECEIVETH MY FATHER;

'AND HE THAT RECEIVETH MY FATHER RECEIVETH MY FATHER'S KINGDOM; THEREFORE ALL THAT MY FATHER HATH SHALL BE GIVEN UNTO HIM.

'AND THIS IS ACCORDING TO THE OATH AND COVENANT WHICH BELONGETH TO THE PRIESTHOOD.'[568]

The priesthood is the power and authority to act in God's name in performing various ordinances here upon the earth.

Our Heavenly Father has great power. By His priesthood power, the heavens and earth were created and the universe is kept in perfect order. The priesthood can only be used on principles of righteousness.

Baptism, confirmation, the administration of the sacrament and temple marriage are a few of the ordinances which require the authority of the

---

[568] D&C 84:33, 35-39

priesthood. They can only be performed on the earth. For those who have passed beyond the veil, their work can be done by proxy in the temples. In this way, the Lord has provided that each of his children may receive the ordinances necessary for salvation and exaltation. It is up to each individual to accept or reject these blessings. Everyone will have that opportunity, whether here or in the next world.

The Lord first gave Adam the Melchizedek priesthood. Prophets and patriarchs in every dispensation have had this priesthood. The Lord took it away from the children of Israel when they failed to live up to the privileges and covenants. They were then given the lesser priesthood and lesser law. This is known as the Aaronic Priesthood and the Law of Moses. The Aaronic Priesthood is not a different priesthood, but rather a lesser portion of it dealing with the introductory ordinances and the preparatory commandments. Jesus restored the Melchizedek priesthood among the Jews with his earthly ministry. After his crucifixion, it was eventually lost with the death of each of the apostles and taken from the earth.

Joseph Smith had been translating the gold plates. 'Among the doctrines taught in the ancient record was that of baptism for the remission of sins. As Joseph Smith had not joined any church, he was not baptized. Wanting to know what he should do, he was resolved to ask the Lord pertaining to the ordinance of baptism.

'Joseph Smith and Oliver Cowdery retired to seclusion of the woods along the banks of the Susquehanna River. It was on the 15th of May 1829. While they were engaged in prayer a light appeared above them, and in it a heavenly messenger descended. He announced himself to them as John, known in scripture as John the Baptist.

'He said he had come under the authority of Peter, James, and John, Apostles of the Lord, who held the keys of the priesthood, and that he had been sent to confer upon them the priesthood of Aaron with authority to administer in the temporal affairs of the gospel. He then laid his hands upon their heads and ordained them, saying, "Upon you my fellow servants, in the name of Messiah I confer the Priesthood of Aaron, which holds the keys of

PRIESTHOOD

the ministering of angels, and of the gospel of repentance, and of baptism by immersion for the remission of sins."[569]

'It was not long thereafter that another remarkable and even more significant event occurred. It took place "in the wilderness between Harmony, Susquehanna County [Pennsylvania], and Colesville, Broome County [New York], on the Susquehanna river." The ancient Apostles Peter, James, and John appeared to and conferred upon Joseph Smith and Oliver Cowdery the higher powers of the priesthood and they became "apostles and special witnesses" of Christ. With this ordination there was restored to earth the same authority to act in God's name that had been enjoyed in the primitive Church.[570]

From there, it was conferred upon men who were worthy. In order for the sacred name of Jesus Christ to be kept from being used on a daily basis, Melchizedek was honoured to have his name represent the higher priesthood.

Men need the priesthood to perform the sacred ordinances needed and to preside and direct the Church of Jesus Christ of Latter-day Saints. Through the priesthood, we can learn and understand the will of our Heavenly Father, thereby carrying out his purposes.

There are several things that can only be accomplished through worthy men holding the priesthood:

1. The naming and blessing of children
2. Baptism
3. Confirmation and bestowal of the Holy Ghost
4. Blessing the sacrament
5. Conferring the priesthood and ordaining to an office therein
6. Consecrating with oil
7. Administering to the sick
8. Dedication of graves
9. Father's blessing and blessing of comfort and counsel
10. Dedication of homes
11. Temple marriage for time and eternity

---

569 *Truth Restored, 1979 Edition, The Church of Jesus Christ of Latter-Day Saints*, p. 20; D&C 13
570 *Truth Restored, 1979 Edition, The Church of Jesus Christ of Latter-Day Saints*, p.22; D&C 128:20

Without the priesthood, the work of the Lord could not be accomplished.

'Behold, there are many called, but few are chosen. And why are they not chosen?

'Because their hearts are set so much upon the things of this world, and aspire to the honours of men, that they do not learn this one lesson...

'That the rights of the priesthood are inseparably connected with the powers of heaven, and that the powers of heaven cannot be controlled nor handled only upon the principles of righteousness.

'...when we undertake to cover our sins, or to gratify our pride, our vain ambition, or to exercise control or dominion or compulsion upon the souls of the children of men, in any degree of unrighteousness, behold, the heavens withdraw themselves; the Spirit of the Lord is grieved; and when it is withdrawn, Amen to the priesthood or the authority of that man.

'Behold, ere he is aware, he is left unto himself, to kick against the pricks, to persecute the saints, and to fight against God.

'...it is the nature of almost all men, as soon as they get a little authority, as they suppose, they will immediately begin to exercise unrighteous dominion.

'No power or influence can or ought to be maintained by virtue of the priesthood, only by persuasion, by long-suffering, by gentleness and meekness, and by love unfeigned;

'By kindness, and pure knowledge, which shall greatly enlarge the soul without hypocrisy, and without guile...

'Let thy bowels also be full of charity towards all men, and to the household of faith, and let virtue garnish thy thoughts unceasingly; then shall thy confidence wax strong in the presence of God; and the doctrine of the priesthood shall distil upon thy soul as the dews from heaven.

'The Holy Ghost shall be thy constant companion, and thy sceptre an unchanging sceptre of righteousness and truth; and thy dominion shall be an everlasting dominion, and without compulsory means it shall flow unto thee forever and ever.'[571]

What beautiful promises await the faithful! There are many cautions that we need to be aware of. The Lord loves us and wants us to succeed.

---

571 D&C 121:34-46

CHAPTER THIRTY SIX

Testimony

A testimony is a sacred gift from God. Through the Holy Ghost he has given us the knowledge that he lives, that Jesus Christ lives and that He is our Saviour and Redeemer. Jesus Christ is the Son of the Living God.

Apostle Melvin J. Ballard received a foretaste of the joys of eternal life promised to those who are valiant in their testimony of the Saviour. He recalls:

"I found myself one evening in the dreams of the night, in that sacred building, the temple. After a season of prayer and rejoicing, I was informed that I should have the privilege of entering into one of those sacred rooms to meet a glorious Personage, and, as I entered the door I saw seated on a raised platform, the most glorious Being my eyes have ever beheld or that I ever conceived existed in all the eternal worlds. As I approached to be introduced, He arose and stepped toward me with extended arms, and He smiled and He softly spoke my name. If I shall live to be a million years old I shall never forget that smile. He took me into His arms and kissed me, until the marrow of my bones seemed to melt. When he had finished I fell at His feet, and as I bathed them with my tears and kisses, I saw the prints of the nails in the feet of the redeemer of the world.

"The feeling that I had in the presence of Him who hath all things in His hands --- to have His love, His affection and His blessings was such that if I ever can receive that of which I had but a foretaste, I would give all that I am, all that I ever hope to be, to feel what I then felt."[572]

If the only source of a person's knowledge or assurance that the gospel is true comes from persuasion, reason, or logic, then that person does not have a testimony of the gospel and the Lord's work. It is contrary to the

---

[572] *Apostle Melvin J. Ballard*

nature of what a testimony is. A testimony consists of knowledge gained through revelation, for as is stated in Revelations 19:10, "The testimony of Jesus is the spirit of prophecy." If the Lord desired and willed, any person could receive knowledge of future events and prophecy of them through the power of the Holy Ghost.

Therefore, a testimony of the gospel is the sure knowledge received by revelation from the Holy Ghost of the divinity of the latter-day work. It also includes the knowledge that the gospel has been the same in all former ages when it has been upon the earth.

To those seeking the truth, logic and reason will lead an individual towards the path of a testimony. They are simply a means to an end. The sure knowledge which constitutes "the testimony of Jesus" must come by the "spirit of prophecy". When the Holy Ghost speaks to the spirit of men, it comes as the whisperings of a still small voice which is heard within the inner man. When a testimony is felt, it is accompanied by a feeling of calm, unwavering certainty.

For a testimony to be valid, it must be to know and believe these four basic great truths:

1. Jesus Christ is the Son of the Living God and the Saviour of the world.

2. Joseph Smith is a true prophet through whom the gospel has been restored in these latter days.

3. The Church of Jesus Christ of Latter-day Saints is "the only true and living church upon the face of the whole earth.

4. The Book of Mormon is true. It is scripture written for us in our day.

Among these are many other truths that are testified to such as:

5. The priesthood is the authority to act in the name of God. The keys and authority have been restored by holy messengers of God and that the present leadership of the Church has the right and power to direct the Lord's work upon the earth.

6. Personal revelation has been received certifying the truth of the realities which comprise a testimony.

Anyone who has a desire to gain a testimony may by obedience to the law upon which such knowledge is predicated. First, he must **desire** to

TESTIMONY

know the truth of the gospel, the Book of Mormon, the Church, or whatever it is the individual is seeking. Second, he must **study** and learn the basic facts about the matter involved. The Lord has said "**Search the scriptures.**"[573]"**Search these commandments.**"[574] Third, he must **practice** those principles and things which he has learned by conforming his life to them. "**My doctrine is not mine, but his that sent me. If any man will do his will, he shall know of the doctrine, whether it be of God, or whether I speak of myself.**"[575] Fourth, he must **pray** to the Father in the name of Jesus Christ, **in faith**, and the truth will then be made known by the "power of the Holy Ghost. And by the power of the Holy Ghost ye may know the truth of all things."[576]

Once the gift of a testimony has been granted, the individual has an obligation to bear witness of the divinity of the Lord's work to the world.

As testimonies are born, great blessings are promised.

'Nevertheless, ye are blessed, for the testimony which ye have borne is recorded in heaven for the angels to look upon; and they rejoice over you, and your sins are forgiven you.'[577]

'For I will forgive you of your sins with this commandment - that you remain steadfast in your minds in solemnity and the spirit of prayer, in bearing testimony to all the world of those things which are communicated to you.'[578]

'Let him that is ignorant learn wisdom by humbling himself and calling upon the Lord his God, that his eyes may be opened that he may see, and his ears opened that he may hear;

'For my Spirit is sent forth into the world to enlighten the humble and contrite, and to the condemnation of the ungodly.

---

573 *John 5:39*
574 *D&C 1:37*
575 *John 7:16-17*
576 *Moroni 10:3-5; 1 Corinthians 2*
577 *D&C 62:3*
578 *D&C 84:61*

'Thy brethren have rejected you and your testimony, even the nation that has driven you out;

'And now cometh the day of their calamity, even the days of sorrow, like a woman that is taken in travail; and their sorrow shall be great unless they speedily repent, yea, very speedily.

'For they killed the prophets, and them that were sent unto them; and they have shed innocent blood, which crieth from the ground against them.

'Therefore, marvel not at these things, for ye are not yet pure; ye can not yet bear my glory; but ye shall behold it if ye are faithful in keeping all my words that I have given you, from the days of Adam to Abraham, from Abraham to Moses, from Moses to Jesus and his apostles, and from Jesus and his apostles to Joseph Smith, whom I did call upon by mine angels, my ministering servants, and by mine own voice out of the heavens, to bring forth my work; 'Which foundation he did lay, and was faithful; and I took him to myself.

'Many have marvelled because of his death; but it was needful that he should seal his testimony with his blood, that he might be honoured and the wicked might be condemned.

'Be diligent in keeping all my commandments, lest judgements come upon you, and your faith fail you, and your enemies triumph over you.'[579]

Upon baptism, part of the covenant is to "stand as a witness of God at all times and in all things, and in all places that ye may be in, even until death."[580] "It becometh every man who hath been warned to warn his neighbour."[581]

Every person will have an opportunity to hear the gospel before the resurrection, either in this life or in the spirit world.[582] For those individuals who have the opportunity in this life but choose not to listen, may have a second opportunity in the spirit world. However, they will not have a second chance to gain salvation by belatedly accepting the truth. They have forfeited

---

579 D&C 136:32-39, 42
580 Mosiah 18:9
581 D&C 88:81
582 D&C 1:2

their reward of exaltation. Rather, they will go to a terrestrial kingdom because they "received not the testimony of Jesus in the flesh, but afterwards received it."[583]

A testimony alone will not save an individual.[584] However, real spiritual progress does begin with a testimony. Once a testimony has been gained, we have a greater obligation to keep the commandments, serve God, and live by the light of truth and knowledge which we have received.[585] As we are valiant in our testimonies, we work out our salvation. Those who are not valiant in the testimony of Jesus are assigned an inheritance, not in the celestial kingdom, but rather in the terrestrial kingdom.[586]

---

583   D&C 76:73-79
584   D&C 3:4
585   D&C 82:2-4
586   D&C 76:79

CHAPTER THIRTY SEVEN

Tithing

'BRING YE ALL THE TITHES INTO THE STOREHOUSE, THAT THERE MAY BE MEAT IN MINE HOUSE, AND PROVE ME NOW HEREWITH, SAITH THE LORD OF HOSTS, IF I WILL NOT OPEN YOU THE WINDOWS OF HEAVEN, AND POUR YOU OUT A BLESSING, THAT THERE SHALL NOT BE ROOM ENOUGH TO RECEIVE IT.'[587]

'Those who have thus been tithed shall pay one-tenth of all their interest annually; and this shall be a standing law unto them forever, for my holy priesthood, saith the Lord.'[588]

At Far West, Missouri, July 8, 1838, the Lord answered Joseph Smith's prayer when he asked, "O Lord, show unto thy servants how much thou requirest of the properties of thy people for a tithing."

'Verily, thus saith the Lord, I require all their surplus property to be put into the hands of the bishop of my church in Zion,

'For the building of mine house and for the laying of the foundation of Zion and for the priesthood...

'And this shall be the beginning of the tithing of my people.

'And after that, those who have thus been tithed shall pay one-tenth of all their interest annually; and this shall be a standing law unto them forever, for my holy priesthood, saith the Lord.

'Verily I say unto you, it shall come to pass that all those who gather unto the land of Zion shall be tithed of their surplus properties, and shall observe this law, or they shall not be found worthy to abide among you.

---

587 *Malachi 3:10:*
588 *D&C 119:4*

'And I say unto you, if my people observe not this law, to keep it holy, and by this law sanctify the land of Zion unto me, that my statutes and my judgments may be kept thereon, that it may be most holy, behold, verily I say unto you, it shall not be a land of Zion unto you.

'And this shall be an ensample unto all the stakes of Zion. Even so. Amen.'[589]

The term 'tithing' in the above prayer and in previous revelations meant not just one-tenth but all free-will offerings, or contributions, to the Church funds. The question presented in the petition to the Almighty was not how much a tenth part of the property of the people amounted to, but how much of that property He required for sacred purposes. The answer was this Revelation on the Law of Tithing. The Lord required first, "all the surplus property" (v.1), for the building of temples, etc. (v.2); this is the "beginning of tithing" (v.3); then He required one-tenth of all the interest annually (v. 4). This law was to become obligatory upon all who gathered to Zion (v. 5-7).[590]

The Prophet Joseph Smith and Oliver Cowdery, on the 29th of November 1834, entered into a covenant with the Lord as follows:

"That if the Lord will prosper us in our business and open the way before us that we may obtain means to pay our debts, that we be not troubled nor brought into disrepute before the world, nor His people; after that, of all that He shall give unto us, we will give a tenth to be bestowed upon the poor in His Church, or as He shall command; and that we will be faithful over that which He has entrusted to our care, that we may obtain much; and that our children after us shall remember to observe this sacred and holy covenant, and that our children, and our children's children may know of the same, we have subscribed our names with our own hands."[591]

The law of tithing is of very ancient origin. How early it was observed by the people of God is not clearly set forth in the Scriptures, but we have an

---

589 D&C 119
590 *Doctrine and Covenants Commentary*, 1951 Edition, Deseret Book Company, University Press, Winchester, Massachusetts, p. 749
591 *History of the Church*, Vol. 11, p. 175

account of its observance as early as the days of Abraham and Melchizedek. We have also, anterior to that, an account given us in the Scriptures of the bringing forward of offerings of Cain and Abel, one bringing the first fruits of the earth, and the other the first fruits of his flocks, as offering unto the Lord their God. From the days of Abraham down to the days of Jesus the law of tithing was observed by the people of God."[592]

"In the year 1831 the Lord revealed certain laws by which the Saints would have been made one in temporal, as well as spiritual affairs. But they did not comply with that celestial law. Then the Lord decided to give them a new, less exacting law. This has been called the Order of Enoch, or the law of Enoch.

"The law of Enoch is so named in the Book of Doctrine and Covenants, but, in other words, it is the law given by Joseph Smith, Jr. The word 'Enoch' did not exist in the original copy; neither did some other names. The names that were incorporated when it was printed did not exist there, when the manuscript revelations were given, for I saw them myself. Some of them I copied. And when the Lord was about to have the Book of Covenants given to the world, it was thought wisdom, in consequence of the persecutions of our enemies in Kirtland and some of the regions around, that some of the names should be changed, and Joseph was also called Enoch and the Revelation where it read so many dollars into the treasury was changed to talents.

"Therefore, when I speak of the Order of Enoch, I do not mean the Order of ancient Enoch; I mean the Order that was given to Joseph Smith in 1832-1834, which is a law inferior to the celestial law, because the celestial law required the consecration of all that a man had. The law of Enoch only required a part. The law of consecration in full required that all the people should consecrate everything that they had; and none were exempt.

The law of Enoch called upon certain men only to consecrate." [593]

"Now, did the people keep this second law, inferior to the first? The Lord picked out some of the best men in the Church, and tried them, if they

---

592 *George Q. Cannon, Journal of Discourses, Vol. XV., p. 145*
593 *Orson Pratt, Journal of Discourse, Vol. XVI, p. 156; Doctrine & Covenants Commentary, 1951 Edition, Deseret Book Company, University Press, Winchester, Massachusetts, p. 492*

would keep it. "Now I will,' says He, 'try the best men I have in the Church, not with the celestial law, but they shall consecrate in part, and have a common stock property among them.' In order to stir them up in diligence, He fixed certain penalties to this law, such as, 'he shall be delivered up to the buffetings of Satan'; 'sins that have been remitted shall return to him and be answered upon his head.' How did they get along then? The Lord tells us that the covenant had been broken. And consequently it remained with Him to do with them as seemed to Him good. Many have apostatized since that day, Sidney Rigdon for one, Oliver for another, and John Johnson for another. Why have they apostatized? They did not comply with the covenant that they made in regard to the law given to Joseph Smith that was afterwards called the Law of Enoch."[594]

"Behold, now it is call today until the coming of the Son of Man, and verily it is a day of sacrifice and a day for the tithing of my people; for he that is tithed shall not be burned at his coming."[595]

"It is contrary to the will and commandment of God that those who receive not their inheritance by consecration, agreeable to his law, which he has given, that he may tithe his people, to prepare them against the day of vengeance and burning, should have their names enrolled with the people of God."[596]

The Lord had previously given to the Church the law of consecration and stewardship of property, which members (mostly the leading elders) entered into by a covenant that was to be everlasting. Because of failure on the part of many to abide by this covenant, the Lord withdrew it and gave instead, the law of tithing as we know it today. Previous to this revelation, the law of tithing as we understand it had not been given to the Church.

Upon the withdrawal of the higher law of consecration, the lesser law of tithing was given wherein one-tenth of all interest and income annually would be given to the Lord for the building up of the Lord's kingdom upon the earth.

---

[594] *Doctrine and Covenants Commentary*, 1951 Edition, Deseret Book Company, University Press, Winchester, Massachusetts, p. 492-493
[595] D&C 64:23
[596] D&C 85:3

TITHING

Temples are built from the funds available from tithing donations. Here, ordinances are performed for the living and the dead, enabling them to continue to progress towards eternal life and exaltation. Without the ordinances that are available only in the temple to those who are worthy, progression is barred at death. No further work can be accomplished on the other side. The saving ordinances **must** be done in the temples on the earth. Time is of the essence.

'Verily I say unto you, that it is my will that a house should be built unto me, in the land of Zion, like unto the pattern which I have given you.

'Yea, let it be built speedily, by the tithing of my people.

'Behold, this is the tithing and the sacrifice which I, the Lord, require at their hands, that there may be a house built unto me for the salvation of Zion...

'For a place of thanksgiving for all saints, and for a place of instruction for all those who are called to the work of the ministry in all their several callings and offices;

'That they may be perfected in the understanding of their ministry, in theory, in principle, and in doctrine, in all things pertaining to the kingdom of God on the earth, the keys of which kingdom have been conferred upon you.'[597]

'Alma stated that the law of tithing was the economic "order" of Christ, being "a type of his order" in eternity, or "it being his order" by which men could enter "into the rest of the Lord their God."[598]

'Now they, after being sanctified by the Holy Ghost, having their garments made white, being pure and spotless before God, could not look upon sin save it were with abhorrence; and there were many exceedingly great many who were made pure and entered into the rest of the Lord their God.

'Now these ordinances were given after this manner, that thereby the people might look forward on the Son of God, it being a type of his order, or

---

[597] D&C 97:10-14
[598] *Doctrines of the Kingdom*, Hyrum L. Andrus, 1973 Edition, Bookcraft Inc., Salt Lake City, Utah, p. 253; Alma 13:11-16

it being his order, and this that thy might look forward to him for a remission of their sins, that they might enter into the rest of the Lord.'[599]

When Jesus instituted the full law of Zion among the Nephites after His resurrection, including the divine economic order by which "they had all things common among them," he quoted the law of tithing which Malachi delivered to ancient Israel and commanded the Nephites to obey it.[600]

"These scriptures, which ye had not with you," the Master said of Malachi's writings, "the Father commanded that I should give unto you; for it was wisdom in him that they should be given unto future generations."[601] The future generations among the Nephites of whom Jesus spoke, were those who had the full economic law of Zion. Being under the law of consecration and stewardship, they were also to obey the law of tithing.[602]

Early information on the law of tithing in this dispensation indicates that it had a companion relationship to the law of consecration and stewardship. A revelation in 1831 mentioned both laws as essential parts of the economic program of Zion. Having referred to the law of consecration and stewardship, the Lord declared: "Verily it is a day of sacrifice, and a day for the tithing of my people."[603]

The next year another revelation declared that under the law of consecration the Lord would "tithe his people."[604]

It is the fixed purpose of our God, and has been so from the testimony of the ancient prophets, that the great work of the last days was to be accomplished by the tithing of his saints. The saints were required to bring their tithes into the storehouse, and after that, not before; they were to look for a blessing that there should not be room enough to receive it.[605, 606]

---

599   *Alma 13:12, 16*
600   *3 Nephi 26:19; 4 Nephi 1:2, 3, 25, 26*
601   *3 Nephi 26:2*
602   *4 Nephi*
603   *D&C 64:23*
604   *D&C 85:3*
605   *Malachi 3:10*
606   *Doctrines of the Kingdom, Hyrum L. Andrus, 1973 Edition, Bookcraft Inc., Salt Lake City, Utah p. 253-255*

TITHING

We are promised that when we pay our tithes and offerings, the windows of heaven will be opened. When we put the Lord first, there will be enough left to pay all of our other obligations.

'Payment of an honest tithing is essential to the attainment of those great blessings which the Lord has in store for his faithful saints. Indeed, the law of consecration itself is the celestial law of property and money, and to gain the celestial world man must be able to abide this higher law, to say nothing of the lesser law of tithing.'[607]

'For he who not able to abide the law of a celestial kingdom cannot abide a celestial glory.'[608]

"By this principle," President Joseph F. Smith says, "the loyalty of the people of this Church shall be put to the test. By this principle it shall be known who is for the kingdom of God and who is against it."[609]

There is a great deal of importance connected with this principle, for by it, it shall be known whether we are faithful or unfaithful. In this respect it is as essential as faith in God, as repentance of sin, as baptism for the remission of sin, or as the laying on of hands for the gift of the Holy Ghost. For if a man keep all the law save one point, and he offend in that, he is a transgressor of the law, and he is not entitled to the fullness of the blessings of the gospel of Jesus Christ.

But when a man keeps all the law that is revealed, according to his strength, his substance, and his ability, though what he does may be little, it is just as acceptable in the sight of God as if he were able to do a thousand times more.

"The law of tithing is a test by which the people as individuals shall be proved. Any man who fails to observe this principle shall be known as a man who is indifferent to the welfare of Zion, who neglects his duty as a member

---

607 *Mormon Doctrine*, Bruce R. McConkie, 1979 Edition, Bookcraft Inc., Publishers Press, Salt Lake City, Utah, p. 787

608 D&C 88:22

609 *Mormon Doctrine*, Bruce R. McConkie, 1979 Edition, Bookcraft Inc., Publishers Press, Salt Lake City, Utah, p. 797

of the Church. . . . He neglects to do that which would entitle him to receive the blessings and ordinances of the gospel."[610]

Both temporal and spiritual blessings are poured out upon the honest tithe payer as a result of his obedience to that law. By such obedience he gains the spirit of inspiration in temporal and spiritual pursuits so that in the end he is ahead financially and temporally, to say nothing of the spiritual growth that always attends such a course.[611]

"Bring ye all the tithes into the storehouse, that there may be meat in mine house, and prove me now herewith, saith the Lord of hosts, if I will not open you the windows of heaven, and pour you out a blessing, that there shall not be room enough to receive it. And I will rebuke the devourer for your sakes, and he shall not destroy the fruits of your ground; neither shall your vine cast her fruit before the time in the field, saith the Lord of hosts. And all nations shall call you blessed: for ye shall be a delightsome land, saith the Lord of hosts."[612]

---

610 *Gospel Doctrine*, 5th *Edition, p. 225-226*
611 *Gospel Doctrine*, 5th *Edition, p. 226-22*
612 *Malachi 3:10-12*

TITHING

THE CHURCH OF JESUS CHRIST OF LATTER-DAY SAINTS

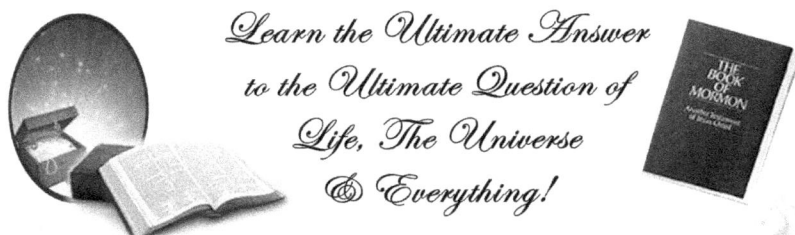

Learn the Ultimate Answer to the Ultimate Question of Life, The Universe & Everything!

For your free copy of the Book of Mormon
Contact the Canada Calgary Mission Office
403-252-1141

HAVE BOOK OF MORMON WILL TRAVEL
The Church of Jesus Christ of Latter-Day Saints

CHAPTER THIRTY EIGHT

Scriptures

'SEARCH THE SCRIPTURES...THEY ARE THEY WHICH TESTIFY OF ME.'[613]

'...FOR I DID LIKEN ALL SCRIPTURE UNTO US, THAT IT MIGHT BE FOR OUR PROFIT AND LEARNING.'[614]

'AND WHATSOEVER THEY SHALL SPEAK WHEN MOVED UPON BY THE HOLY GHOST SHALL BE SCRIPTURE, SHALL BE THE WILL OF THE LORD, SHALL BE THE MIND OF THE LORD, SHALL BE THE WORD OF THE LORD, SHALL BE THE VOICE OF THE LORD, AND THE POWER OF GOD UNTO SALVATION.'[615]

'Wherefore, I said unto you, feast upon the words of Christ; for behold, the words of Christ will tell you all things what ye should do.'[616]

'For my soul delighteth in the scriptures, and my heart pondereth them, and writeth them for the learning and the profit of my children.'[617]

Why are the scriptures so important? What is in them that they should be so valuable?

President Ezra Taft Benson has admonished the saints to study and ponder the Book of Mormon daily, to sup from its pages. As we do so, he

---

613   *John 5:39*
614   *1 Nephi 19:23*
615   *D&C 68:4*
616   *2 Nephi 32:3*
617   *2 Nephi 4:15*

has promised peace and greater love within our families and wisdom and understanding.

In today's perilous times, we need the nourishment and strength the scriptures can give us.

The Prophet Joseph Smith said, "...The Book of Mormon is the most correct of any book on earth, and the keystone of our religion, and a man would get nearer to God by abiding by its precepts, than any other book".

Nephi tells us that the Bible has had many precious parts removed. The Eighth Article of Faith says, "We believe the Bible to be the word of God as far as it is translated correctly; we also believe the Book of Mormon to be the word of God."

The scriptures can be likened to a matreska doll; it is a hollow wooden doll with several smaller hollow dolls that fit inside each one until you reach the smallest, which is solid. The Holy Ghost will enlighten our minds, layer by layer, as we study and pray and ponder the scriptures, until finally, we reach the heart. Some people feel they know all that there is that the scriptures have to offer. They don't feel that they need to put forth the effort and study as they have learned it all. They are missing out on the "heart" of the doctrine. The Holy Ghost is the key to unlocking the messages of the scriptures. To enjoy the Holy Ghost as a constant companion, we must keep the commandments, pray, and study the scriptures daily. In them, the Lord tells us what we must do. He gives us answers to our daily problems.

Let us examine closely what it is that makes the Book of Mormon so important.

WHAT IS THE BOOK OF MORMON?

"Wherefore, it is an abridgment of the record of the people of Nephi, and also of the Lamanites---Written to the Lamanites, who are a remnant of the house of Israel; and also to Jew and Gentile---Written by way of commandment, and also by the spirit of prophecy and of revelation---Written and sealed up, and hid up unto the Lord, that they might not be destroyed---To come forth by the gift and power of God unto the interpretation thereof---Sealed by the hand of Moroni, and hid up unto the Lord, to come forth in due time by way of the Gentile---The interpretation thereof by the gift of God.

SCRIPTURES

"An abridgment taken from the Book of Ether also, which is a record of the people of Jared, who were scattered at the time the Lord confounded the language of the people, when they were building a tower to get to heaven--- Which is to show unto the remnant of the House of Israel what great things the Lord hath done for their fathers; and that they may know the covenants of the Lord, that they are not cast off forever---And also to the convincing of the Jew and Gentile that JESUS is the CHRIST, the ETERNAL GOD, manifesting himself unto all nations---And now, if there are faults they are the mistakes of men; wherefore, condemn not the things of God, that ye may be found spotless at the judgement-seat of Christ."[618]

The Book of Mormon is a priceless spiritual treasure of Holy Scriptures comparable to the Holy Bible. It is a record of God's dealings with ancient inhabitants of the Americas who came from the eastern hemisphere. It contains the everlasting gospel of Jesus Christ. It was recorded by prophets who testified of Jesus Christ and the way to salvation.

The Prophet Joseph Smith brought forth the Book of Mormon. The angel Moroni, the last prophet to write in the book, directed Joseph Smith to the hill Cumorah where it had lain hidden and protected.

The Book of Mormon is the word of God. "And gave him power from on high, by the means which were before prepared, to translate the Book of Mormon;

"Which contains a record of a fallen people, and the fullness of the gospel of Jesus Christ to the Gentiles and to the Jews also;

"Which was given by inspiration, and is confirmed to others by the ministering of angels, and is declared unto the world by them--- "Proving to the world that the holy scriptures are true, and that God does inspire men and call them to his holy work in this age and generation, as well as in generations of old;"

"Thereby showing that he is the same God yesterday, today, and forever. Amen."[619]

---

618 *Translated by Joseph Smith, Jun.; Published by The Church of Jesus Christ of Latter-day Saints, Salt Lake City, Utah, U.S.A.*
619 D&C 20:8-12

In section 20 of the Doctrine and Covenants, the Lord said that he gave Joseph Smith the power from on High to translate the Book of Mormon which contains the fullness of the Gospel of Jesus Christ, which was given by inspiration.

Nephi, one of the prophet-writers of the Book of Mormon, testifies that the book contains the words of Christ. Moroni, the last writer in the book testifies that these things are true.[620]

The Book of Mormon was written for us today. God is the author of the book. It is a record of a fallen people compiled by inspired men for our blessing today. People of ancient times never had the book - it was meant for us.

Mormon, the ancient prophet, after whom the book was named, abridged centuries of records. God, who knows the end from the beginning, told him what to include in his abridgement that we would need for our days.

Mormon turned the records over to his son Moroni, the last recorder. Mormon, writing over 1500 years ago, but speaking to us today, states, "Behold, I speak unto you as if ye were present, and yet ye are not. But behold, Jesus Christ hath shown you unto me, and I know your doing."[621]

Moroni adds his voice to that of his father Mormon, "And I exhort you to remember these things; for the time speedily cometh that ye shall know that I lie not, for ye shall see me at the bar of God; and the Lord God will say unto you: did I not declare my words unto you, which were written by this man, like as one crying from the dead, yea, even as one speaking out of the dust?"[623]

The purpose of the Book of Mormon is the show unto the remnant of the house of Israel the great things which the Lord has done for their fathers; to teach them the covenants of the Lord so that they will know they are not cast off forever. It is also to convince the Jew and Gentile that Jesus is the Christ, the Eternal God, manifesting himself unto all nations.

---

620 *Moroni 10:4-5*
621 *Mormon 8:35*
623 *Moroni 10:27*

SCRIPTURES

The Book of Mormon is the personal ministry of Jesus Christ. The Book of Mormon brings men to Christ through two basic means: First, it tells in a plain manner of Christ and his gospel; it testifies of his divinity and of the necessity for a redeemer and the need of putting our trust in him. It bears witness of the fall and the atonement and the first principles of the gospel, including our need of a broken heart and a contrite spirit and a spiritual rebirth. It proclaims we must endure to the end in righteousness.

Second, the Book of Mormon exposes the enemies of Christ.

It confounds false doctrines and lays down contention, "Wherefore, the fruit of thy loins shall write (Book of Mormon); and the fruit of the loins of Judah shall write (The Holy Bible); and that which shall be written by the fruit of thy loins, and also that which shall be written by the fruit of the loins of Judah, shall grow together, unto the confounding of false doctrines and laying down of contentions, and establishing peace among the fruit of thy loins, and bringing them to the knowledge of their fathers in the latter days, and also to the knowledge of my covenants, saith the Lord."[624] It fortifies the humble followers of Christ against the evil designs, strategies and doctrines of the devil in our day. God, with His infinite foreknowledge, so moulded the Book of Mormon, that we might see the errors and know how to combat them.

'He commandeth that there shall be no priestcrafts; for, behold, priestcrafts are that men preach and set themselves up for a light unto the world, that they may get gain and praise of the world; but thy seek not the welfare of Zion.

'Behold, the Lord hath forbidden this thing; wherefore, the Lord God hath given a commandment should do none of these things; for whoso doeth them shall perish.

'For none of these iniquities come of the Lord; for he doeth that which is good among the children of men; and he doeth nothing save it be plain unto the children of men; and he inviteth them all to come unto him and partake of his goodness; and he denieth none that come unto him, black and

---

624 2 Nephi 3:12

white, bond and free, male and female; and he remembereth the heathen; and all are alike unto God...'[625]

'Thus we see how quick the children of men do forget the Lord their God, yea, how quick to do iniquity, and to be led away by the evil one.'[626]

Flattery and cunning devices are other weapons that the adversary uses.

'And he was learned, that he had a perfect knowledge of the language of the people, wherefore, he could use much flattery, and much power of speech, according to the power of the devil.'[627]

'...And he was a man of many words, and did speak much flattery to the people; therefore he led many of the people to do after the manner of his iniquities.'[628]

'...for they have used great flattery, and they have led away the hearts of many people, which will be the cause of sore affliction among us...'[629]

Many wicked men use flattery today to appeal to our vain side. They want us to think that we can disobey the commandments and that everything will be all right. They tell us,

'...Eat, drink, and be merry, for tomorrow we die; and it shall be well with us.

'And there shall also be many which shall say: Eat, drink, and be merry; nevertheless, fear God - he will justify in committing a little sin; yea, lie a little, take the advantage of one because of his words, dig a pit for thy neighbour; there is no harm in this; and do all these things, for tomorrow we die; and if it so be that we are guilty, God will beat us with a few stripes, and at last we shall be saved in the kingdom of God.

'Yea, and there shall be many which shall teach after this manner, false and vain and foolish doctrines, and shall be puffed up in their hearts, and shall seek deep to hide their counsels from the Lord; and their works shall be in the dark.

---

625   *2 Nephi 26:29-33*
626   *Alma 46:8*
627   *Jacob 7:4*
628   *Mosiah 27:8*
629   *Alma 61:4*

'Because of pride, and because of false teachers, and false doctrine, their churches have become corrupted, and their churches are lifted up; because of pride they are puffed up.

'They rob the poor because of their fine sanctuaries; they rob the poor because of their fine clothing; and they persecute the meek and the poor in heart, because in their pride they are puffed up.

'They wear stiff necks and high heads; yea, and because of pride and wickedness and abominations, and whoredoms, they have all gone astray save it be a few, who are the humble followers of Christ; nevertheless, they are led, that in many instances they do err because they are taught by the precepts of men.'[630]

The Lord is explicit in his instructions to us on what to be aware of.

'And now, behold...I have spoken unto you, according as the Spirit hath constrained me; wherefore, I know that they must surely come to pass. 'And the things which shall be written out of the book shall be of great worth unto the children of men...

'For it shall come to pass in that day that the churches which are built up, and not unto the Lord, when the one shall say unto the other: Behold, I, I am the Lord's; and the others shall say: I, I am the Lord's; and thus shall every one say that hath built up churches, and not unto the Lord-

'And they shall contend one with another; and their priests shall contend one with another, and they shall teach with their learning, and deny the Holy Ghost, which giveth utterance.

'And they deny the power of God, the Holy One of Israel; and they say unto the people: Hearken unto us, and hear ye our precept; for behold there is no God today, for the Lord and the Redeemer hath done his work, and he hath given his power unto men;

'Behold, hearken ye unto my precept; if they shall say there is a miracle wrought by the hand of the Lord, believe it not; for this day he is not a God of miracles; he hath done his work.

'O the wise, and the learned, and the rich, that are puffed up in the pride of their hearts, and all those who preach false doctrines, and all those who commit whoredoms, and pervert the right way of the Lord, wo, wo, wo

---

630   2 Nephi 28:7-9, 12-14

be unto them, saith the Lord God Almighty, for they shall be thrust down to hell!

'Wo unto them that turn aside the just for a thing of naught and revile against that which is good and say that it is of no worth! For the day shall come that the Lord God will speedily visit the inhabitants of the earth; and in that day that they are fully ripe in iniquity they shall perish.

'But behold, if the inhabitants of the earth shall repent of their wickedness and abominations they shall not be destroyed, saith the Lord of Hosts.

'For the kingdom of the devil must shake, and they which belong to it must needs be stirred up unto repentance, or the devil will grasp them with his everlasting chains, and they be stirred up to anger and perish;

'For behold, at that day shall he rage in the hearts of the children of men, and stir them up to anger against that which is good.

'And others will he pacify, and lull them away into carnal security, and they will say: All is well in Zion; yea, Zion prospereth, all is well - and thus the devil cheateth their souls, and leadeth them away carefully down to hell.

'And behold, others he flattereth away, and telleth them there is no hell; and he saith unto them: I am no devil, for there is none - and thus he whispereth in their ears, until he grasps them with his awful chains, from whence there is no deliverance.

'Yea, they are grasped with death, and hell; and death, and hell, and the devil, and all that have been seized therewith must stand before the throne of God, and be judged according to their works, from whence they must go into a place prepared for them, even a lake of fire and brimstone, which is endless torment.

'Yea, wo be unto him that hearkeneth unto the precepts of men, and denieth the power of God, and the gift of the Holy Ghost!

'Wo be unto him that shall say: We have received the word of God, and we need no more of the word of God, for we have enough.'[631]

God expects us to use the Book of Mormon in several ways. We are to read it ourselves - carefully, prayerfully, and ponder it as we read as to

---

631   2 Nephi 28

whether this book is the word of God. Then when we are finished reading the things in the book, Moroni exhorts us to put them to the test in these words:

'AND WHEN YE SHALL RECEIVE THESE THINGS, I WOULD EXHORT YOU THAT YE WOULD ASK GOD THE ETERNAL FATHER, IN THE NAME OF JESUS CHRIST, IF THESE THINGS ARE NOT TRUE, AND IF YE SHALL ASK WITH A SINCERE HEART, WITH REAL INTENT, HAVING FAITH IN CHRIST, HE WILL MANIFEST THE TRUTH OF IT UNTO YOU BY THE POWER OF THE HOLY GHOST.

'AND BY THE POWER OF THE HOLY GHOST, YE MAY KNOW THE TRUTH OF ALL THINGS.'[632]

We are to use the Book of Mormon for the basis for our teaching. In section 42 of the Doctrine and Covenants, the Lord states, "And again the elders, priests and teachers of this church shall teach the principles of my gospel, which are in the Book of Mormon in the which is the fullness of the gospel."[633]

As we read and teach, we are to liken the Book of Mormon scriptures unto us that it might be for our profit and learning.

The Bible testifies of the Book of Mormon on several occasions. For example, the Book of Mormon people were some of the other sheep Christ spoke of in John 10:16. "And other sheep I have which are not of this fold: them also I must bring, and they shall hear my voice; and there shall be one fold and one shepherd. Also, the Lord told Ezekiel how the writings of the Bible and the Book of Mormon would be joined together when He said, "Take thee one stick (wooden tablet) and write upon it for Judah (the Bible), then take another stick

---

[632] *Moroni 10:4-5*
[633] *D&C 42:12*

and write upon it for Joseph (the Book of Mormon) and join them one to another into one stick and they shall be one in thine hand."[634]

The Book of Mormon is to be used for a standard unto my people.[635]

"And for this cause, that men might be made partakers of the glories which were to be revealed, the Lord sent forth the fullness of his gospel, his everlasting covenant, reasoning in plainness and simplicity---"[636]

We, the members of the church and particularly the missionaries, have to be tellers and testifiers of the Book of Mormon unto the ends of the earth.

The Book of Mormon is the great standard we are to use. It shows that Joseph Smith was a prophet. It contains the words of Christ and its great mission is to bring men to Christ and all other things are secondary.

The golden question of the Book of Mormon is "Do you want to learn more of Christ?" The Book of Mormon is the great finder of the golden contact. It does not contain things which are pleasing unto the world and so the worldly are not interested.

Any one who has diligently sought to know the doctrines and teachings of the Book of Mormon, and has used it in missionary work, knows within his soul that this is the instrument which God has given to the missionaries to convince the Jew, Gentile and the Lamanites of the truthfulness of the Book of Mormon.

'...Feast upon the words of Christ; for behold, the words of Christ will tell you all things what ye should do.'[637]

'Wherefore, ye must press forward with a steadfastness in Christ, having a perfect brightness of hope, and a love of God and of all men. Wherefore, if ye shall press forward, feasting upon the word of Christ, and endure to the end, behold, thus saith the Father: Ye shall have eternal life.'[638]

---

634   *Ezekiel 37:16*
635   *D&C 45:9*
636   *D&C 133:57*
637   *2 Nephi 32:3*
638   *2 Nephi 31:20*

SCRIPTURES

'For I command all men, both in the east and in the west, and in the north, and in the south, and in the islands of the sea, that they shall write the words which I speak unto them; for out of the books which shall be written I will judge the world, every man according to their works, according to that which is written.

'For behold, I shall speak unto the Jews and they shall write it; and I shall also speak unto the Nephites and they shall write it; and I shall also speak unto the other tribes of the house of Israel, which I have led away, and they shall write it; and I shall also speak unto all nations of the earth and they shall write it.

'And it shall come to pass that the Jews shall have the words of the Nephites, and the Nephites shall have the words of the Jews; and the Nephites and the Jews shall have the words of the lost tribes of Israel; and the lost tribes of Israel shall have the words of the Nephites and the Jews. 'And it shall come to pass that my people, which are of the house of Israel, shall be gathered home unto the lands of their possessions; and my word also shall be gathered in one. And I will show unto them that fight against my word and against my people, who are of the house of Israel, that I am God, and that I covenanted with Abraham that I would remember his seed forever.'[639]

How precious and priceless are the scriptures! We have the Bible, the Book of Mormon, the Doctrine and Covenants, and the Pearl of Great Price. These are truly more valuable than rubies or diamonds or gems of any kind which will one day disintegrate into dust. On the other hand, the treasures in the scriptures will enable us, if we are wise, to gain eternal life and exaltation.

The Lord has promised us that we will yet be entitled to more scripture, giving us more light and knowledge. How do we treat what we presently have? Do we let them sit on our shelves gathering dust? Do we browse through them now and again just to say that we are reading them? Or do we reverently handle the pages, devouring and searching for the hidden treasures of knowledge that Heavenly Father wants to give us.

'For behold, thus saith the Lord God: I will give unto the children of men line upon line, precept upon precept, here a little and there a little; and

---

[639] 2 Nephi 29:11-14

blessed are those who hearken unto my precepts, and lend an ear unto my counsel, for they shall learn wisdom; for unto him that receiveth I will give more; and from them that shall say, We have enough, from them shall be taken away even that which they have.

'Cursed is he that putteth his trust in man, or maketh flesh his arm, or shall hearken unto the precepts of men, save their precepts shall be given by the power of the Holy Ghost.'[640]

'And now, whoso readeth, let him understand; he that hath the scriptures, let him search them.'[641]

---

640 *2 Nephi 28:30-31*
641 *3 Nephi 10:14*

CHAPTER THIRTY NINE

Temples

"HEARTS MUST BE PURE TO COME WITHIN THESE WALLS,
WHERE SPREADS A FEAST UNKNOWN TO FESTIVE HALLS.

"FREELY PARTAKE, FOR FREELY GOD HATH GIVEN,
AND TASTE THE HOLY JOYS THAT TELL OF HEAVEN.

"HERE LEARN OF HIM WHO TRIUMPHED O'ER THE GRAVE,
AND UNTO MEN THE KEYS, THE KINGDOM GAVE:

"JOINED HERE BY POWERS THAT PAST AND PRESENT BIND,
THE LIVING AND THE DEAD PERFECTION FIND."[642]

'KNOW YE NOT THAT YE ARE THE TEMPLE OF GOD,
AND THAT THE SPIRIT OF GOD DWELLETH IN YOU?
IF ANY MAN DEFILE THE TEMPLE OF GOD,
HIM SHALL GOD DESTROY;
FOR THE TEMPLE OF GOD IS HOLY, WHICH TEMPLE YE ARE.'[643]

Since the beginning, the Lord has commanded that men build temples. When the Israelites were wandering in the desert for forty years, they had a temple which was able to be moved from location to location as they travelled. What is the importance of temples? We know that our bodies are temples because the spirit of God dwells in us as we strive to be righteous.

---

642 *Orson F. Whitney*

643 *1 Corinthians 3:16-17*

The Lord has commanded that we build earthly temples to prepare his people to return home. We need the ordinances that are therein to enable us to bypass the angels.

Here we will not only lay aside the clothing of the street, but the thoughts of the streets. Not only will we clothe our bodies in white, but also our minds in purity of thought.

In the temple, the Lord uses symbols for the truths given. As worthy individuals receive temple recommends to enter the holy temple, the Holy Ghost reveals the meaning of those truths. We need the Holy Ghost as our companion. The endowment, which was given by revelation, can best be understood by revelation. To those who seek diligently, with pure hearts, will the revelation be greatest.

The **endowment** is a gift from our Heavenly Father. It is the story of man's progression from the past to the future if he is worthy. The instructions and conditions give us the knowledge which is necessary to have eternal increase and eternal progression. The covenants give life to the knowledge we are given, by our voluntarily obligating ourselves to obedience to the fullness of the law. As we keep our covenants, we are showing that we are willing and fit for exaltation which shall be granted to all those who keep and honour their covenants.

You cannot receive an exaltation until you have made covenants in the House of the Lord and received the keys and authorities that are there bestowed and which cannot be given in any other place on earth.

A **covenant** is a bond or solemn agreement involving at least two individuals. Both parties must abide by the conditions set forth. As we keep our covenants with our Heavenly Father, he has promised that we will qualify for the fullness of joy in our Father's kingdom. He has also promised that we will come forth in the resurrection of the just with our husbands or wives as our companions along with our children.

Man does not have the right to change in any degree whatsoever or to reject in the slightest, any part of the covenant which the Lord presents for the benefit and salvation of his children, which are all of us.

If you keep God's commandments, He will not let you fail.

'The season of the world before us will be like no other in the history of mankind. Satan has unleashed every evil, every scheme, and every blatant, vile perversion ever known to man in any generation. Just as this is the dispensation of the fullness of times, so it is also the dispensation of the fullness of evil. We and our wives and husbands, our children, and our members must find safety. There is no safety in the world; wealth cannot provide it, enforcement agencies cannot assure it, membership in this Church alone cannot bring it.

'As the evil night darkens upon this generation, we must come to the temple for light and safety. In our temples we find quiet, sacred havens where the storm cannot penetrate to us. There are hosts of unseen sentinels watching over and guarding our temples. Angels attend every door. As it was in the days of Elisha so it will be for us, "Those that be with us are more than they that be against us."

'Before the Saviour comes, the world will darken. There will come a period of time where even the elect will lose hope if they do not come to the temples. The world will be so filled with evil that the righteous will only feel secure within these walls. The Saints will come here not only to do vicarious work, but to find a haven of peace. They will long to bring their children here for safety sake.

'I believe we may well have living on the earth now or very soon when the boy or babe who will be the prophet of the Church when the Saviour comes. Those who will sit in the Quorum of Twelve Apostles are here. There are many in our homes and communities who will have apostolic callings. We must keep them clean, sweet, and pure in an, oh, so wicked world.

'There will be greater hosts of unseen beings in the temple. Prophets of old as well as those in this dispensation will visit the temples. Those who attend will feel their strength and feel their companionship. We will not be alone in our temples.

'The covenants and ordinances will fill us with faith as a living fire. In a day of desolating sickness, scorched earth, barren wastes, sickening plagues, disease, destruction, and death, we as a people will rest in the shade of trees, we will drink from the cooling fountains. We will abide in places of refuge from the storm; we will mount up as on eagle's wings, we will be lifted out of an insane and evil world. We will be as fair as the sun and clear as the moon.

'The Saviour will come and will honour His people. Those who are spared and prepared will be a temple loving people. They will know Him. They will cry out "blessed be the name of He that cometh in the name of the Lord; thou art my God and I will bless thee; thou art my God and I will exalt thee."

'Our children will bow down at His feet and worship Him as the Lord of Lords, the King of Kings. They will bathe His feet with their tears and He will weep and bless them for having suffered through the greatest trials ever known to man. His bowels will be filled with compassion and His heart will swell wide as eternity and He will love them. He will bring peace that will last a thousand years and they will receive their reward to dwell with Him.

'Let us prepare them with the faith to surmount every trial and every condition. We will do it in these holy, sacred temples. Come, come, oh come up to the temples of the Lord and abide in His presence.'[644]

President Darryl Nilsson stated, "**The temple is the grand classroom for perfecting the saints.**" As we attend the temple, it will bring great blessings into our lives. Within its holy walls we will find peace and a closeness to our Heavenly Father which is unsurpassed in any other earthly dwelling for it is here in which the Lord resides. As long as the temple is kept holy and sacred, his Spirit will continue to dwell there, bringing peace to all who enter. The cares of the world are cast away, leaving us free to learn and ponder upon spiritual matters.

It is here, within these sacred walls, that ordinances are done for the living as well as the dead, thus enabling them to gain salvation and exaltation.

'**My people are always commanded to build temples for the glory, honour, and endowment of all saints.**'[645]

The design of the eternal family was to give every worthy man a fullness of the priesthood.[646]

---

644 *Vaughn J. Featherston, reproduced by the Seattle Temple with permission of the author, June 1, 1987*
645 *D&C 124:39-40* [642] *Doctrine of the Kingdom, Volume 11, and the section in chapter eleven entitled "Temple and the Fullness of the Priesthood."*
646 *Doctrine of the Kingdom, Volume 11, and the section in chapter eleven entitled "Temple and the Fullness of the Priesthood."*

This is the highest order of the Melchizedek Priesthood, by which the faithful could 'secure the fullness of those blessings . . . and abide in the presence of the Eloheim [the Gods] in the eternal worlds.' The Lord informed the Prophet Joseph Smith that the temples were the places to receive 'the fullness of the priesthood." These additional powers included all of the keys that belong to the holy priesthood on the earth, or were ever revealed to man in any dispensation, and which admit men and women within the veil. They enable them to pass by the angels and the gods, until they get into the presence of the Father and the Son. They make of them kings and priests, queens and priestesses to God, to rule and reign as such over their posterity and those who may be given to them by adoption.

. . . It gives them the right to the tree of life, and the "seal of the living God in their foreheads," spoken of by John the Revelator. No marvel, then, that the Lord requires sacred places for such great and glorious things---"the fullness of the holy priesthood" to be restored.[647]

This kingdom in which each worthy man could receive the keys referred to by the Prophet, and a fullness of the priesthood, was based on several concepts:

First the Patriarchal Order is God's work and the means by which He continually increases in glory to bring to pass the immortality and eternal life of man.[648]

Second, to realize his full potential as an exalted being in this eternal family, man must be organized as a personage of spirit, tabernacled in a body of flesh and bones, and endowed with the full glory and power of the Man of Holiness, including the power to beget children in the resurrection and develop glory in them through the same divine plan.

Third, before the Saints could become like the exalted Man of Holiness in every way, they had to be organized into an eternal family order under the Father and His Only Begotten Son, Jesus Christ. This eternal family was a continuous, on-going priesthood organization called the divine patriarchal order.

---

647 *Juvenile Instructor, XV (May 1, 1880), p. 111; Doctrine of the Kingdom, Hyrum L. Anders, 1973 Edition, Bookcraft Inc., Salt Lake City, Utah, p. 404-405*

648 *Doctrines of the Kingdom, Hyrum L. Andrus, 1973 Edition, Deseret Inc., Salt Lake City, Utah, p.406*

It had its origin in eternity before the earth was formed, and it came down by generation from God through Adam to the great patriarchs of this earth.[649]

Each ordinance by which the eternal order was established was a dynamic, life-giving function by which man could acquire divine attributes and powers of life through the Holy Spirit. The symbolic elements of gospel ordinances represented significant phases of earth life or some prominent feature of the program by which the plan of eternal life was given to men, such as the experiences of birth, death, the atonement, and the resurrection.

Fourth, the Saints were expected to develop Zion's economic and social programs and, eventually, to establish the government of God in their midst as features of the law of the divine patriarchal order.

Fifth, by applying the principles and laws of the gospel to their lives, the Saints could make sure their calling and election to the sacred family relationships of the patriarchal order in eternity.[650] Only by doing this and by being sealed in the marriage and family relationship could they become priests and kings (and priestesses and queens) in the celestial order in eternity. The power to seal was held by the living prophet and president of the Church.[651]

Finally, when the Saints applied celestial law and were united as heirs with the greater eternal family in the presence of God, they would receive a fullness of the priesthood and be made recipients of the glory that those exalted beings possess, to the degree the Saints were able to receive and apply it to their good.[652]

Brigham Young expressed the basic idea of the eternal family in the following statement:

'When the Holy Priesthood, which is after the order of the Son of God, is upon the earth, and its organizations, ordinances, gospel, powers, authorities and blessings, are enjoyed by the children of men; then by means of sealing powers and keys, and an everlasting covenant, the sons of men become

---

649 *Doctrine of the Kingdom, Volume 11, and the section in chapter twelve entitled "Antiquity of Divine Patriarchal Order,"* Hyrum L. Andrus, 1973 Edition, Deseret Inc., Salt Lake City, Utah

650 *Doctrine of the Kingdom, Volume 11, the section in chapter thirteen entitled "Sealing Family Units Together,"* Hyrum L. Andrus, 1973 Edition, Deseret Inc., Salt Lake City, Utah, p.407

651 See MS, V (March, 1845), p. 151

652 *Doctrine of the Kingdom, Volume 11, the section in chapter eleven entitled "Endowment of Zion with Glory*

the sons of God by regeneration, and are entitled, every man in his order, to the privileges, exaltations, principalities and powers, kingdoms and thrones, which are held and enjoyed by the Great Father of our race; and all these are obtained through the law of natural increase, and the saving of that which the Father puts in our power.'[653]

The Lord loves us. He has shown us the way. All things are prepared for them that love him and follow his commandments. He wants us to return home. **"This is my work and my glory, to bring to pass the immortality and eternal life of man."**[654] He will not let us fail if we obey him and follow his commandments.

JUST A CARD

We are individuals in the Third Estate
Represented on earth by a card
We had no chance to get the keys while on the earth;
So alas, our progress is barred.

There are millions of us waiting here,
And forward we cannot go.
How despondent we get waiting for years,
You mortals have no way to know.
For years I have prayed and waited here
And no encouragement came.
With the Church of England I had cast my lot,
And I hoped that they still had my name.

In an old English church in a little town
Lay old church records stacked in a pile.
A young Mormon boy was looking for names
And he looked through the books for a while.

---

653 *Doctrine of the Kingdom*, Hyrum L. Andrus, 1973 Edition, Deseret Inc., Salt Lake City, Utah, p. 407-408

654 *Moses 1:39*

BEYOND THE SUNSET

He copied some names, and some he passed by,
When he got through he had quite a list.
There was much disappointment and sorrow for some
Of the spirits whose names he had missed.

As for me, I was joyous and full of new hope
And to shout I could hardly resist.
My prayer and my hopes were rewarded at last,
The boy had my name on the list.
The boy sent our names to the Index Bureau
I hope he will get a reward.
We were full of much joy and rejoicing that day,
When they wrote each one's name on a card.

We are individuals on earth once again
Our soul and our hopes in a card.
And, oh for the joy no mortals can know
They've been sent to the House of the Lord.

I am just a card in a pile of cards,
You may think of me just as a name,
But I have lived on earth the same as you
But my chances were not just the same.

I cannot do my own work on earth,
How can you mortals be so at ease?
Please drop your work for half a day,
And get me those precious keys.

That reassured card there in that pile
Should move you mortals to tears.
I have waited and longed for this day to come
For more than a hundred years.

TEMPLES

If you take my name through the Temple to-day,
Pay strict attention, Please.
I have waited so long, so don't fail to get
A single one of the keys.[655]

MY DREAM

I dreamed my Father called me home across the Great Divide.
I was very much bewildered – I thought that I had died.
Saint Peter met me at the gate; he said, "Come, follow me"

Then I saw rows of people standing in a line;
When I looked them over, they were relatives of mine.
Some among the massive crowd I remembered well;
Some of them had lived on earth long before my time.
There were my great grandparents, whom I was pleased to see;
But when I walked toward them they turned away from me.

Then I saw my cousins, my uncles and my aunts.
They said to me accusingly, "We never had a chance
To do the work that must be done to start us on our way
–To give to us eternal life – so here we have to stay."

My Father and my Mother too were standing far apart
They looked so disappointed it made the teardrops start.
I turned and saw my Saviour – On his face there was a frown–
"I died upon the cross for them, and you have let them down.
Behold your noble ancestors waiting for the day
When you would open up the gates to help them on their way."

My heart was very heavy as I looked those people over;
The blinding tears ran down my face. I turned to Him once more,
Please, blessed Saviour, send me back; I'll make another try;

---

655 *Author unknown*

BEYOND THE SUNSET

"There's something I must show you – Something you must see."
I'll do the work for all my kin; I'm not prepared to die.
I'll not miss a single one; I'm so ashamed, dear Lord;
I'll try to do each ordinance according to Thy word."

Then I awoke, the dream was gone; I had not passed away;
But I made a resolution: to start that very day:
Baptisms, endowments, sealings – I found are but a few.
The more I searched – and searched –
The more I found to do;
But I will keep on hunting, searching all the while –
Next time I meet my ancestors,
I'll meet them with a smile.[656]

---

[656] Mr. Hillman, (Maxwell Hartline, 1ˢᵗ Counselor, Colton Ward Bishopric)

CHAPTER FORTY

Celestial Kingdom

'FOR IF YOU WILL THAT I GIVE UNTO YOU A PLACE IN THE CELESTIAL WORLD, YOU MUST PREPARE YOURSELVES BY DOING THE THINGS WHICH I HAVE COMMANDED YOU AND REQUIRED OF YOU.'[657]

"IF YE ARE PREPARED, YE SHALL NOT FEAR.'[658]

What does this mean to you? I have two dishes, one is a dish of wheat kernels and the other is a dish of pinto beans. Neither one has had any processing. They are simply, just wheat and beans. In this stage, they are very difficult to eat. We could eat them, but they would not be very tasty. Here are an additional two bowls, one of cooked wheat and the other of cooked beans. Neither has had anything else added. As yet, they are still edible, but not very tasty. We continue adding spices and other ingredients until we have the final products, delicious dishes of baked beans or bean tarts and pineapple wheat fluff or whole wheat bread. The ingredients added determine what the end product will be. The wheat and beans are now ready to eat, a delicious meal or desert. A lot of preparation goes into bringing them from the basic wheat and beans to the delicious meals and deserts.

The wheat and beans can be likened to us. When we are born, we are babies. We know absolutely nothing. As we grow and learn, we are like a sponge, absorbing everything.

The trials and tribulations that we endure prepare us and teach us things that we would never know otherwise. As we determine what it is we

---

657 D&C 78:7
658 D&C 38:30

are to learn from each trial we pass through, our characters grow and develop. As we continue to learn, we become softened and pliable, blending our will with that of our Heavenly Father. He gives us experiences that will teach us what we need to know to reach our potential. Our experiences and how we deal with the trials and tribulations that we pass through are the ingredients that are added to us. If we become bitter, then the end result is one of bitterness.

However, if the ingredients we add are faith, virtue, knowledge, temperance, patience, brotherly kindness, godliness, charity, humility, diligence, we are learning the attributes of God. To that we add honesty, benevolence, doing good to all men, and long-suffering. We learn these through that which we suffer. **The Lord tells us, "Peace be unto thy soul; thine adversity and thine afflictions shall be but a small moment; And then, if thou endure it well, God shall exalt thee on high; thou shalt triumph over all thy foes."**[659]

There are many areas in which we can be prepared; food storage, clothing, water, 72 hour emergency pack, etc. We have been counselled for many years to have at least a year's supply of food and other items needed for our families in case of disasters or emergencies. Are there any that have that supply in? Or are we procrastinating? We need to have a goal on what we will be putting into our food storage.

We need to plan and then carry it out. "There is no royal road to anything; careful planning, hard work, and determination to reach an objective is the path to success."[660]

'All scripture is given by inspiration of God, and is profitable for doctrine, for reproof, for correction, for instruction in righteousness.'[661]

If you want to go where God is, you must be like God. You need to study the scriptures to know how to become as God would have you become. We all have desires for our children to become like us. So too, does our Heavenly Father desire that we become like Him. As we search the

---

659 *D&C 121:7-8*
660 *Unknown author*
661 *2 Timothy 3:16*

scriptures, we will discover the attributes that we may attain to in order to become like God. Search your heart to see how many attributes you have which are God-like. All the commandments point the way toward our goal of one day entering the Celestial Kingdom where our Heavenly Parents and Jesus Christ dwell. No unclean thing can dwell with God. Jesus told us to **"Be ye therefore perfect, even as your Father which is in Heaven is perfect."**[662] If this was not possible, He would not have told us.

Nephi goes on to tell us that "I will go and do the things that the Lord hath commanded, for I know that the Lord giveth no commandments unto the children of men, save he shall prepare a way for them that they may accomplish the thing which he commandeth them."[663]

We cannot achieve perfection in one day, one week or one month or a year. However, we can work on things one at a time. For example, we can pay a perfect tithing, we can attend our meetings weekly, and we can have our daily family and personal prayers.

Our Father in Heaven and Jesus Christ have not left us alone to grope in the dark. They have shown us the way. Jesus Christ came into this world to atone for the sins of mankind so that if they would repent and follow Jesus Christ, they would be able to return to our heavenly home. They are anxiously waiting for us. Just as we worry about our children and want them to come home, so too, do our Heavenly Father and Jesus Christ. They have shown us what we need to do.

I AM A CHILD OF GOD

I am a child of God,
And he has sent me here,
Has given me an earthly home
With parents kind and dear.
I am a child of God
And so my needs are great;
Help me to understand his words
Before it grows too late.

---

662 *Matthew 5:48*
663 *1 Nephi 3:7*

I am a child of God,
Rich blessings are in store;
If I but learn to do his will
I'll live with him once more.

Lead me guide me, walk beside me
Help me find the way,
Teach me all that I must do,
To live with Him someday. [664]

Exalted beings are: "These are they who came through much tribulation". (Unknown author)

'Blessed is the man that endureth temptation: for when he is tried, he shall receive the crown of life, which the Lord hath promised to them that love him.'[665]

'For after much tribulation come the blessings. Wherefore the day cometh that ye shall be crowned with much glory; the hour is not yet, but is nigh at hand.'[666] Each time that we make the right choice, the spirit becomes more and more beautiful. We are learning. It does not happen overnight. Many times we may not choose the correct way. However, we repent of those things which are taking us away from our goal of returning home to our Father in Heaven and Jesus Christ in the Celestial kingdom. We know that this is possible because they have told us. They have shown us they way and what we need to do.

Exaltation in the celestial kingdom will be granted to those only who enter and faithfully observe the covenant of celestial marriage.

'And in order to obtain the highest, a man must enter into this order of the priesthood [meaning the new and everlasting covenant of marriage.

'In the celestial glory there are three heavens, or degrees;

'And if he does not, he cannot obtain it.

---

664 *Hymns of the Church of Jesus Christ of Latter-day Saints, 1985 Edition, p. 301*
665 *James 1:12*
666 *D&C 58:4*

'He may enter into the other, but that is the end of his kingdom; he cannot have an increase.'[667]

He cannot have an increase! That means worlds without end. Once a person has been assigned to his place, his assignment is eternal, be it telestial, terrestrial or celestial, he cannot advance. Only in the highest degree of the Celestial kingdom can one advance. Our decisions we make now are vital. They will determine where our final eternal lot has been assigned. We **must** make right decisions.

The Lord makes clear to us, his children that we cannot afford to make mistakes in the decisions we make when it comes to our eternal destination. Those who keep his laws are promised untold glory.

'...If a man marry a wife by my word, which is my law, and by the new and everlasting covenant, and it is sealed unto them by the Holy Spirit of promise, by him who is anointed, unto whom I have appointed this power and the keys of this priesthood...it...shall be of full force when they are out of the world; and they shall pass by the angels, and the gods, which are set there, to their exaltation and glory in all things...which glory shall be a fullness and a continuation of the seeds forever and ever.

'Then shall they be gods, because they have no end... then shall they be above all, because all things are subject unto them. They shall then be gods, because they have all power, and the angels are subject unto them.'[668]

'Verily, verily, I say unto you, except ye abide my law ye cannot attain to this glory.'[669]

Attaining eternal life is not a matter of goodness only. Not only must we make right decisions, but we must also practice those things we know are right. We must also receive all the ordinances of the gospel. If a person does not bring their lives into harmony with the laws of God either in this life (if that is impossible) or the next, he will remain single and separate in the eternities. They will have no spouses or children. If one is to be in God's kingdom of exaltation, it will be as husband and wife. No single person can

---

667 D&C 131:1-4
668 D&C 132:19-20
669 D&C 132:21

be exalted. Nor can people married for this life only. It doesn't matter how good a life they have led. Brigham Young says, "No man can be perfect without the woman, so no woman can be perfect without a man to lead her. I tell you the truth as it is in the bosom of eternity. If he wishes to be saved, he cannot be saved without a woman by his side."

Celestial marriage is extremely important.

Lorenzo Snow emphasized the importance and blessing of celestial marriage:

"When two Latter-day Saints are united together in marriage, promises are made to them concerning their offspring that reach from eternity to eternity. They are promised that they shall have the power and the right to govern and control and administer salvation and exaltation and glory to their offspring, worlds without end. And what offspring they do not have here, undoubtedly there will be opportunities to have them hereafter. What else could man wish? A man and a woman, in the other life, having celestial bodies, free from sickness and disease, glorified and beautified beyond description, standing in the midst of their posterity, governing and controlling them, administering life, exaltation and glory, worlds without end."

Only righteous members of the Church of Jesus Christ can receive exaltation. They must accept the gospel and be baptised; receive their endowments in the holy temples of our God, are sealed for eternity; then continue to live righteously for the rest of their lives. All will fail these blessings if they do not live worthy lives even though their temple ordinances have been done.

Procrastination is a tool of Satan. Many times people will delay their decision to marry in the temple. They think that they need to finish their education, get a bigger home, and become successful in their careers. **This is wrong! The time to act is now!** All contracts not made under the sealing power of the priesthood terminate when one is dead.

People who have never heard the gospel will have the opportunity to hear it on the other side. The necessary work can then be done vicariously for them.

However, for those of us who have heard the voice of the Lord, we who have the scriptures; we who have had many witnesses and have been informed

- there is no tomorrow. Tomorrow is too late! If we are worthy enough, we may be angels. Even unmarried, we may reach the lower realms of the celestial kingdom, but we will be ministering angels only, "...which angels are ministering servants, to minister for those who are worthy of a far more, and an exceeding, and an eternal weight of glory." The Lord continues: "For these angels did not abide my law; therefore, they cannot be enlarged, but remain separately and singly, without exaltation, in their saved condition, to all eternity; and from henceforth are not gods, but are angels of God forever and ever."[670]

The same revelation emphasizes the need for celestial marriage now, in this life:

"...Except ye abide my law [celestial marriage] ye cannot attain to this glory.

"For strait is the gate, and narrow the way that leadeth unto the exaltation and continuation of the lives, and few there be that find it, because ye receive me not in the world neither do you know me.

"But if ye receive me in the world, then shall ye know me, and shall receive your exaltation; that where I am ye shall be also."[671]

Joseph Smith added, "Except a man and his wife enter into an everlasting covenant and be married for eternity, while in this probation, by the power and authority of the Holy Priesthood, they will cease to increase when they die; that is they will not have any children after the resurrection.

Those who are married by the power and authority of the priesthood in this life, and continue without committing the sin against the Holy Ghost, will continue to increase and have children in the celestial glory."

The Lord's program is unchangeable. His laws are immutable. They will not be modified. Your opinion or mine does not alter the laws. Many people seem to think that eventually the Lord will be merciful and give them the unearned blessing. But the Lord cannot be merciful at the expense of justice.

Qualify yourself by obedience and the Lord is bound.[672] **Don't take your eyes off your goal.**[673]

---

670 *D&C 132:16-17*
671 *D&C 132:21-23*
672 *D&C 82:10*
673 *Philippians 3:14; Matthew 17:22; Matthew 14:28-31*

Avoid distractions – Satan will do all he can to distract us. He wants us to fail. He wants to give us feelings of low self-worth, discouragement and failure. When we give in to these feelings, we find it much more difficult to keep our eyes on the goals we have set.

As we continually strive towards the Celestial Kingdom, our trials, like these bowls of wheat and beans will become something very desirable as we prepare ourselves worthy for entrance into the Celestial Kingdom. Jesus when He meets us will say, "Well done, thou good and faithful servant." The prophet Joseph Smith explains to us:

'God himself was once as we are now, and is an exalted man, and sits enthroned in yonder heavens! That is the great secret. If the veil were rent today, and the Great God who holds this world in its orbit, and who upholds all worlds in its orbit, and who upholds all worlds and all things by his power, was to make himself visible,---I say, if you were to see him today, you would see him like a man in form---like yourselves in all the person, image, and very form as a man; for Adam was created in the very fashion, image and likeness of God, and received instruction from, and walked, talked and conversed with him, as one man talks and communes with another.

'In order to understand the subject of the dead, for consolation of those who mourn for the loss of their friends, it is necessary we should understand the character and being of God and how he came to be so; for I am going to tell you how God came to be God. We have imagined and supposed that God was God from all eternity. I will refute that idea, and take away the veil, so that you may see.

'These are incomprehensible ideas to some, but they are simple. It is the first principle of the Gospel to know for a certainty the Character of God, and to know that we may converse with him as one man converses with another, and that he was once a man like us; that God himself, the Father of us all, dwelt on an earth, the same as Jesus Christ himself did; and I will show it from the Bible.'[674]

Because Heavenly Father once went through trials and tribulations, and is an exalted being, He knows that it is possible for us to accomplish

---

[674] *Teachings of the Prophet Joseph Smith, 1977 Edition, Deseret Book Company, Salt Lake City, Utah,* p. 345-346

this as well. Therefore He says: "Be ye therefore perfect, even as your Father in Heaven which is perfect." **"This is my work and my glory, to bring to pass the immortality and eternal life of man."**

To those who have chosen to be married in the temple, they have already established a pattern for righteous living when they find the right partner. When their partner is found, they should sit down together and chart their life. To this end they will achieve exaltation in the kingdom of God.

Some of the goals they may decide on are as follows:

1. The husband will attend priesthood meeting every week of the year, every year of his life.

2. They will both attend Sunday school and Sacrament meeting every Sabbath, bringing their children with them. In this way, they are teaching their children the importance of the Sabbath.

3. Another commitment is to pay an honest tithe, no matter what the circumstances. In this way, they are trusting in the Lord when he says that he will open the windows of heaven.

Many times in the scriptures, the Covenant of Abraham is referred to. What is it and how does it pertain to us?

Latter-day revelation has clarified the significance of the Abrahamic covenant and other aspects of Abraham's life and ministry. We learn that he was greatly blessed with divine revelation concerning the planetary system, the creation of the earth and the pre-mortal activities of the spirits of mankind. One of the most valiant spirits in the pre-mortal life, he was chosen to be a leader in the kingdom of God before he was born into this world.[675]

We also learn from latter-day revelation that because of Abraham's faithfulness, he is now exalted and sits upon a throne in eternity.[676]

COVENANT OF ABRAHAM

Abraham first received the gospel by baptism, (which is the covenant of salvation). Then he had conferred upon him the higher priesthood, and he entered into celestial marriage (which is the covenant of exaltation) gaining

---

675   Abraham 3:23
676   D&C 132:29, 37

assurance that he would have eternal increase. Finally he received a promise that all of these blessings would be offered to all of his mortal posterity.[677]

'My name is Jehovah, and I know the end from the beginning; therefore my hand shall be over thee.

'And I will make of thee a great nation, and I will bless thee above measure, and make thy name great among all nations, and thou shalt be a blessing unto thy seed after thee, that in their hands they shall bear this ministry and Priesthood unto all nations;

'And I will bless them through thy name; for as many as receive this Gospel shall be called after thy name, and shall be accounted thy seed, and shall rise up and bless thee, as their father; 'And I will bless them that bless thee, and curse them that curse thee; and in thee (that is, thy Priesthood), for I give unto thee a promise that this right shall continue in thee, and in thy seed after thee (that is to say, the literal seed of the body) shall all the families of the earth be blessed, even with the blessings of the Gospel, which are the blessings of salvation, even life eternal.'[678]

Included in the divine promises to Abraham were the assurances that:

1. Christ would come through his lineage, and

2. That Abraham's posterity would receive certain lands as an eternal inheritance.[679]

These promises taken together are called the <u>Abrahamic Covenant.</u> It was renewed with Isaac and again with Jacob.

The portions of the covenant that pertain to personal salvation and eternal increase are renewed with each individual who receives the ordinance of celestial marriage.[680]

Those of non-Israelite lineage, commonly known as gentiles, are adopted into the house of Israel, and become heirs of the covenant and the seed of Abraham through the ordinances of the gospel.[681] Being an heir to the

---

677 *D&C 132:29-50*
678 *Abraham 2:8-11*
679 *Genesis 17; Genesis 22:15-18; Galatians 3; Abraham 2*
680 *D&C 132:29-33*
681 *Galatians 3:26-29*

Abrahamic covenant does not make one a "chosen person" per say, but does signify that such are chosen to responsibly carry the gospel to all the peoples of the earth. Abraham's seed have carried out the missionary activity in all the nations since Abraham's day.

To fulfil the covenant God made with Abraham - having particular reference to the fact that the literal seed of his body would be entitled to all of the blessings of the gospel;[682] a number of specific and particular things must take place in the last days.

The gospel must be restored, the priesthood must be conferred again upon man, the keys of the sealing power must be given again to mortals, Israel must be gathered, and the Holy Ghost must be poured out upon the Gentiles. All this has already taken place or is in process of fulfilment.

The Lord wants all of His children to return home. He has provided the way.

---

682 *Abraham 2:10-11*

CHAPTER FORTY ONE

Heavenly Father

'If ye then...know how to give good gifts unto your children: how much more shall your Heavenly Father give the Holy Spirit to them that ask him?'[683]

'Eye hath not seen, nor ear heard, neither have entered into the heart of man, the things which God hath prepared for them that love him.'[684]

'I declare with all the strength I possess that we have a Heavenly Father who claims and loves all of us regardless of where our steps have taken us. You are his son and you are his daughter, and he loves you.'[685]

We will be startled to see how familiar the face of our Heavenly Father is when we see Him again.

Without God, repentance would be meaningless; life would be meaningless. We must believe in God. We must want to be with him; to be purified and sanctified.

When we are distant from loved ones, we find a way to reach out to them. We may write a letter, or telephone. The more we reach out and keep in touch, the stronger and closer the bond becomes.

If our Heavenly Father were to write a letter to us, it might read: "My Dearest Child, "Remember who you are. You are a child of God. Your mother and I love you very much. When you dwelt with us, we taught you all that you now know. In order for you to continue your progression, you needed to go away to continue your learning and growth. We want you to come back home when your time is finished upon the earth. Enjoy your sojourn upon the earth. It was created for you.

---

683   Luke 11:13
684   1 Corinthians 2:9
685   Marvin J. Ashton

"We are sending you off to school so that you may learn how to become like us. It is necessary that a veil would be drawn across your mind, so that you would not remember your life here. In this way, you would be tested to see if you would do all things that your Father commanded.

"You will have many joys and sorrows; many trials and tribulations. These will give you experience and knowledge. However, you will not be left alone. You will have the Holy Ghost to be your constant companion. You will have the scriptures to guide you and to teach you.

"When you want to talk to us, you can pray and we will answer you. We love you and are anxiously waiting for your return. As you obey the commandments, and learn and grow in wisdom and understanding, you will have eternal life and exaltation.

"Love your Heavenly Father"

Our Heavenly Father has reached out to us. It is up to us to catch hold. How do we do this?

Pray always. We are told to pray always lest we be tempted by the devil. Our Father hears and answers our prayers. We must be ready to listen to that still small voice.

Keep the commandments.

Study the scriptures.

Often times we will have answers to our prayers in conference addresses, or through speakers in church. We need to be in tune with the Spirit.

The Spirit beareth record that the things which we hear are from God. God speaks directly to your heart. The Spirit whispers to us.

Fast when you want to listen; be willing to accept and say, 'Father, Thy will be done.' As you listen, you need to be prepared that it may not be the answer that you are seeking. You must be willing to accept the answer and act upon it. The answer may be a rebuke. You may need to have a mighty change of heart before the answer will come. But come it will.

We need to recognize that each individual is a child of God. When we offend one another, we offend our Father in Heaven. We need to learn to live as God would have us live.

'For behold, thus saith the Lord God: I will give unto the children of men line upon line, precept upon precept, here a little and there a little; and blessed are those who hearken unto my precepts, and lend an ear unto my counsel, for they shall learn wisdom; for unto him that receiveth I will give more; and from them that shall say, We have enough, from them shall be taken away even that which they have.

'Cursed is he that putteth his trust in man, or maketh flesh his arm, or shall hearken unto the precepts of men, save their precepts shall be given by the power of the Holy Ghost.'[686]

'Wherefore, do the things which I have told you I have seen that your Lord and your Redeemer should do; for, for this cause have they been shown unto me, that ye might know the gate by which ye should enter. For the gate by which ye should enter is repentance and baptism by water; and then cometh a remission of your sins by fire and by the Holy Ghost.

'And then are ye in this strait and narrow path which leads to eternal life; yea, ye have entered in by the gate, ye have done according to the commandments of the Father and the Son; and ye have received the Holy Ghost, which witnesses of the Father and the Son, unto the fulfilling of the promise which he hath made, that if ye entered in by the way ye should receive.

'And now, my beloved brethren, after ye have gotten into this strait and narrow path, I would ask if all is done? Behold, I say unto you, Nay; for ye have not come thus far save it were by the word of Christ with unshaken faith in him, relying wholly upon the merits of him who is mighty to save. 'Wherefore, ye must press forward with a steadfastness in Christ, having a perfect brightness of hope, and a love of God and of all men, Wherefore, if ye shall press forward, feasting upon the word of Christ, and endure to the end, behold, thus saith the Father: Ye shall have eternal life.

'And now, behold, my beloved brethren, this is the way; and there is none other way nor name given under heaven whereby man can be saved in

---

686 2 Nephi 28:30-31

the kingdom of God. And now, behold, this is the doctrine of Christ, and the only and true doctrine of the Father and of the Son, and of the Holy Ghost, which is one God. Amen.'[687]

When the scriptures refer to God the Father, Jesus Christ and the Holy Ghost as being one God, it is in reference to their being united in purpose for the salvation of mankind. They are three distinct persons, God the Father and Jesus Christ having a body of flesh and bones, and the Holy Ghost being a personage of spirit.

'The Father has a body of flesh and bones as tangible as man's' the Son also; but the Holy Ghost has not a body of flesh and bones, but is a personage of Spirit. Were it not so, the Holy Ghost could not dwell in us.'[688]

'I will go back to the beginning before the world was, to show what kind of being God is. What sort of a being was God in the beginning? Open your ears and hear, all ye ends of the earth, for I am going to prove it to you by the Bible, and to tell you the designs of God in relation to the human race, and why He interferes with the affairs of man.

'God himself was once as we are now, and is an exalted man, and sits enthroned in yonder heavens! That is the great secret. If the veil were rent today, and the great God who holds this world in its orbit, and who upholds all worlds and all things by his power, was to make himself visible,---I say, if you were to see him today, you would see him like a man in form---like yourselves in all the person, image, and very form as a man; for Adam was created in the very fashion, image and likeness of God, and received instruction from, and walked, talked and conversed with him, as one man talks and communes with another.

'In order to understand the subject of the dead, for consolation of those who mourn for the loss of their friends, it is necessary we should understand the character and being of God and how he came to be so; for I am going to tell you how God came to be God. We have imagined and supposed that God was God from all eternity. I will refute that idea, and take away the veil, so that you may see.

---

687 *2 Nephi 31:17-21*
688 *D&C 130:22*

HEAVENLY FATHER

'These are incomprehensible ideas to some, but they are simple. It is the first principle of the Gospel to know for a certainty the Character of God, and to know that we may converse with him as one man converses with another, and that he was once a man like us; that God himself, the Father of us all, dwelt on an earth, the same as Jesus Christ himself did; and I will show it from the Bible.'[689]

Because Heavenly Father once went through trials and tribulations, the same as we, and is now an exalted being, He knows that it is possible for us to accomplish as well. Therefore, he says, "Be ye therefore perfect, even as your Father which is in Heaven is perfect."[690] **"This is my work and my glory, to bring to pass the immortality and eternal life of man."**[691]

It is up to us to listen and follow. He loves us and wants us to come home.

---

689 *Teachings of the Prophet Joseph Smith*, 1977 Edition, Deseret Book Company, Salt Lake City, Utah, p. 345-346
690 Matthew 5:48
691 Moses 1:39

CHAPTER FORTY TWO

Truth

'He that keepeth his commandments receiveth truth and light, until he is glorified in truth and knoweth all things.'[692] 'And truth is knowledge of things as they are, and as they were, and as they are to come.'[693]

There are many truths in the world. The sun rises and sets every day. There are twelve months to a year. To gain entrance into a college or university, you must first pass an entrance exam. To gain entrance into the temple, you must be worthy and have a current temple recommend.

In science the 'truths' often change as new discoveries are made. At one time, it was believed that the earth was flat. Anyone daring to venture out would eventually fall off the end of the earth. Columbus set sail to prove that the earth was not flat, but was instead, round. Everyone mocked him. However, to the astonishment of everyone, he returned with items to show he had found a 'new world'. That new world was the Americas.

As important as each of the truths of the world are, there are some that are so vital, that without our possessing their knowledge, we will be forever closed off to the rest of eternity. Some people want to discover and learn all they can of the mysteries and things this world and universe have to offer. They put off the things of God, thinking that it is of no consequence. They may feel that they need to gain all the earthly knowledge now and when they reach the other side of the veil, they can then delve into the mysteries of God.

Unfortunately, it does not work that way. We need to gain the saving truths now. There will come a time and place to learn everything else, but if we put off learning the saving truths, receiving the saving ordinances here in

---

692   D&C 93:28
693   D&C 93:24

this life, we will not be able to progress any further in the worlds to come. Our progress will be banned.

If we have opportunities in this life to accept the gospel and the ordinances and refuse to do so, we will not be allowed to receive them on the other side. However, if we have not had the opportunity to learn about the gospel of Jesus Christ, we will be given that opportunity in the spirit world.

This life is the time to prepare to meet God. We cannot procrastinate our repentance. The time will come when we die, that we can no longer perform any work; then comes the night of darkness.

'FOR BEHOLD, THIS LIFE IS THE TIME FOR MEN TO PREPARE TO MEET GOD; YEA, BEHOLD THE DAY OF THIS LIFE IS THE DAY FOR MEN TO PERFORM THEIR LABOURS.

'AND NOW, AS I SAID UNTO YOU BEFORE, AS YE HAVE HAD SO MANY WITNESSES, THEREFORE, I BESEECH OF YOU THAT YE DO NOT PROCRASTINATE THE DAY OF YOUR REPENTANCE UNTIL THE END; FOR AFTER THIS DAY OF LIFE, WHICH IS GIVEN US TO PREPARE FOR ETERNITY, BEHOLD, IF WE DO NOT IMPROVE OUR TIME WHILE IN THIS LIFE, THEN COMETH THE NIGHT OF DARKNESS WHEREIN THERE CAN BE NO LABOUR PERFORMED.

'YE CANNOT SAY, WHEN YE ARE BROUGHT TO THAT AWFUL CRISIS, THAT I WILL REPENT, THAT I WILL RETURN TO MY GOD. NAY, YE CANNOT SAY THIS; FOR THAT SAME SPIRIT WHICH DOTH POSSESS YOUR BODIES AT THE TIME THAT YE GO OUT OF THIS LIFE, THAT SAME SPIRIT WILL HAVE POWER TO POSSESS YOUR BODY IN THAT ETERNAL WORLD.

'FOR BEHOLD, IF YE HAVE PROCRASTINATED THE DAY OF YOUR REPENTANCE EVEN UNTIL DEATH, BEHOLD, YE HAVE BECOME SUBJECTED TO THE SPIRIT OF THE DEVIL, AND HE

TRUTH

DOTH SEAL YOU HIS; THEREFORE, THE SPIRIT OF THE LORD HATH WITHDRAWN FROM YOU, AND HATH NO PLACE IN YOU AND THE DEVIL HATH ALL POWER OVER YOU; AND THIS IS THE FINAL STATE OF THE WICKED.'[694]

'Verily, thus saith the Lord: It shall come to pass that every soul who forsaketh his sins and cometh unto me, and calleth on my name, and obeyeth my voice, and keepeth my commandments, shall see my face and know that I am; [695]

'And that I am the true light that lighteth every man that cometh into the world;'[696]

'The Father because he gave me of his fullness, and the Son because I was in the world and made flesh my tabernacle, and dwelt among the sons of men.

'The light and the Redeemer of the world; the Spirit of truth, who came into the world, because the world was made by him, and in him was the life of men and the light of men.

'The worlds were made by him; men were made by him; all things were made by him, and through him and of him.

'And I John, bear record that I beheld his glory, as the glory of the Only Begotten of the Father, full of grace and truth, even the Spirit of truth, which came and dwelt among us.

'And I, John, saw that he received not of the fullness at the first, but received grace for grace;

'And he received not of the fullness at first, but continued from grace to grace, until he received a fullness;

'And thus he was called the Son of God, because he received not of the fullness at the first.

---

694 Alma 34:32-35
695 D&C 93:1
696 D&C 93:2

'And I, John, bear record, and lo, the heavens were opened, and the Holy Ghost descended upon him in the form of a dove, and sat upon him, and there came a voice out of heaven saying: This is my beloved Son.

'And I, John, bear record that he received a fullness of the glory of the Father;

'And he received all power, both in heaven and on earth, and the glory of the Father was with him, for he dwelt in him.

'And it shall come to pass, that if you are faithful you shall receive the fullness of the record of John.

'I give unto you these sayings that you may understand and know how to worship and know what you worship, that you may come unto the Father in my name, and in due time receive of his fullness.

'For if you keep my commandments you shall receive of his fullness, and be glorified in me as I am in the Father; therefore, I say unto you, you shall receive grace for grace.'[697]

'And truth is knowledge of things as they are, and as they were, and as they are to come;'[698]

'The Spirit of truth is of God. I am the Spirit of truth, and John bore record of me, saying: He received a fullness of truth, yea, even of all truth;

'And no man receiveth a fullness unless he keepeth his commandments.

'He that keepeth his commandments receiveth truth and light, until he is glorified in truth and knoweth all things.

'Man was also in the beginning with God. Intelligence, or the light of truth, was not created or made, neither indeed can be.

'All truth is independent in that sphere in which God has placed it, to act for itself, as all intelligence also; otherwise there is no existence.

'Behold, here is the agency of man, and here is the condemnation of man; because that which was from the beginning is plainly manifest unto them, and they receive not the light.

'And every man whose spirit receiveth not the light is under condemnation.

---

697 *D&C 93:9-20*
698 *D&C 93:24*

'For man is spirit. The elements are eternal, and spirit and element, inseparably connected, receive a fullness of joy;

'And when separated, man cannot receive a fullness of joy.

'The elements are the tabernacle of God; yea, man is the tabernacle of God, even temples; and whatsoever temple is defiled, God shall destroy that temple.

'The glory of God is intelligence, or, in other words, light and truth.

'Light and truth forsake that evil one.

'Every spirit of man was innocent in the beginning; and God having redeemed man from the fall, men became again, in their infant state, innocent before God.

'And that wicked one cometh and taketh away light and truth through disobedience, from the children of men, and because of the tradition of their fathers.

'But I have commanded you to bring up your children in light and truth.'[699]

'You have not taught your children light and truth, according to the commandments; and that wicked one hath power, as yet, over you, and this is the cause of your affliction.'[700]

'WHAT I SAY UNTO ONE I SAY UNTO ALL; PRAY ALWAYS LEST THAT WICKED ONE HAVE POWER IN YOU, AND REMOVE YOU OUT OF YOUR PLACE.'[701]

With all of the different professions and the knowledge in the world, how can we know which are those of 'scientific value' where their truths may change as new discoveries are made; or which are the priceless truths to be had that are precious gems?

Bruce R. McConkie tells us that the truth of all things, (spiritual or temporal) is measured by the scriptures.

---

699   D&C 93:26-40
700   D&C 93:42
701   D&C 93:49

Therefore, if we have doubts about something, all we need to do is to study it out in the scriptures. If it is true, the Lord will cause that our bosoms will burn within us, and if it is not, then darkness will cover our minds and we will forget the things which we sought.

The Lord has said, "Behold, you have not understood; you have supposed that I would give it unto you, when you took no thought save it was to ask me.

"But, behold, I say unto you, that you must study it out in your mind; then you must ask me if it be right, and if it is right I will cause that your bosom shall burn within you; therefore, you shall feel that it is right."[702]

Even though the veil has been drawn across our minds, the Lord has not left us to wander about in the dark. He has given us scriptures, prophets and leaders to guide us to the truth. We must take the initiative to look. It is up to us to have the desire and begin the search for truth.

As we ask and knock upon the door, Heavenly Father will open the door.[703] He will not force us. It is our choice.

'Ask, and ye shall receive; knock, and it shall be opened unto you. Amen.'[704]

---

702 D&C 9:7-8
703 2 Nephi 9:42
704 D&C 4:7

CHAPTER FORTY THREE

Faith

'WE BELIEVE THAT THE FIRST PRINCIPLES AND ORDINANCES OF THE GOSPEL ARE: FIRST, FAITH IN THE LORD JESUS CHRIST; SECOND, REPENTANCE; THIRD, BAPTISM BY IMMERSION FOR THE REMISSION OF SINS; FOURTH, LAYING ON OF HANDS FOR THE GIFT OF THE HOLY GHOST.'[705]

There are many things in the world today which will try and test our faith. What is faith?

Faith is to hope for things which are not seen, but which are true [706] and must be centred in Jesus Christ in order to produce salvation. To have faith is to have confidence in something or someone. The Lord has revealed himself and his perfect character, possessing in their fullness all the attributes of love, knowledge, justice, mercy, unchangeableness, power and every other needful thing, so as to enable the mind of man to place confidence in him without reservation. Faith is kindled by hearing the testimony of those who have faith. Miracles do not produce faith but strong faith is developed by obedience to the gospel of Jesus Christ; in other words, faith comes by righteousness, although miracles often confirm one's faith.

Faith is a principle of action and of power, and by it one can command the elements and/or heal the sick, or influence any number of circumstances when occasion warrants. Even more important, by faith one obtains a remission of sins and eventually can stand in the presence of God.

All true faith must be based upon correct knowledge or it cannot produce the desired results. Faith in Jesus Christ is the first principle of the gospel and is more than belief, since true faith always moves its possessor to

---

705 *Fourth Article of Faith*
706 *Hebrew 11:1; Alma 32:21*

some kind of physical and mental action; it carries an assurance of the fulfilment of the things hoped for. A lack of faith leads one to despair, which comes because of iniquity.

Although faith is a gift, it must be cultured and sought after until it grows from a tiny seed to a great tree.[707] The effects of true faith in Jesus Christ include (1) an actual knowledge that the course of life one is pursuing is acceptable to the Lord; (2) a reception of the blessings of the Lord that are available to man in this life; and (3) an assurance of personal salvation in the world to come. These things involve individual and personal testimony, guidance, revelation and spiritual knowledge. Where there is true faith there are miracles, visions, dreams, healings, and all the gifts of God that he gives to his saints. Jesus pointed out some obstacles to faith.

Satan tries to blind us spiritually and harden our hearts so that we will not receive the blessings. Satan wants us to doubt the Lord and his goodness. He wants us to believe that evil is good and good is evil.

Faith without works is dead.[708]

'Seest thou how faith wrought with his works, and by works was faith made perfect?'[709]

'For as the body without the spirit is dead, so faith without works is dead also.'[710] When we have a desire to do something or go somewhere, it will not happen unless we put into action those thoughts. For example, if we desire to have grilled cheese sandwiches for lunch, it will not happen unless we butter two slices of bread for each sandwich, cut the cheese and put it on the bread, heat the frying pan to the proper temperature. Will we have grilled cheese sandwiches then? No. We must still continue. We need to put the buttered bread with the cheese on the grill. When the bottom of the bread is toasty brown, we then turn the sandwich over in order to toast the other side.

Once the other side is also toasted, we then remove the grilled cheese sandwich from the frying pan. We now have a grilled cheese sandwich. Could

---

707 *Luke 17:6*
708 *James 2:20*
709 *James 2:22*
710 *James 2:26*

FAITH

we have had the sandwich without the necessary preparations? No. We could wish all we wanted, but unless we did the preparations ourselves, it would not have happened.

We can have a desire to know Jesus Christ, to learn about Him, but if we do nothing more, it will not happen. We cannot just have a desire to know about Jesus Christ and then wait for knowledge to be poured down upon our heads. We need to study the scriptures, pray, and fast.

'Now faith is the substance of things hoped for, the evidence of things not seen.'[711]

'If ye have faith as a grain of mustard seed, ye shall say unto this mountain, remove hence to yonder place; and it shall remove; and nothing shall be impossible unto you.'[712]

How can we turn faith into works? We can put on the whole armour of God. As we go about our daily activities, we will be protected against the adversary. 'For we wrestle not against flesh and blood, but against principalities, against powers, against the rulers of the darkness of this world, against spiritual wickedness in high places.'[713] We will have confidence to move forward. What is the whole armour of God?

"Wherefore take unto you the whole armour of God that ye may be able to withstand in the evil day, and having done all, to stand.

"Stand therefore, having your loins girt about with truth, and having on the breastplate of righteousness; "And your feet shod with the preparation of the gospel of peace;

"And above all, taking the shield of faith, wherewith ye shall be able to quench all the fiery darts of the wicked.

"And take the helmet of salvation, and the sword of the Spirit, which is the word of God:

"Praying always..."[714]

---

711 *Hebrews 11:1*
712 *Mathew 17:20*
713 *Ephesians 6:12*
714 *Ephesians 6:13-18*

Jesus Christ has told us "If ye will have faith in me ye shall have power to do whatsoever thing is expedient in me."[715] If we have faith in Jesus Christ and believe Him, we can do anything. There is nothing that is impossible for Him. He went on to say, "Repent all ye ends of the earth, and come unto me, and be baptized in my name; and have faith in me; that ye may be saved."[716]

We need to have faith that we can accomplish anything. Our Saviour Jesus Christ and Heavenly Father want us to be able to come home. They have shown us the way and what we need to do in order to succeed. They will help us along the way. The road will not be easy, but it will be worth it. The path that we choose is up to us.

---

715 *Moroni 7:33*
716 *Moroni 7:34*

CHAPTER FORTY FOUR

Endurance

'SEEK TO BRING FORTH AND ESTABLISH MY ZION. KEEP MY COMMANDMENTS IN ALL THINGS.

'AND, IF YOU KEEP MY COMMANDMENTS AND ENDURE TO THE END YOU SHALL HAVE ETERNAL LIFE, WHICH GIFT IS THE GREATEST OF ALL THE GIFTS OF GOD.'[717]

THE MONUMENT
By Blaine M. Yorgason

God, Before He sent His children to the Earth
Gave each of them
A very carefully selected package
Of problems.

These, He promised, smiling
Are yours alone. No one
Else may have the blessings
These problems will bring you.

And only you
Have the special talents and abilities
That will be needed
To make these problems
Your servant.

---

[717] D&C 14:6-7

Now go down to birth
And to your forgetfulness. Know that
I love you beyond measure.
These problems I give you
Are a symbol of that love.

The monument you make of your life
With the help of your problems
Will be a symbol of your
Love for me,
Your Father.

All of the varieties of problems we face throughout this life require endurance. Sometimes it seems that we face the same problems over again. When this happens, we need to ask ourselves what it is the Lord would have us learn from this particular problem. When the lesson is learned, we are then able to go on to new trials and tribulations. What are some of the things the Lord would have us learn? Compassion, patience, understanding, empathy, and trust are some of the jewels that the Lord would have us learn. We ask for strength and we are given weaknesses.

As we conquer these, we have been given strength. We ask for patience, and we are given situations which are very trying. We ask for empathy and we are given sorrow in our lives to understand that which someone else is suffering. Often because of our natures, we need to go through many of the lessons again and again. It takes many times for us to learn these Godlike attributes. Those things which we persist in doing, whether they are right or wrong, becomes easier to do, not because the nature of the things have changed, but because our ability to do those things have increased. Therefore, we need to learn to be persistent in doing right. When we choose wrong, it is more difficult to change our attitudes. When we do, and repent, we have learned humility.

The Lord has told us that everything that we endure shall be for our good. All our trials are for our benefit. We are like work-horses with blinkers on. We can only see immediately in front of us. The Lord, on the other hand, can see for eternity. He knows what each of us needs to perfect ourselves to reach our goal. We need to trust him that no matter what we may face, he will not give us more than we can handle. All commandments are given with a way open to us to obey them.

Nephi says, "I will go and do the things which the Lord hath commanded, for I know that the Lord giveth no commandments unto the children of men save he shall prepare a way that they may accomplish them."[718] The Lord gives us days, weeks, months, and years in which to prefect ourselves. Through Holy Scriptures and a living prophet, he directs us to do specific things each day, small things that are well within our reach.

Today, for example, we can pray fervently, read the scriptures thoughtfully, and reach out to others through acts of charitable service.

This week, we can observe a sacred Sabbath, plan a more effective family home evening, work on our personal journals, and share the gospel with a friend.

This month, we can increase our temple attendance, pay an honest tithe and generous fast offering, and complete our visiting and home teaching with enthusiasm.

This year, we can make greater strides in all areas of family preparedness.

Line upon line, precept upon precept, we learn.

'Eternal life means eternal growth. It means endless progression. It is not possible through one outburst of religious zeal to meet the foe, fight the battle, and win the victory once and for all in a single encounter.' (Sterling W. Sill)

'And ye cannot bear all things now; nevertheless, be of good cheer, for I will lead you along.'[719] 'For verily I say unto you, blessed is he that keepeth my commandments, whether in life or in death; and he that is faithful in tribulation, the reward of the same is greater in the kingdom of heaven,[720]

'Ye cannot behold with your natural eyes, for the present time, the design of your God concerning those things which shall come hereafter, and the glory which shall follow after much tribulation.'[721]

718　1 Nephi 3:7
719　D&C 78:18
720　D&C 58:2
721　D&C 58:3

'For after much tribulation come the blessings. Wherefore the day cometh that ye shall be crowned with much glory; the hour is not yet, but is nigh at hand.'[722]

As we progress through this life, we need to be thankful that the Lord has blessed us with the trials and tribulations which we face. In this way, we learn and we prepare to return to our Heavenly home. Just as we prepare for eligibility and entrance into schools, colleges, universities and vocations, so do we prepare for entrance back to our Heavenly Father in the Celestial Kingdom. Each of the experiences we pass through brings us that much closer to our goal.

'...Peace be unto thy soul; thine adversity and thine afflictions shall be but a small moment;

'And then, if thou endure it well, God shall exalt thee on high; thou shalt triumph over all thy foes.'[723]

---

722 *D&C 58:4*
723 *D&C 121:7-8*

CHAPTER FORTY FIVE

Zion

'AND THE LORD CALLED HIS PEOPLE ZION, BECAUSE THEY WERE OF ONE HEART AND ONE MIND, AND DWELT IN RIGHTEOUSNESS.'[724]

'FOR I WILL RAISE UP UNTO MYSELF A PURE PEOPLE THAT WILL SERVE ME IN RIGHTEOUSNESS.'[725]

'MY PEOPLE MUST BE TRIED IN ALL THINGS, THAT THEY MAY BE PREPARED TO RECEIVE THE GLORY THAT I HAVE FOR THEM, EVEN THE GLORY OF ZION; AND HE THAT WILL NOT BEAR CHASTISEMENT IS NOT WORTHY OF MY KINGDOM.'[726]

All tenets of the gospel are woven together to make of our lives a beautiful pattern. They each overlap. It is not impossible to become a Zion people here, in this life. The City of Enoch was translated.

'And the Lord called his people Zion, because they were of one heart and one mind, and dwelt in righteousness; and there was no poor among them.'[727]

'And Enoch continued his preaching in righteousness unto the people of God. And it came to pass in his days, that he built a city that was called the City of Holiness, even ZION.'[728]

---

724 *Moses 7:18*
725 *D&C 100:16*
726 *D&C 136:31*
727 *Moses 7:18*
728 *Moses 7:19*

'And it came to pass that Enoch talked with the Lord; and he said unto the Lord: Surely Zion shall dwell in safety forever.

'But the Lord said unto Enoch: Zion have I blessed, but the residue of the people have I cursed.[729]

'And it came to pass that the Lord showed unto Enoch all the inhabitants of the earth; and he beheld, and lo, Zion, in process of time, was taken up into heaven. And the Lord said unto Enoch: Behold mine abode forever.[730]

'And all the days of Zion, in the days of Enoch, were three hundred and sixty-five years.[731]

'And Enoch and all his people walked with God, and he dwelt in the midst of Zion; and it came to pass that Zion was not, for God received it up into his own bosom; and from thence went forth the saying, ZION IS FLED.[732]

Can you imagine a whole city so worthy as to be lifted out of this polluted world? As we all enter this life, God asks no one whether he will accept life. We made the choice in the pre-existence when we fought on the side of the Lord. This is not the choice now. The only choice you have as you go through life is how you will live it.

Do we have specific tasks to do to become a Zion people? Are we doing them?

'Verily I say unto you who have assembled yourselves together that you may learn my will concerning the redemption of mine afflicted people-'Behold, I say unto you, were it not for the transgressions of my people, speaking concerning the church and not individuals, they might have been redeemed even now.

'But behold, they have not learned to be obedient to the things which I required at their hands, but are full of all manner of evil, and do not impart of their substance, as becometh saints, to the poor and afflicted among them;

---

729 *Moses 7:20*
730 *Moses 7:21*
731 *Moses 7:68*
732 *Moses 7:69*

ZION

'And are not united according to the union required by the law of the celestial kingdom;

'And Zion cannot be built up unless it is by the principles of the law of the celestial kingdom; otherwise I cannot receive her unto myself.

'And my people must needs be chastened until they learn obedience, if it must needs be, by the things which they suffer.

'That they may be prepared, and that my people may be taught more perfectly, and have experience, and know more perfectly concerning their duty, and the things which I require at their hands.

'For behold, I have prepared a great endowment and blessing to be poured out upon them, inasmuch as they are faithful and continue in humility before me.

'But inasmuch as there are those who have hearkened unto my words, I have prepared a blessing and an endowment for them, if they continue faithful.

'I have heard their prayers, and will accept their offering; and it is expedient in me that they should be brought thus far for a trial of their faith.

'And let those commandments which I have given concerning Zion and her law be executed and fulfilled, after her redemption.

'There has been a day of calling, but the time has come for a day of choosing; and let those be chosen that are worthy.

'And it shall be manifest unto my servant, by the voice of the Spirit, those that are chosen; and they shall be sanctified;

'And inasmuch as they follow the counsel which they receive, they shall have power after many days to accomplish all things pertaining to Zion.

'And again I say unto you, sue for peace, not only to the people that have smitten you, but also to all people;

'And lift up an ensign of peace, and make a proclamation of peace unto the ends of the earth;

'And make proposals for peace unto those who have smitten you according to the voice of the spirit which is in you and all things shall work together for your good.

'Therefore, be faithful; and behold, and lo, I am with you even unto the end. Amen.'[733]

'The children of Zion love in proportion to the heavenly knowledge which they have received - for love keeps pace with knowledge - and as one increases, so does the other. When knowledge is perfected, love will be perfected also.'[734]

We will see the day when we live on what we can produce. We have to be prepared for the future. Soon we will be asked to live the Law of Consecration. We need to live the Celestial law. As we do so, we are becoming prepared for the Second Coming of our Saviour, Jesus Christ. We need to strive to become worthy to be called His people.

How can we become a Zion people? How can we overcome Satan? As we live the commandments the Lord has given to us, we become stronger and more righteous.

'And because of the righteousness of his people, Satan has no power; wherefore, he cannot be loosed for the space of many years; for he hath no power over the hearts of the people, for they dwell in righteousness, and the Holy One of Israel reigneth.'[735]

This scripture has reference to the Millennium when Jesus Christ will come and reign personally upon the Earth for a thousand years. Satan will be bound, and there will be peace. However, if we study it more closely, we can discover how we can personally bind and ban Satan from our lives now. When we are righteous, then Satan has no power over us. That is why he tries so hard to get us to disobey the commandments. As we obey the commandments, we are living righteously. As we disobey them, we are unrighteous and Satan therefore has power over us.

The above scripture states that 'he hath no power over the hearts of the people for they dwell in righteousness.' The heart of the people refers to that

---

733 *D&C 105*
734 *Orson Pratt*
735 *1 Nephi 22:26*

ZION

frame of mind which each of us has wherein we think thoughts which no one but the Lord knows. As we think, so we are.[736]

The thoughts which we have are manifest in our actions and choices. As we strive to have pure thoughts, we will better be able to live the commandments, having peace in this life and eternal life in the world to come.

'For behold, ye are free; ye are permitted to act for yourselves; for behold, God hath given unto you a knowledge and he hath made you free.'[737]

"For behold, this is my work and my glory-- to bring to pass the immortality and eternal life of man."[738]

It is my hope and prayer that we can strive to follow the teachings of Jesus Christ. As we live the teachings of Jesus Christ we become righteous, achieving happiness and peace for ourselves and our families here in this life and immortality and eternal life in the life to come.

---

736 *Proverbs 23:7*
737 *Helaman 14:30*
738 *Moses 1:39*

CHAPTER FORTY SIX

Resurrection

'And when the time cometh when all shall rise, then shall they know that God knoweth all the times which are appointed unto man.[739]

'Now there must needs be a space betwixt the time of death and the time of the resurrection.[740]

'Now, concerning the state of the soul between death and the resurrection---Behold, it has been made known unto me by an angel, that the spirits of all men, as soon as they are departed from this mortal body, yea, the spirits of all men, whether they be good or evil, are taken home to that God who gave them life.[741]

'And then shall it come to pass that the spirits of those who are righteous are received into a state of happiness, which is called paradise, a state of rest, a state of peace, where they shall rest from all their troubles and from all care, and sorrow.[742]

'And then shall it come to pass that the spirits of the wicked, yea, who are evil—for behold, they have no part nor portion of the Spirit of the Lord; for behold, they chose evil works rather than good; therefore the spirit of the devil did enter into them, and take possession of their house—and these shall be cast out into outer darkness; there shall be weeping, and wailing, and gnashing of teeth, and this because of their own iniquity, being led captive by the will of the devil.[743]

---

739 Alma 40:10
740 Alma 40:6
741 Alma 40::11
742 Alma 40:12
743 Alma 40:13

'Now this is the state of the souls of the wicked, yea, in darkness, and a state of awful, fearful looking for the fiery indignation of the wrath of God upon them; thus they remain in this state, as well as the righteous in paradise, until the time of their resurrection.[744]

'Now there are some that have understood that this state of happiness and this state of misery of the soul, before the resurrection, was a first resurrection. Yea, I admit it may be termed a resurrection, the raising of the spirit or the soul and their consignation to happiness or misery, according to the words which have been spoken.[745]

'And behold, again it hath been spoken, that there is a first resurrection, a resurrection of all those who have been, or who are, or who shall be, down to the resurrection of Christ from the dead.[746]

'Now, we do not suppose that this first resurrection, which is spoken of in this manner, can be the resurrection of the souls and their consignation of happiness or misery. Ye cannot suppose that this is what it meaneth.[747]

'Behold, I say unto you, Nay; but it meaneth the reuniting of the soul with the body, of those from the days of Adam down to the resurrection of Christ.[748]

'Now, whether the soul and the bodies of those of whom has been spoken shall be reunited at once, the wicked as well as the righteous, I do not say; let it suffice, that I say that they all come forth; or in other words, their resurrection cometh to pass before the resurrection of those who die after the resurrection of Christ.[749]

'Now, my son, I do not say that their resurrection cometh at the resurrection of Christ; but behold, I give it as my opinion, that the souls and the bodies are reunited, of the righteous, at the resurrection of Christ, and his ascension into heaven.[750]

---

744   *Alma 40:14*
745   *Alma 40:15*
746   *Alma 40:16*
747   *Alma 40:17*
748   *Alma 40:18*
749   *Alma 40:19*
750   *Alma 40:20*

RESURRECTION

'But whether it be at his resurrection or after, I do not say; but this much I say, that there is a space between death and the resurrection of the body, and a state of the soul in happiness or in misery until the time which is appointed of God that the dead shall come forth, and be reunited, both soul and body, and be brought to stand before God, and be judged according to their works.[751]' Yea, this bringeth about the restoration of those things of which has been spoken by the mouths of the prophets.[752]

'The soul shall be restored to the body, and the body to the soul; yea, and every limb and joint shall be restored to its body; yea, even a hair of the head shall not be lost; but all things shall be restored to their proper and perfect frame.[753]

'And now, my son, this is the restoration of which has been spoken by the mouths of the prophets--[754]

'And then shall the righteous shine forth in the kingdom of God.[755]

'But behold, an awful death cometh upon the wicked; for they die as to things pertaining to things of righteousness; for they are unclean, and no unclean thing can inherit the kingdom of God; but they are cast out, and consigned to partake of the fruits of their labors or their works, which have been evil; and they drink the dregs of a bitter cup.'[756]

'Do not suppose, because it has been spoken concerning restoration, that ye shall be restored from sin to happiness. Behold, I say unto you, wickedness never was happiness.'[757]

Our time here on earth is to prepare ourselves and our families to be able to return home to heaven to dwell with God the Father and his Son Jesus Christ. We have been shown the way – the scriptures give us the direction for our lives here and what we must do to be righteous.

"No unclean thing can dwell in the presence of God."

---

751   *Alma 40:21*
752   *Alma 40:22*
753   *Alma 40:23*
754   *Alma 40:24*
755   *Alma 40:25*
756   *Alma 40:26*
757   *Alma 41:10*

Through the atonement of Jesus Christ, we can become clean from all our sins. The choice is up to us.

"Behold, I am Jesus Christ, whom the prophets testified shall come into the world.

"And behold, I am the light and the life of the world; and I have drunk out of that bitter cup which the Father hath given me, and have glorified the Father in taking upon me the sins of the world, in the which I have suffered the will of the Father in all things from the beginning.

"And it came to pass that when Jesus had spoken these words the whole multitude fell to the earth; for they remembered that it had been prophesied among them that Christ should show himself unto them after his ascension into heaven.

"And it came to pass that the Lord spake unto them saying:

RESURRECTION

"Arise and come forth unto me, that ye may thrust your hands into my side, and also that ye may feel the prints of the nails in my hands and in my feet, that ye may know that I am the God of Israel, and the God of the whole earth, and have been slain for the sins of the world."[758]

---

758 *3 Nephi 11:10-14*

CHAPTER FORTY SEVEN

Conclusion

As we can see, we have not been left to grope in the dark to find our way. We have been given the scriptures, as a set of guidelines to follow as well as living prophets on the earth today.

'WHEREFORE, YE MUST PRESS FORWARD WITH A STEADFASTNESS IN CHRIST, HAVING A PERFECT BRIGHTNESS OF HOPE, AND A LOVE OF GOD AND OF ALL MEN. WHEREFORE, IF YE SHALL PRESS FORWARD, FEASTING UPON THE WORD OF CHRIST, AND ENDURE TO THE END, BEHOLD, THUS SAITH THE FATHER: YE SHALL HAVE ETERNAL LIFE.[759]

'Wherefore, do the things which I have told you I have seen that your Lord and our Redeemer should do; for, for this cause have they been shown unto me, that ye might know the gate by which ye should enter. For the gate by which ye should enter is repentance and baptism by water; and then cometh a remission of your sins by fire and by the Holy Ghost.[760]

'And then are ye in this strait and narrow path which leads to eternal life; yea, ye have entered in by the gate; ye have done according to the commandments of the Father and the Son; and ye have received the Holy Ghost, which witnesses of the Father and the Son, unto the fulfilling of the promise which he hath made, that if ye entered in by the way ye should receive.[761]

'And now my beloved brethren, after ye have gotten into this strait and narrow path, I would ask if all is done? Behold, I say unto you, Nay; for

---

759 *2 Nephi 31:20*
760 *2 Nephi 31:17*
761 *2 Nephi 31:18*

ye have not come thus far save it were by the word of Christ with unshaken faith in him, relying wholly upon the merits of him who is mighty to save.[762]

'And now, behold, my beloved brethren, this is the way; and there is none other way nor name given under heaven whereby man can be saved in the kingdom of God.[763]

Through the sealing power, families can be sealed for time and all eternity, and sacred ordinances can be performed for the dead in the Temples which is the House of the Lord.

The Lord says in Malachi, "I will send you Elijah the prophet before the coming of the great and dreadful day of the Lord: and he shall turn the heart of the fathers to the children, and the heart of the children to their fathers, lest I come and smite the earth with a curse."[764]

The spirit, power, and calling of Elijah is, that ye have power to hold the key of the revelation, ordinances, oracles, powers and endowments of the fullness of the Melchizedek Priesthood and of the kingdom of God on the earth; and to receive, obtain, and perform all the ordinances belonging to the kingdom of God, even unto the turning of the hearts of the fathers unto the children, and the hearts of the children unto the fathers, even those who are in heaven.[765]

What is this office and work of Elijah? It is one of the greatest and most important subjects that God has revealed. He should send Elijah to seal the children to the fathers, and the fathers to the children.[766]

In the days of Noah, God destroyed the world by a flood, and He has promised to destroy it by fire in the last days: but before it should take place, Elijah should first come and turn the hearts of the fathers to the children and the hearts of the children to the fathers. Was this merely confined to the living, to settle difficulties with families on earth? By no means. It was a far greater work. Elijah! What would you do if you were here? Would you confine your work to the living alone? No: I would refer you to the Scriptures,

---

762 *2 Nephi 31:19*
763 *2 Nephi 31:21*
764 *Malachi 4:5-6*
765 *Teachings of Presidents of the Church, Joseph Smith p.311*
766 *Teachings of Presidents of the Church, Joseph Smith p. 311*

where the subject is manifest: that is, without us, they could not be made perfect, nor we without them; the fathers without the children, nor the children without the fathers.'[767]

'This is the spirit of Elijah, that we redeem our dead, and connect ourselves with our fathers which are in heaven, and seal up our dead to come forth in the first resurrection; and here we want the power of Elijah to seal those who dwell on earth to those who dwell in heaven. This is the power of Elijah and the keys of the kingdom of Jehovah…

'Again: The doctrine or sealing power of Elijah is as follows: ---If you have power to seal on earth and in heaven, then we should be wise. The first thing you do, go and seal on earth your sons and daughters unto yourself, and yourself unto your fathers in eternal glory.'[768]

'The hearts of the children of men will have to be turned to the fathers, and the fathers to the children, living or dead, to prepare them for the coming of the Son of Man. If Elijah did not come, the whole earth would be smitten.'[769]

Families are forever.

As we read and study the scriptures, and ponder and pray, the Lord gives us direction in all areas of our lives. From how to live to enjoy peace and happiness, to having a joyful marriage and happy children, and to all other areas in our personal lives, we are given guidance. We learn where we came from, why we are here and where we are going. We are given a purpose to our lives.

'Do not suppose, because it has been spoken concerning restoration, that ye shall be restored from sin to happiness. Behold, I say unto you, wickedness never was happiness.'[770]

'FOR BEHOLD, THIS IS MY WORK AND MY GLORY--- TO BRING TO PASS THE IMMORTALITY AND ETERNAL LIFE OF MAN.'[771]

---

767 *Hebrews 11:40*
768 *History of the Church, 6:251-53*
769 *History of the Church, 3:390*
770 *Alma 41:10*
771 *Moses 1:39*

APPENDIX

The Consequences If There Had Been No Atonement

A Life Without Hope

"How would it be if the sacrament table was empty because there were no atonement? What would it be like if there were no bread because there had been no crucifixion, no water because there had been no shedding of blood? If there had been no Atonement, what would the consequences be to us? As we know that there was an atonement, it puts into perspective our total dependence on the Lord. To ask and answer this question only heightens our awareness of, and appreciation for, the Savior. What might have been, even for the "righteous", if there had been no atoning sacrifice, stirs the very depths of human emotion.

First, there would be no resurrection or as suggested in the explicit language of Jacob: "This flesh must have laid down to rot and to crumble to its mother earth, to rise no more."

Second, our spirits would become subject to the devil. He would have "all power over you: and "seal you his". In fact we would become like him, even "angels to a devil".

Third, we would be "shut out from the presence of our God" to remain forever with the father of lies.

Fourth, we would "endure a never-ending torment."

Fifth, we would be without hope, for "if Christ be not risen, then is our preaching vain, and your faith is also vain...If in this life only we have hope in

Christ, we are of all men most miserable." The poet, John Fletcher, captures the desperate lot of the individual who inherits Lucifer's life:

Life's but a walking shadow, a poor player
That struts and frets his hour upon the stage
And then is heard no more. It is a tale
Told by an idiot, full of sound and fury,
Signifying nothing.

Life would signify nothing without Christ's redemptive act. The Book of Mormon prophet Jacob, asked, "Why not speak of the atonement of Christ?"[2] The third article of faith states: "We believe that through the Atonement of Christ, all mankind may be saved, by obedience to the laws and ordinances of the Gospel."[3]

WHO IS JESUS CHRIST?

Meeting with the Twelve at Caesarea Philippi, Jesus asked, "Whom say ye that I am?" Simon Peter, the chief Apostle answered, "Thou art the Christ, the Son of the living God."[4] Peter later testified that Jesus "was foreordained before the foundation of the world."[5] He was "in the beginning with the Father, and is the Firstborn."[6]

When the Father's plan—the plan of salvation and happiness[7]—was presented,[8] one was required to atone to provide redemption and mercy to all those who accepted the plan.[9] The Father asked, "Whom shall I send?" He who was to be known as Jesus freely and willingly chose to answer, "Here am I, send me."[10] "Father, thy will be done, and the glory be thine forever."[11]

In preparation, the earth was created: "By the Son I created the earth, which is mine Only Begotten," declared the Father.[12]

He was known as **Jehovah** by the Old Testament prophets.[13] The prophets were shown of His coming: "Behold the Lamb of God, yea, even the Son of the Eternal Father!"[14] His mother was told, "Call his name Jesus. ... He shall be ... called the Son of the Highest."[15]

At the last day, "God shall judge ... men by Jesus Christ according to the gospel."[16] "God so loved the world, that he gave his only begotten Son;"[17]

"wherefore, redemption cometh in and through the Holy Messiah; for he is full of grace and truth."[18]

The Lord had come from Gethsemane; before Him was His crucifixion. At the moment of betrayal, Peter drew his sword against Malchus, a servant of the high priest. Jesus said:

"Put up again thy sword into his place. ...

"Thinkest thou that I cannot now pray to my Father, and he shall presently give me more than twelve legions of angels?"[19] During all of the taunting, the abuse, the scourging, and the final torture of crucifixion, the Lord remained silent and submissive. Except, that is, for one moment of intense drama which reveals the very essence of Christian doctrine.

That moment came during the trial. Pilate, now afraid, said to Jesus: "Speakest thou not unto me? Knowest thou not that I have power to crucify thee, and have power to release thee?"[20]

One can only imagine the quiet majesty when the Lord spoke. "Thou couldest have no power at all against me, except it were given thee from above."[21]

Pilate had power to impose it, but the Lord had the will to accept it.

"I lay down my life," the Lord said, "that I might take it again.

"No man taketh it from me, but I lay it down of myself. I have power to lay it down, and I have power to take it again."[22]

Atonement of Jesus Christ

Before the Crucifixion and afterward, many men have willingly given their lives in selfless acts of heroism. But none faced what Christ endured. Upon Him was the burden of all human transgression, all human guilt.

Hanging in the balance was the Atonement. Through His willing act, mercy and justice could be reconciled, eternal law sustained, and that mediation achieved without which mortal man could not be redeemed.

He by choice accepted the penalty in behalf of all mankind for the sum total of all wickedness and depravity; for brutality, immorality, perversion, and corruption; for addiction; for the killings and torture and terror—for all of it that ever had been or all that ever would be enacted upon this earth.

In so choosing He faced the awesome power of the evil one, who was not confined to flesh nor subject to mortal pain. That was Gethsemane!

How the Atonement was wrought we do not know. When what was done was done, the ransom had been paid. Both death and hell forsook their claim on all who would repent. Men at last were free. Then every soul who ever lived could choose to touch that Light and be redeemed.[23]

By this infinite sacrifice, "through this Atonement of Christ, all mankind may be saved, by obedience to the laws and ordinances of the Gospel."[24]

It was all planned before the world was. Events from the Creation to the final, winding-up scene are not based on *chance;* they are based on *choice!* It was planned that way.

Had there been no Creation, no Fall, there should have been no need for any Atonement, neither a Redeemer to mediate for us. Then Christ need not have been.

At Gethsemane and Golgotha the Savior's blood was shed. Centuries earlier the Passover had been introduced as a symbol and a type of things to come. It was an ordinance to be kept forever.

When the plague of death was decreed upon Egypt, each Israelite family was commanded to take a lamb, firstborn, male, without blemish. This paschal lamb was slain without breaking any bones, its blood to mark the doorway of the home. The Lord promised that the angel of death would *pass over* the homes so marked and not slay those inside. They were saved by the blood of the lamb.

After the crucifixion of the Lord, the law of sacrifice required no more shedding of blood. For that was done, as Paul taught the Hebrews, "once for all, ... one sacrifice for sins forever."[25] The sacrifice thenceforth was to be a broken heart and a contrite spirit—repentance.

The Passover would be commemorated forever as the sacrament, in which we renew our covenant of baptism and partake in remembrance of the body of the Lamb of God and of His blood, which was shed for us.

It is no small thing that this symbol reappears in the Word of Wisdom. Beyond the promise that Saints in this generation, who obey, will receive health and great treasures of knowledge is this: "I, the Lord, give unto them a promise, that the destroying angel shall pass by them, as the children of Israel, and not slay them."[26] He is our Lord, our Redeemer, our advocate with the Father. He ransomed us with His blood.

Before we can comprehend the Atonement of Christ, we must first understand the Fall of Adam. And before we can understand the Fall of Adam, we must first understand the Creation. These three crucial components of the plan of salvation relate to each other.[27]

The Creation

The Creation culminated with Adam and Eve in the Garden of Eden. They were created in the image of God, with bodies of flesh and bone.[28] Created in the image of God and not yet mortal, they could not grow old and die.[29] "They would have had no children"[30] nor experienced the trials of life. The creation of Adam and Eve was a *paradisiacal creation,* one that required a significant change before they could fulfill the commandment to have children[31] and thus provide earthly bodies for premortal spirit sons and daughters of God.

The cost of the Atonement was borne by the Lord without compulsion, for agency is a sovereign principle. According to the plan, agency must be honored. It was so from the beginning, from Eden.

"The Lord said unto Enoch: Behold these thy brethren; they are the workmanship of mine own hands, and I gave unto them their knowledge, in the day I created them; and in the Garden of Eden, gave I unto man his agency."[32]

Whatever else happened in Eden, in his supreme moment of testing, Adam made a choice.

After the Lord commanded Adam and Eve to multiply and replenish the earth and commanded them *not* to partake of the tree of knowledge of good and evil, He said: "Nevertheless, thou mayest choose for thyself, for it is given unto thee; but, remember that I forbid it, for in the day thou eatest thereof thou shalt surely die."[33]

There was too much at issue to introduce man into mortality by force. That would contravene the very law essential to the plan. The plan provided that each spirit child of God would receive a mortal body and each would be tested. Adam saw that it must be so and made his choice. "Adam fell that men might be; and men are, that they might have joy."[34]

Adam and Eve ventured forth to multiply and replenish the earth as they had been commanded to do. The creation of their bodies in the image of God, as a separate creation, was crucial to the plan. Their subsequent fall was essential if the condition of mortality was to exist and the plan to proceed.

Because of the Fall, the Atonement was absolutely essential for resurrection to proceed and overcome mortal death.

The Atonement was absolutely essential for men to cleanse themselves from sin and overcome the second death, which is the spiritual death, which is separation from our Father in Heaven.

No unclean thing may enter the presence of God.

"Thou mayest choose for thyself, for it is given unto thee,"[35] introduced Adam and Eve and their posterity to all the risks of mortality. In mortality men are free to choose, and each choice begets a consequence. The choice Adam made energized the law of justice, which required that the penalty for disobedience would be death.

Those words spoken at the trial, "Thou couldest have no power at all against me, except it were given thee from above,"[36] proved mercy was of equal rank. A redeemer was sent to pay the debt and set men free. That was the plan.

Alma's son Corianton thought it unfair that penalties must follow sin, that there need be punishment. Alma spoke of the Atonement and said, "Now, repentance could not come unto men except there were a punishment."[37]

If punishment is the price repentance asks, it comes at bargain price. Consequences, even painful ones, protect us. As simple a thing as a child's cry of pain when his finger touches fire, can teach us that. Except for the pain, the child might be consumed.

An atonement was made. Ever and always it offers amnesty from transgression and from death if we will but repent. Repentance is the escape clause in it all. Repentance is the key with which we can unlock the prison from inside. We hold that key within our hands, and agency is ours to use it.

How supernally precious freedom is; how consummately valuable is the agency of man.

Lucifer in clever ways manipulates our choices, deceiving us about sin and consequences. He, and his angels with him, tempt us to be unworthy, even wicked. But he cannot, in all eternity he cannot, with all his power he cannot completely destroy us; not without our own consent. Had agency come to man without the Atonement, it would have been a fatal gift.

The Fall

"Adam fell that men might be; and men are, that they might have joy."[38] The Fall of Adam (and Eve) constituted the *mortal creation* and brought about the required changes in their bodies, including the circulation of blood and other modifications as well.[39] They were now able to have children. They and their posterity also became subject to injury, disease, and death. A loving Creator blessed them with healing power by which the life and function of precious physical bodies could be preserved. For example, bones, if broken, could become solid again. Lacerations of the flesh could heal themselves. And miraculously, leaks in the circulation could be sealed off by components activated from the very blood being lost.

Think of the wonder of that power to heal! If you could create anything that could repair itself, you would have created life in perpetuity. For example, if you could create a chair that could fix its own broken leg, there would be no limit to the life of that chair. Many of you walk on legs that were once broken and do so because of your remarkable gift of healing.

Even though our Creator endowed us with this incredible power, He consigned a counterbalancing gift to our bodies. It is the blessing of *aging,* with visible reminders that we are mortal beings destined one day to leave this "frail existence."[40] Our bodies change every day. As we grow older, our broad chests and narrow waists have a tendency to trade places. We get wrinkles, lose color in our hair—even the hair itself—to remind us that we are mortal children of God, with a "manufacturer's guarantee" that we shall not be stranded upon the earth forever.

Adam and Eve, as mortal beings, were instructed to "worship the Lord their God, and ... offer the firstlings of their flocks, for an offering unto the Lord."[41] They were further instructed that "the life of the flesh is in the blood: ... for it is the blood that maketh an atonement for the soul."[42] Probation, procreation, and aging were all components of—and physical death was essential to—God's "great plan of happiness."[43]

But mortal life, glorious as it is, was never the *ultimate* objective of God's plan. Life and death here on planet Earth were merely *means* to an end—not the *end* for which we were sent.

The Atonement

Paul said, "As in Adam all die, even so in Christ shall all be made alive."[44] The Atonement of Jesus Christ became the *immortal creation*. He volunteered to answer the ends of a law previously transgressed.[45] By the shedding of His blood, His[46] and our physical bodies could become perfected. They could again function without blood, just as Adam's and Eve's did in their *paradisiacal* form. Paul taught that "flesh and blood cannot inherit the kingdom of God; ... this mortal must put on immortality."[47]

Meaning of Atonement

To be redeemed is to be atoned—received in the close embrace of God with an expression not only of His forgiveness, but of our oneness of heart and mind. What a privilege! And what a comfort to those of us with loved ones who have already passed from our family circle through the gateway we call death!

The Old Testament has many references to atonement, which called for animal sacrifice. Not any animal would do.
- the selection of a firstling of the flock, without blemish,[48]
- the sacrifice of the animal's life by the shedding of its blood,[49]
- death of the animal without breaking a bone, and [50]
- one animal could be sacrificed as a vicarious act for another.[51]

The Atonement of Christ fulfilled these prototypes of the Old Testament. He was the firstborn Lamb of God, without blemish. His sacrifice occurred by the shedding of blood. No bones of His body were broken—noteworthy in that both malefactors crucified with the Lord had their legs broken.[52] And His was a vicarious sacrifice for others.

Infinite Atonement

In preparatory times of the Old Testament, the practice of atonement was finite—meaning it had an end. It was a symbolic forecast of the definitive Atonement of Jesus the Christ. His Atonement is infinite—without an end.⁵³ It was also infinite in that all humankind would be saved from never-ending death. It was infinite in terms of His immense suffering. It was infinite in time, putting an end to the preceding prototype of animal sacrifice. It was infinite in scope—it was to be done once for all.⁵⁴ The mercy of the Atonement extends not only to an infinite number of people, but also to an infinite number of worlds created by Him.⁵⁵ It was infinite beyond any human scale of measurement or mortal comprehension.

Jesus was the only one who could offer such an infinite atonement, since He was born of a mortal mother and an immortal Father. Because of that unique birthright, Jesus was an infinite Being.

The Ordeal of the Atonement

The ordeal of the Atonement centered about the city of Jerusalem. There the greatest single act of love of all recorded history took place.⁵⁶ Leaving the upper room, Jesus and His friends crossed the deep ravine east of the city and came to a garden of olive trees on the lower slopes of the Mount of Olives. There in the garden bearing the Hebrew name of *Gethsemane*—meaning "oil-press"—olives had been beaten and pressed to provide oil and food. There at Gethsemane, the Lord "suffered the pain of all men, that all … might repent and come unto him." ⁵⁷

He took upon Himself the weight of the sins of all mankind, bearing its massive load that caused Him to bleed from every pore.⁵⁸

Later He was beaten and scourged. A crown of sharp thorns was thrust upon His head as an additional form of torture.⁵⁹ He was mocked and jeered. He suffered every indignity at the hands of His own people. "I came unto my own," He said, "and my own received me not."⁶⁰ Instead of their warm embrace, He received their cruel rejection. Then He was required to carry His own cross to the hill of Calvary, where He was nailed to that cross and made to suffer excruciating pain.

Later He said, "I thirst."⁶¹ When a person goes into shock because of blood loss, invariably that person—if still conscious—with parched and shriveled lips cries for water.

Even though the Father and the Son knew well in advance what was to be experienced, the actuality of it brought indescribable agony. "And Jesus said, "Abba, Father, all things are possible unto thee; take away this cup from me: nevertheless not what I will, but what thou wilt." [62] Jesus then complied with the will of His Father.

Through this suffering, Jesus redeemed the souls of all men, women, and children "that his bowels may be filled with mercy, according to the flesh, that he may know according to the flesh how to succor his people according to their infirmities."[63] In doing so, Christ "descended below all things"—including every kind of sickness, infirmity, and dark despair experienced by every mortal being—in order that He might "comprehend all things, that he might be in all and through all things, the light of truth."[64]

The utter loneliness and excruciating pain of the Atonement begun in Gethsemane reached its zenith when, after unspeakable abuse at the hands of Roman soldiers and others, Christ cried from the cross, "Eli, Eli, lama sabachthani? that is to say, My God, my God, why hast thou forsaken me?"[65] In the depths of that anguish, even nature itself convulsed. "There was a darkness over all the earth. ... And the sun was darkened."[66] "And, behold, the veil of the temple was rent in twain from the top to the bottom; and the earth did quake, and the rocks rent,"[67] causing many to exclaim, "The God of nature suffers."[68] Finally, even the seemingly unbearable had been borne.[69]

Jesus said, "It is finished."[70] "Father, into thy hands I commend my spirit."[71]

Three days later, precisely as prophesied, He rose from the grave. He became the firstfruits of the Resurrection. He had accomplished the Atonement, which could give immortality and eternal life to all obedient human beings. All that the Fall allowed to go awry, the Atonement allowed to go aright.

The Savior's gift of *immortality* comes to all who have ever lived. But His gift of *eternal life* requires repentance and obedience to specific ordinances and covenants. Essential ordinances of the gospel symbolize the Atonement. Baptism by immersion is symbolic of the death, burial, and Resurrection of the Redeemer. Partaking of the sacrament renews baptismal covenants and also renews our memory of the Savior's broken flesh and of the blood He shed for us. Ordinances of the temple symbolize our reconciliation with the Lord and seal families together forever. Obedience to the sacred covenants made in temples qualifies us for eternal life—the greatest gift of God to man[72]—the "object and end of our existence."[73]

The Atonement Enabled the Purpose of the Creation to Be Accomplished

The Creation required the Fall. The Fall required the Atonement. The Atonement enabled the purpose of the Creation to be accomplished. Eternal life, made possible by the Atonement, is the supreme purpose of the Creation. To phrase that statement in its negative form, if families were not sealed in holy temples, the whole earth would be utterly wasted.[74]

The purposes of the Creation, the Fall, and the Atonement all converge on the sacred work done in temples of The Church of Jesus Christ of Latter-day Saints. The earth was created and the Church was restored to make possible the sealing of wife to husband, children to parents, families to progenitors, worlds without end.

The Atonement of Jesus Christ was indispensable because of the separating transgression, or Fall, of Adam, which brought two kinds of death into the world when Adam and Eve partook of the fruit of the tree of knowledge of good and evil.[75] Physical death brought the separation of the spirit from the body, and spiritual death brought the estrangement of both the spirit and the body from God. As a result of the Fall, all persons born into mortality would suffer these two kinds of death. But we must remember the Fall was an essential part of Heavenly Father's divine plan. Without it no mortal children would have been born to Adam and Eve, and there would have been no human family to experience opposition and growth, moral agency, and the joy of resurrection, redemption, and eternal life.[76]

The need for this Fall and for an atonement to compensate for it was explained in a premortal Council in Heaven at which the spirits of the entire human family attended and over which God the Father presided. It was in this premortal setting that Christ volunteered to honor the moral agency of all humankind even as He atoned for their sins. In the process, He would return to the Father all glory for such redemptive love.[77]

This is the great latter-day work of which we are a part. That is why we have missionaries; that is why we have temples—to bring the fullest blessings of the Atonement to faithful children of God. That is why we respond to our own calls from the Lord. When we comprehend His voluntary Atonement, any sense of sacrifice on our part becomes completely overshadowed by a profound sense of gratitude for the privilege of serving Him.

The Atonement of the Only Begotten Son of God is the crucial foundation upon which all Christian doctrine rests and the greatest expression of divine love this world has ever been given.

As a young missionary, Elder Orson F. Whitney (1855–1931), who later served in the Quorum of the Twelve Apostles, had a dream so powerful that it changed his life forever. He later wrote:

"One night I dreamed ... that I was in the Garden of Gethsemane, a witness of the Savior's agony. ... I stood behind a tree in the foreground. ... Jesus, with Peter, James, and John, came through a little wicket gate at my right. Leaving the three Apostles there, after telling them to kneel and pray, He passed over to the other side, where He also knelt and prayed ...: 'Oh my Father, if it be possible, let this cup pass from me; nevertheless not as I will but as Thou wilt.'

"As He prayed the tears streamed down His face, which was [turned] toward me. I was so moved at the sight that I wept also, out of pure sympathy with His great sorrow. My whole heart went out to Him. I loved Him with all my soul and longed to be with Him as I longed for nothing else.

"Presently He arose and walked to where those Apostles were kneeling—fast asleep! He shook them gently, awoke them, and in a tone of tender reproach, untinctured by the least show of anger or scolding, asked them if they could not watch with Him one hour. ...

"Returning to His place, He prayed again and then went back and found them again sleeping. Again He awoke them, admonished them, and returned and prayed as before. Three times this happened, until I was perfectly familiar with His appearance—face, form, and movements. He was of noble stature and of majestic mien ... the very God that He was and is, yet as meek and lowly as a little child.

"All at once the circumstance seemed to change. ... Instead of before, it was after the Crucifixion, and the Savior, with those three Apostles, now stood together in a group at my left. They were about to depart and ascend into heaven. I could endure it no longer. I ran from behind the tree, fell at His feet, clasped Him around the knees, and begged Him to take me with Him.

"I shall never forget the kind and gentle manner in which He stooped and raised me up and embraced me. It was so vivid, so real that I felt the very warmth of His bosom against which I rested. Then He said: 'No, my son; these have finished their work, and they may go with me; but you must stay and finish yours.' Still I clung to Him. Gazing up into His face—for He was taller than I—I besought Him most earnestly: 'Well, promise me that I will come to You at the last.' He smiled sweetly and tenderly and replied: 'That will depend entirely upon yourself.' I awoke with a sob in my throat, and it was morning."[78]

Someday, somewhere, every human tongue will be called upon to confess as did a Roman centurion who witnessed all of this, "Truly this was the Son of God."[79]

To the thoughtful woman and man, it is "a matter of surpassing wonders"[80] that the voluntary and merciful sacrifice of a single being could satisfy the infinite and eternal demands of justice, atone for every human transgression and misdeed, and thereby sweep all humankind into the encompassing arms of His merciful embrace. But so it is.

To quote President John Taylor (1808–87): "In a manner to us incomprehensible and inexplicable, He bore the weight of the sins of the whole world; not only of Adam, but of his posterity; and in doing that, opened the kingdom of heaven, not only to all believers and all who obeyed the law of God, but to more than one-half of the human family who die before they come to years of maturity, as well as to [those] who ... [die] without [the] law."[81]

As Elder Whitney felt regarding this majestic gift and the giver of it, may we so feel: "I was so moved at the [gift] that I wept ... out of pure sympathy. My whole heart went out to Him. I loved Him with all my soul and longed to be with Him as I longed for nothing else." Having already offered the Atonement in our behalf, Christ has done His part to make that longing a reality. The rest will depend entirely upon ourselves.

Notes:
1. *"The Infinite Atonement," Tad R. Callister page 53, 54*
2. *Jacob 4:12*
3. *Articles of Faith 1:3*
4. *Matthew 16:15–16*
5. *1 Peter 1:20*
6. *D&C 93:21*
7. *Alma 34:9*
8. *Alma 42:5, 8*
9. *Alma 34:16; 39:18; 42:15*
10. *Abraham 3:27*
11. *Moses 4:2*
12. *Moses 1:33; Ephesians 3:9; Helaman 14:12; Moses 2:1*
13. *Abraham 1:16; Exodus 6:3*
14. *1 Nephi 11:21; John 1:14*
15. *Luke 1:31–32*
16. *Romans 2:16; Mormon 3:20*
17. *John 3:16*
18. *2 Nephi 2:6*
19. *Matthew 26:52–53*
20. *John 19:10*
21. *John 19:11*
22. *John 10:17–18*
23. *"Atonement, Agency, Accountability," Elder Boyd K. Packer, May 1988 Ensign*
24. *Articles of Faith 1:3*
25. *Hebrews 10:10, 12*
26. *D&C 89:21*
27. *Alma 18:34-39; Mormon 9:12; D&C 20:17-24*
28. *They were created as amortal beings "without mortality" – not at that time subject to death)*

29. Alma 12:21-23
30. 2 Nephi 2:23
31. Genesis 1:28; Moses 2:28
32. Moses 7:32
33. Moses 3:17
34. 2 Ne. 2:25
35. Moses 3:17
36. John 19:11
37. Alma 42:16
38. 2 Nephi_2:25
39. Moses_6:53
40. Eliza R. Snow, 'O My Father" Hymns, no 292
41. Moses 5:5
42. Leviticus 17:11
43. Alma 42:8
44. 1 Corinthians 15:22; Mosiah 16:7-8
45. 2 Nephi 2:7; "Behold the Great Redeemer Die" Hymns, no 191
46. Luke 13:32
47. 1 Corinthians 15:50-53
48. Leviticus 5:18; Leviticus 27:26
49. Leviticus 9:18
50. Exodus 12:46; Numbers 9:12
51. Leviticus 16:10
52. John 19:31-33
53. 2 Nephi 9:7
54. Hebrews 10:10
55. D&C 76:24; Moses 1:33
56. John 3:16
57. D&C 18:11
58. Luke 22:44; D&C 19:18
59. Matthew 27:29; Mark 15:17; John 19:2, 5
60. 3 Nephi 9:16; D&C 6:21; D&C 10:57; D&C 11:29; D&C 39:3; D&C 45:8; D&C 133:66

61. *John 19:28*
62. *Mark 14:36; The word Abba is significant. Ab means "father"; Abba is an endearing and tender form of that term. The nearest English equivalent might be Daddy.*
63. *Alma 7:12*
64. *D&C 88:6*
65. *Matthew 27:46*
66. *Luke 23:44-45*
67. *Matthew 27:51*
68. *1 Nephi 19:12*
69. *D&C 19 Centuries later, the Lord shared innermost recollections of this experience with the Prophet Joseph Smith, the record of which we read in Doctrine and Covenants 19.*
70. *John 19:30*
71. *Matthew 27:54*
72. *D&C 14:7*
73. *Bruce R. McConkie, "The Promised Messiah" (1978), 568*
74. *D&C 2:3; D&C 138:48*
75. *Genesis 2:9; 3*
76. *2 Nephi 2:22-27; Moses 5:11*
77. *Revelation 13:8; Moses 4:1-2; Abraham 3:22-27*
78. *"The Divinity of Jesus Christ", Improvement Era, January 1926, 224-225; Liahona, December 2003, 16*
79. *Matthew 27:54*
80. *James E. Talmage, The Articles of Faith, 12th ed. (1924), 77*
81. *"The Mediation and Atonement" (1882), 148-49*

Additional Reading:

"Atonement, Agency, Accountability," Boyd K. Packer, May 1988 Ensign

"The Atonement," Russell M. Nelson, November 1996 Ensign

"The Infinite Atonement," Tad R. Callister

"The Mediation and Atonement," John Taylor, 1882

WHAT IS LOVE?

True Love

True love is a total giving of oneself without expecting anything in return. There are many different kinds of love, but the most important is selfless love.

In families where there is selfless love, there will be very little contention and bickering because each individual is doing things for the other members of the family. They know and understand how each individual feels about different things and what is important to them. Therefore they empathize with their happiness, sorrows, and joys.

Each member of the family takes into consideration other members feelings in the things he does and says. Each person endeavors to do and say things which will bring happiness and contentment. I know this type of love exists because my children do these things. When we reach out of ourselves, our capacity to love and bring joy to others increases. Our feelings of self-worth, peace and contentment increase as we endeavor to build up and encourage one another.

Wanda Thompson

List of Previous Publications

"**What is Love?**" Fort Macleod Gazette, Wednesday, February 20, 1985, page 7© Copyright 1985

"**For My Grandson Seth Eric Want**" July 2005 © Copyright

"**Seth Eric Want**" May 2006 © Copyright 2006

"**Happy Father's Day Dad**" June 2006© Copyright 2006

"**A New Beginning**" 2009 © Copyright

"**The Mighty Transformer**" 2011 © Copyright

"**The Adventures of Princess Jasmine**" 2011 © Copyright

"**Brian: A New Beginning**" 2012 © Copyright

"**My ABC's Seth Want**" 2012 © Copyright

"**My ABC's Jasmine Want**" 2012 © Copyright

"**Beyond The Sunset – Life's Journey Now and Forever**" 2013 © Copyright

"**My ABC's Wyatt Thompson**" 2013 © Copyright

COMING SOON!

1924 Wembley Rodeo

Mart's Adventures take him from the prairies of Southern Alberta; Across the Atlantic Ocean to London, England where he competes before King George V, Queen Mary and the Prince of Wales at the British Imperial Exhibition at the Wembley Rodeo, the First International Rodeo ever held.

"Twisting, turning, Leaping, and Balling Backward! The Wiles of the Buckjumper as in the Wembley Rodeo Portion of Advertisement for the Wembley Rodeo.

At the time, the Exhibition was the largest show of its kind ever held. A number of American and Wyoming cowboys joined their Canadian, South African, and Australian counterparts at the Exhibition. Not counting American cowboys, 56 of the nations of the British Commonwealth and Empire were represented. The purposes of the Exhibition was to "stimulate trade, strengthen bonds that bind mother Country to her Sister States and Daughters, to bring into closer contact the one with each other, to enable all who owe allegiance to the British flag to meet on common ground and learn to know each other." Even though wireless service was in its infancy, the opening by HM King George V was heard by an estimated ten million listeners.

The cowboys made a distinct impression on usual staid Londoners.

As *Time Magazine*, June 16, 1924, observed:

American rodeo cowboys and cowgirls made a lasting impression upon Londoners when they arrived at the capital of the British Commonwealth en route for the Wembley Exhibition. One cowboy, sitting on the hood of an automobile, yelled: "I want to rope a red-headed goil." He did, but she turned out to be a blonde, so he let her go. Every silk hat within a rope's length was regarded as legitimate prey and Londoners took it all with marked good humor. One body of men who quite overawed the excited "cow people" were the London "bobbies;" they were not molested.

Thousands filled the stands as cowboys straight from American and Canadian ranches gave demonstrations of roping, bronco busting, trick riding, wild horse racing, and bulldogging. Canadian cowboys entered the contest, including Mart Thompson, Jack Purnell, Elmer Jameson, Francis Hutchinson, Arthur Lund, Andrew Lund, Charles Donovan Perrin, Ed Perrin, Walter Armsdon, Russell Drury, Pete Vandemeer, Harry Knight, Earl Havens, Harold Walsh, Calvin Lish, Roland Hayes, Walter Whitney, O. Haynes, and Pete Knight, Canadian Bronco Busting Champion.

Americans included cowgirls Mabel Strickland, Donnie Glover, Fox Hastings, Helen Elliot, Ruth Wheat, Florence Hughes, Donna Glover, Vera McGinnis, Ruth Roach, Tad Lucas, Bea Kirnan, Florence Fenton and Bonnie McCarrol. Judges included Tom B. Hickman. G.M. Jones, Phil Yoder and Tex Austin, who was the general manager. Cowboys included bareback bronco rider Frank Studenick, trick and fancy ropers, Jack McCaleb, Chester Beyers who used two ropes, Tommy Kirnan who roped his wife and pony and repeated the trick standing on his head, Buck Lucas, rodeo clown Red Sublett, and Mike Hastings to whom the Prince of Wales, later Edward VIII, presented a thoroughbred horse.

About The Author

Wanda Thompson was raised in Fort Macleod, Alberta, Canada. She has four children; Jerry, Jennifer, Mary and Brian. Brian is married to Lisa. They have three children, Seth, Jasmine and Spencer. Jerry is married to Crystal. They have two children, Wyatt and Emma.

Wanda Thompson has been published in newspapers and has written several books among which are **Brian - A New Beginning; Beyond The Sunset – Life's Journey Now and Forever; The Mighty Transformer** and **The Adventures of Princess Jasmine.** She has won literary contests and has studied with the Institute of Children's Literature in Redding Ridge, Connecticut. She has also attended the Writing with Style (Historical Fiction) residency workshop at the Banff Fine Arts Centre. Wanda is also interested in photography. She is a photographer and works with her own photos.

Wanda has written additional books, among which are one for her father and mother for Father's Day; one for her grandchild Seth's first birthday and one for her sister Darlene.

Wanda is currently working on *1924 **Wembley Rodeo*** which will soon be available.

Wanda is member of The Church of Jesus Christ of Latter-day Saints. She has taught Nursery, Sunbeams, CTR classes and music in Primary. She has been in the Primary Presidency and has taught home, family and personal enrichment. Wanda has also worked in public relations serving the single adults in the Lethbridge region.

www.ingramcontent.com/pod-product-compliance
Lightning Source LLC
Chambersburg PA
CBHW071016240426
43661CB00073B/2331